BICHITRA RAMAYANA

Bichitra Ramayana

A VOICE FROM WILDERNESS

SIDDHESWAR DAS

Translated by
BASANT KUMAR TRIPATHY

ADIKABI SARALA DAS
CHAIR OF ODIA STUDIES
Jawaharlal Nehru University,
New Delhi

MANOHAR
2020

First published 2020

ISBN 978-93-88540-98-8

Published by
Adikabi Sarala Das Chair of Odia Studies
Jawaharlal Nehru University,
New Delhi 110 067
&
Ajay Kumar Jain *for*
Manohar Publishers & Distributors
4753/23 Ansari Road, Daryaganj
New Delhi 110 002

Printed at
Replika Press Pvt. Ltd.

This book is dedicated to the sacred memory of Sacchidananda Mishra (1930-2015), an ardent scholar of Ancient and Medieval Odia literature, who is credited with discovering two palm-leaf manuscripts of the *Bichitra Ramayana*: one from Chhatrapur of Odisha in 1967, and, sometime later, another from Srikakulam of Andhra Pradesh, which he edited and published in 1980. He had also collected six translations of the text in Telugu language. I feel honoured to dedicate the English version of the book edited by him as a homage to the great soul.

Contents

Foreword

Adikabi Sarala Das Chair of Odia Studies has started its activities at the Jawaharlal Nehru University (JNU) with the financial help of Govt. of Odisha from 25 December 2017 in Centre of Indian Languages (CIL), School of Language, Literature and Culture Studies (SLL&CS). The Chair intends to represent Odisha, its language, literature and culture, in all its multilingual and plural manifestations. The Chair encourages comparative studies across a wide range of domains and also aims at disseminating knowledge of Odia language, literature and culture both at National and International levels.

Odisha was the first Indian State to be formed on a Linguistic basis on 1 April 1936. Odia is the only Indo-European spoken Language in India to be accorded the status of a Classical Language in 2014. So, the Chair has taken translation projects with the objective of rendering into English the classical and non-classical Odia texts. Translating Odia Classical texts into English is a challenge and difficult affair. Prof. Basant Kumar Tripathy has accepted this challenge by translating, *Bichitra Ramayana* by Siddheswar Das, a classic.

Epic writing in Odia language started six hundred years ago, in the fifteenth century, the leading exponent being Siddheswar Das/Sarala Das, the author of *Bichitra Ramayana, Mahabharata* and *Sri Chandi Purana*. His works were a milestone in the history of Odia literature for reasons, more than one. The poet was a Shudra by caste, used the oral tongue and the popular rhyme scale known as *Dandi Brutta*. Though Valmiki's *Ramayana* and Vyasa's *Mahabharata* were the chief sources of his inspiration, he shunned Sanskritization and enriched his works with variations, deletions and additions so as to suit the local environment and mindset. The qualities of Siddheswar's *Bichitra Ramayana* are similar to a secondary epic. It begins in *medias res*, with a hero who is larger than life. The actions are fast-moving and there are elements of anthropomorphism, applied both to the gods and the goddesses. They behave as human beings and participate in human affairs most actively. Action on the earth runs parallel to the action in heaven. To retain the epic qualities, there is a cataloguing of names of kings while describing Dasharatha's family tree. There are epic similes too, though rare. It is surprising to note how Siddheswar, in the long past, was able to construct his epic with such discipline.

The popularity of *the Bichitra Ramayana* is evidenced by the fact that five translations of its palm-leaf manuscripts into Telugu language appeared in the eighteenth and nineteenth centuries, the first one being by the Telugu scholar, Donkad Gopinath. It had a ripple effect on the reading mass of Odisha as soon as it appeared in book form in 1980, edited and published by late Sacchidananda Mishra.

The two declarations Siddheswar makes in the *Bichitra* reveal that he was low born; he did not have either the required scholarship or purity of mind to write a holy text such as that, and second, he wrote it for the lay man. Simple in language, uncomplicated in structure and not adorned with literary ornaments it is easily communicable to the subalterns, who occupy the lower strata of the society. In that sense, it is common man's *Ramayana*. There is no voice of Valmiki's wisdom in it, but the voice of the crowd, not the voice of intellectualism and philosophy, but the voice of emotions and feelings. There is not an event which is unaccompanied by a public response. There is crowd everywhere, forming a sub-plot in the great epic.

Sita's sufferings and sacrifices are central to the text. From the time of her banishment to the forest to the end of her life she passes through insurmountable sufferings. When she is driven away from the human society, the animal kingdom, represented by the wild beasts, come to her help and take her to Valmiki's hermitage. Her obstetric experience is so tragic that it evokes pity in the minds of the readers. While in her father's house, she had to appear at another test by fire to prove her innocence. Denial of justice and unfounded question mark on her character bring an unfortunate end to her life.

Siddheswar's art of characterization is greatly influenced by his humanitarian outlook. Basistha and Valmiki, who belong to the spiritual world, are made to serve human purposes, thus uniting the spiritual world with the day-to-day life of man. Basistha is shown as Rama's conscience keeper throughout the play and the guide of his personal life. Valmiki acts like a mother to Sita, providing her with necessities when she gives birth to her children. Even the character of the milkmaid, who appears only for once in the text, is developed fully to give a true picture of the lives of low caste people in the society.

Though Siddheswar declares Valmiki's *Ramayana* as the source of his work, there is a marked difference between the two. The changes are brought about through additions, deletions and innovations. Kaushalya's long speech in which she launches a tirade of abuses at Rama is not found in any other text with the same subject. That the golden deer has two heads, or Sita going to the forest on foot, or the wild beasts coming to her help are not to be found in Valmiki's epic. Similarly, Sita giving birth to her babies in the forest and Valmiki preparing bed for her babies are new additions. These, however, should not be held as contradictions, but as an example of a creative mind at work.

Siddheswar presents the universe as a single entity, that the worlds of the gods, men, animals and plants are one. They communicate with one another and work for the betterment of the universe as a whole. The divine machinery plays a vital role in shaping the fate of man and the earth. Even the nether world finds a place in the universe where Rama was kept as a captive. What happens in one world, affects the other worlds as they are bound with each other.

Considering the literary merit of the text and its linguistic significance, the Chair of Odia Studies is pleased to select it as their first translation project, with the hope that it will act as a bridge between the classical Odia literature and the international world of literary thought.

Lastly I am thankful to Sri Ajay Kumar Jain of Manohar Publishers & Distributors, New Delhi for taking the onerous task of publishing this translation of the Classical text of Odia Literature jointly with Adikabi Sarala Das Chair of Odia Studies at CIL/SLL&CS, Jawaharlal Nehru University.

PROF. UDAYANATH SAHOO
Chair Professor
Adikabi Sarala Das Chair of Odia Studies
CIL/SLL&CS
JNU

Introduction

Kujantam Rama Rameti madhuram madhuraksharam;
Ahuya kabita sakham vande Valmiki kokilam.

[I bow to Valmiki, the cuckoo, who, sitting on the tree
Of poetry, melodiously sings the sweet syllables – Rama, Rama]

K. SUBRAMANIAM[1]

The increasing popularity of the *Ramayana*, composed by the celebrated Sanskrit poet, Valmiki, had such a ripple effect across the Indian subcontinent that it inspired many regional writers to retell it in their own mother tongue, breaking the mould of the *shastrik* identity of a text of the highest order and substituting it with an indigenous, secular distinctiveness. Towards the end of the sixteenth century the production of the vernacular avatars of the *Ramayana* had been unexpectedly very high. Failing to estimate their exact number, A.K. Ramanujan, in his essay 'Three Hundred Ramayanas',[2] asks,

[1] K. Subramaniam, *Ramayana*, Bharatiya Vidya Bhavan, Mumbai, 2003, 8th edn., p. VII.

[2] A.K. Ramanujan, 'Three Hundred Ramayanas: Five Examples and Three Thoughts on Translation', in Vinaya Dharwadker (ed.), *The Collected Essays of A.K. Ramanujan*, Oxford University Press, New Delhi, 1999, pp. 131-60.

'How many Ramayanas? Three hundred? Three thousand?' In fact, most of the languages had many versions of it; in Odia alone there are as many as thirty Ramayanas[3] in existence. Sage Tulsidas goes a bit forward to say '*Rama Katha Kai Miti jaga nahi*',[4] which implies 'It is not possible to keep count of Ramakathas in the world'. To tell the truth, this exercise of retelling the master text is not confined to the mainland only; it is also found in almost all Southeast Asian languages, such as Burmese, Cambodian, Thai, Javanese, Khotanese Laotian, Malay, Indonesian and Tagalog. In Thailand, it is known as *Ramakein*, in Indonesia *Serat Rama*, in Malaysia *Hikayat Seri Rama*, in Myanmar *Yama Pwe* and in Philippines *Maharadia Lawana*. These localized texts, far from being similar to each other, have distinctive features of their own and the degree of their departure and divergence from the source text varies. Some of them belong to *shruti* which abide by the master text and are allowed to provide it with new interpretations. The others belong to *smruti*, the authors of which are at liberty to administer additions, deletions, changes and innovations into it and give it the look of an original text.

There are three traditions of *Ramayana* writing in India: the *shastrik* tradition, the heterogenous Jain tradition, and the indigenous, folk tradition. The *shastrik* tradition is religious and brahmanical, denoting a social code of conduct and imparting spiritual teachings on the readers. Valmiki's *Ramayana*, *Adhyatma Ramayana*,[5] Tulsidas's *Ramacharitamanas*

[3] Mayadhar Manasingha, *A History of Odia Literature*, Sahitya Akademi, New Delhi, 2005, p. 11.

[4] *Ramcharitmanas*, Gita Press, Gorakhpur, 2013.

[5] The authorship of *Adhyatma Ramayana* in the Sanskrit tradition is yet to be fixed. However, that it was a hugely popular text in Odisha is evident from the number of texts that we find in the name of several authors such as Haladhar Das, Pandit Maheswar Acharya, Narahari Kabichandra

and Balaram Das's *Jagamohan Ramayana* (Odia) are some examples. The heterogenous tradition includes the Jain *Ramayanas* and Buddhist *Ramakathas*. It is conversion of a text written for one religion into another religion. The Jain *Ramayanas* describe Rama as one of the sixty-three salaka-purushas, who are divided into nine sets of Balabhadras, Narayanas and Prati Narayanas. Rama is the eighth Balabhadra, Lakshmana is Narayana and Ravana is Prati-Narayana. Lakshmana kills Ravana and both are conveyed to hell. In the end, Rama becomes a Jain monk and Sita, a Jain nun. There are many divergences from the source text which are necessary to cater to the demands of Jain religious beliefs. The third tradition is the indigenous and folk tradition which breaks itself from the delineations in the master text. It is neither holy nor didactic in nature. It has no religious paradigm; it is folk-oriented and secular. It embraces several variations in the story line and creates multiple story cycles on various characters of the text and adds folklore and legends into it.[6] Siddheswar Das's *Bichitra Ramayana* belongs to this category, but with a difference. In it, there is no conscious rejection of the classical, nor of the heterogenous. It contains all the three traditions, rolled into one.

In 1967, Sacchidananda Mishra (1930-2015) discovered a palm-leaf manuscript of the *Bichitra Ramayana*, written by Siddheswar Das, from Chhatrapur Odisha, and a similar manuscript from Srikakulam in Andhra Pradesh, which he edited and published in book form in 1980.[7] He could also find six translations of the manuscript into Telugu language.

(Gangaram Das), Gopala Telenga, Dewan Suryamani Chau Patnaik, Guru Damodar Das, Parikshit Das, and Sitacharan Das.

[6] W.L. Smith, *Ramayan Traditions in Eastern India*, Munshiram Manoharlal, Delhi, 1995, 2nd rev. edn.

[7] Sacchidananda Mishra (ed.), *Bichitra Ramayana*, Bhubaneswar, 1980.

In the absence of the history of Siddheswar's identity, multiple opinions on his times arose, many of which were unfounded. Artaballabha Mohanty placed him among the writers of the seventeenth century,[8] whereas Benimadhaba Padhi determined his era to be two hundred years after Sarala Das.[9] Placing great emphasis on *Bichitra*'s language, structure, rhyme pattern and grammatical distinctions Sacchidananda Mishra published a series of essays[10] to prove that Siddheswar and Sarala were one and the same. J.M. Mohanty, the compiler of the complete works of Sarala Das, *Sarala Rachana Samgrha* includes this text as one of Sarala's writings. Debendra Kumar Dash and Dipti R. Pattanaik, in one of their essays, 'The Case of Bhasa Literature',[11] write, 'Historians of Odia literature had for long believed that the *Bilanka Ramayana* by one Siddheswar Das was the one Sarala had referred to. But later critics have established that Sarala's first work was the *Bichitra Ramayana* and not the *Bilanka Ramayana*.'

Bichitra Ramayana is said to be the earliest composition by Sarala Das who was known as Siddheswar Das in his early life. The text has been translated into Telugu at least three times by three different people: Donkad Gopinath (first half of eighteenth century), Komnaku Somayya (nineteenth century) Kalepalli Venkat Narasingha Murthy (1864-1911). One comes across several other Telugu translations, mainly of the eighteenth and nineteenth century.

[8] Artaballabha Mohanty, *Journal of Rastrabhasa Rajata Jayanti*, p. 60.

[9] Benimadhaba Padhi, *Jhankar*, February 1971.

[10] Sacchidananda Mishra, *Dagara*, December 1969, November 1970, July 1971, November 1973 and December 1974.

[11] Debendra Kumar Dash and Dipti R. Pattanaik, 'A Local Habitation and a Name for Knowledge: The Case of Odia Bhasa Literature', 2019 (Manuscript).

The fifteenth century marked a turning point in the history of Odisha with the removal of the Ganga dynasty from power and the establishment of the Sun dynasty founded by King Kapilendra Deva (1435-67), who was followed by King Purusottama Deva (1467-97). For the first time Odisha came to be ruled by Odia kings, who enhanced the glory of the land by extending its territory to the Ganga in the north and the Godavari in the south. The rise of Odia nationalism was reflected in the literature of the period as the royal favour was shifted from Sanskrit to the native language, so far treated as *Vibhasa* or a dialect. The dominance of Sanskrit that had sealed the fate of the regional language for centuries was gone forever. Second, the right of authorship of the scripture was no more the monopoly of sages and brahmins; it was now free for all. It is on record that Kapilendra Deva had donated three *parganas* to Sarala Das in recognition of his literary excellence.[12]

The literary movement of this period was pioneered by Siddheswar Das/Sarala Das. Not much is known about Siddheswar except what he said about himself in two places in the *Bichitra Ramayana*. He speaks of his caste and his adherence to Vaishnavism:

(1) A sudra/By caste, I can't keep my mind steady/It is the blessing of Narayana that works/Behind the writing of the scripture. (Laba and Kusha agree to sing together)

(2) How can a feeble man, such as I am, /Fathom out the *Ramayana* which is as/Deep as the ocean? Can a man whose/mind is not steadfast, who is born/Into a sudra family, and whose habits/ And actions are unrefined, produce/such a scripture in its purest form? (Epilogue)

The retelling of the master text is conducted not by the

[12] Baishnab Charan Samal, *Odia Sahityara Itihas*, Friends Publishers, Cuttack, 1994.

author alone; it is done at various levels. Laba and Kusha retell it to Rama in Ayodhya and sage Markanda retells the whole story to the Pandavas in the last year of the twelve-year term of their self-exile. And all that is retold by Laba and Kusha and Markanda is reported by the author to his readers. The same technique is followed in the *Mahabharata*, Agasti retells the story to King Baibaswata Manu, and in *Chandi Purana*, the retelling is done by Sage Shuka for the benefit of King Parikshit.

In opposition to the common belief that the works of Siddheswar/Sarala were epics, the author himself claims them to be nothing more than scriptures. The poet calls his *Mahabharata* as *Mahabharata Purana* and *Ramayana* as *Ramayana Purana*. This shows that he does not altogether reject the *shastrik* value of the master texts, and yet he does not follow them blindly.

II

Notwithstanding Siddheswar's admission that his book is based on the 'Uttarakanda' of *Valmiki Ramayana*, there is a world of difference between the two. It is more a paradigmatic departure than thematic, character-based or situational departure. In Valmiki's *Ramayana,* Sita, after being left alone in the forest, is rescued by the women of Valmiki's hermitage where she gives birth to her babies under their care. Siddheswar mentions Valmiki has no women in his hermitage and the hermitage is a four-month journey from where she is left. In the *Bichitra Ramayana*, Sita is rescued by the wild beasts who lead her the way to Valmiki's place. Siddheswar unites the plant kingdom, the animal kingdom and human kingdom together that points to the Vedic theory[13] of 'Unity of Creation', which tells about the interdependence of all created beings and how everything is related to everything else. Second, Sita gives birth to Laba and Kusha under a tree in the forest, on her way to her father's kingdom. Third, Sita's second trial by fire at her father's house is a new addition. In disagreement with Valmiki's views, Siddheswar withdraws the concessions granted to Sita, such as Sita going to the forest in a chariot or leading her life comfortably during her forest days. In *Bichitra*, Sita goes to the forest on foot, in one set of clothes and her days in her father's house are beset with agony and anxiety. By making her life more difficult, the poet allows a free flow of the tragic sense, long stifled by superficial sympathies. The deer Rama had chased had two heads and Rama's birthday was not on the ninth day of Chaitra, but the eleventh day of Bhadraba.

A major difference between the master text and the *Bichitra Ramayana* lies in the tone and tenor. Valmiki's text is for the sophisticated reader, the literati to chew and digest; Siddheswar's is for the lay man to listen and enjoy. The voice of wisdom that resonates Valmiki's text is transcended to the voice of the common people, the rustics, who occupy the lowest strata of the society. Here, not only the narrator, but also the listeners express their emotion, loud and clear. During the recitation of the *Ramayana* in Ayodhya by Laba and Kusha, there are several interruptions in form of reactions not only by Rama, but also by the listeners, which contribute to the central theme of the text. There is crowd everywhere; they are free to pass their judgements on various situations. Here is a situation, when Sita is leaving for the forest with Lakshmana:

[13] *Atharva Veda*, Verse 19.

Men and women thronged to see them.
'What an irony!' they said to each other,
'It is unbelievable to see Janaka's daughter
Walking on the street like this. She is the one
Whom the sun has never seen. How come,
Like a common woman she is left to the street?'
(Sita's journey to the forest)

And while the *Ramayana* is being read out to Rama by his sons, this is how the people react:

Glory to you, O Kausalya's son!
As a child you killed the great demoness,
Your fame has no bounds.
But why did you diminish your fame,
By banishing Janaki to the forest?
(Ravana blessed with a boon)

This shows that an indigenous text meant for the folk is not only an affair of changing the language or twisting the episodes, but also allowing the folk to be an active participant in it.

The portrayal of women characters in the *Bichitra Ramayana* paves way for a feministic criticism that involves rethinking genre distinctions, humanizing female characters and analyzing patriarchal structures for their effect on relationship between the sexes. Siddheswar projects Sita as the central character instead of Rama who is seen buried in an existential gloom, performing a worrying number of funerals and when, finally, he goes to heaven, he faces the contempt of the gods there. His patriarchal mindset has been the cause of Sita's exile, leading to her intense suffering and humiliation. She represents the idea of 'Indian feminity', true, but contrary to other versions of the *Ramayana*, she no longer acts as a strong moral and socio-cultural rulebook. In the most crucial moments of her life, she does not hesitate to speak out her mind quite freely. A couple of examples will act enough to illustrate the articulation of her feelings, moments before she gives birth to her sons. On her way to her father's place, she slumps onto the ground, beset by severe labour pains. When Valmiki, who was leading her to Bideha, tells her that she is going to be a mother soon, she says:

But I don't know how to do it. Who'll
Hold me during my pains?' The sage
Advised her to hold onto the *siali* creeper
For support. She held the creeper tightly
With both of her hands, waiting for
The fateful moment.
(The birth of Laba and Kusha)

Moments later Laba and Kusha are born. Sage Valmiki collects soft leaves and makes the bed for the new born to sleep. He provides her with grass-blades and asks her to cut the umbilical cords of her sons. This done, he tells her to feed her sons with milk from her breast, to which she replies:

x x x But how can I? I don't
Have any. Having none to assist me,
You're doing the duties of my mother.
How can I go on if I am shy of telling you
What I feel?
(The birth of Laba and Kusha)

The rest of her life is spent in Janaka's house in Bideha. Here, too, her father raises questions on her innocence. Not only that, he wanted her to stand the test by fire so that he will save himself from public ridicule. Her second trial by fire is a new addition in the *Bichitra Ramayana*. Before entering the fire, she unburdens her soul in a rhetoric of protest:

O Fire!
x x x
Here is my humble submission:
A father protects his daughter in childhood
And a husband in her youth.
He may kill her or save her.
But have you ever seen a father deciding
The fate of his married daughter?
(Sita's trial by fire)

At last, when Rama meets her, she scolds her sons 'You've brought the devil to me' and without looking at his face, she invokes the earth to split. Without a word she sinks into the nether world, avenging the injustice inflicted on her by her husband.

Another female character, Kausalya, invites a feministic study for her vehement criticism of Rama, who, according to her, is a part of the patriarchal structure. His insensitivity towards her and Sita has been too unbearable for her to pardon him. The most passive Kaushalya in Valmiki's *Ramayana* challenges Rama's behaviour and his sense of judgement in Siddheswar's work. She launches a tirade of abuse at him, her son, that runs over thirty-three lines and is done at one breath. This is when Rama informs her of Sita's exit from the world forever. The following lines are excerpted from her long dialogue which shows her womanhood superceding to her motherhood:

I had persuaded you to take me
To Sita. But you didn't allow me to go.
As a result, you lost her forever.
I hate to see your face. You never
Obeyed my words.

x x x x

It was stupid of you to go after the deer.

x x x x

Seeing Sita alone in the hut,
Ravana kidnapped her. It is for you
She suffered.

x x x x

On your arrival in Ayodhya
You asked me, in the presence of others,
Why I have not yet consigned myself
To fire.

x x x x

Now I shall do it. Why should I care for
Your request? If you don't arrange
A pyre for me, you'll be held responsible
For my death. I will either jump into
A well or immolate myself.
(Mourning in Ayodhya)

Here Kaushalya, the Woman, is asking for her rights and hitting at Rama, the Man, in a language, as stern as it could be.

In the master text, Rama banishes Sita to the forest, acting on a rumour spread by a washerwoman. In the *Bichitra Ramayana* it is a milkmaid who is overheard by Rama speaking about Sita's scandalous character, and the washerwoman is the second to repeat it on another occasion. Though the milkmaid appears as a link character, she fights for the cause of women during a quarrel with her husband, who catches her redhanded while sleeping with her paramour. This is what she says in her defence:

Look at King Srirama
Whose fame spreads across the world.
The King of Lanka took away his wife
And kept for fourteen months.
Didn't Ravana make love to her, she being
So young and so beautiful?

x x x x

Did he [Rama] complain?
No, he kept it a secret.
(Sita in exile)

Thus, the women in the *Bichitra Ramayana* are fully sensitized; they are able to make out justice from injustice, are conscious of their rights and not mute followers of the whims of men. Basistha has rightly pointed out to Rama: 'Women don't/ change their minds so easily' (Mourning in Ayodhya).

Siddheswar's art of characterization reveals that he has added a new twist to each of the characters to make them appear more lively and more natural. The most affected character, in the process, is that of Valmiki who faces a reassessment of his position and status. Held as the greatest of all sages, he is made to do errands for Sita. Like a mother, he helps her in the process of her giving birth to babies, makes the bed for the babies to sleep on and serves her in every which way. His spiritual powers are pressed into service to relieve her of labour pains and to fill her breasts with milk to feed her babies. Siddheswar unites the spiritual world with the world of common men, which is a feather in his cap.

The importance of the role of divine machinery in the *Bichitra Ramayana* cannot be lost sight of. Actions on the earth run parallel to those in heaven. 'God's Will must prevail' is the explanation given to everything that happens in the world. The gods decide the fate of the earth and those who live in it. The tragedy that overtakes the lives of Rama and Sita brews out of the gods' plan to bring an end to the Tretaya Yuga. They wanted them to be defamed and separated from each other, no matter how much they suffer. Not only the gods, but also the goddesses play a deciding role in the affairs of men. When Rama is caught in the cobra snare set by Indrajita during the battle in Lanka, he invokes Goddess Durga to rescue him.

Saraswati inhabits the people of Ayodhya and motivates them to spread scandal against Sita; she induces Rama to forsake her, she is instrumental in sending Laba and Kusha to Ayodhya and it is she who propels Ravana to ask for a wrong boon.

Saraswati inhabits every soul.
Behind each word a man speaks, there is
The unseen hand of Saraswati.
(Laba and Kusha leave for Ayodhya)

Thus, to Siddheswar, the whole creation was a single entity in which the plant kingdom, the animal kingdom, the kingdoms of men and the gods are bound to each other with a golden chain, and that disturbance in one kingdom affects the whole creation.

III

From the end of the eleventh century until the third decade of the fifteenth century, the Ganga rulers of Odisha accepted Odia as the language of the people and Telugu as the language of the state. It was during those times that Odia language moved from the tradition of orality to literarization. The literary output was not much, but it laid the foundation for the emergence of Odia literature. When Kapilendra Deva became the King of Odisha replacing the Gangas, the political and literary domain of Odisha felt a wind of change. With the Mughal invaders occupying most parts of north India and Bengal, the importance of Sanskrit, 'the language of Gods', began to dwindle. Considering that it was the need of the time to bring about the unification of the Odias and to create a separate identity for them, Kapilendra held the cult of Jagannath as the state religion and developed a caste-based society in Odisha and used Odia language in rock-edicts and official matters. He himself authored a Sanskrit text, *Parasuram Vijaya*, with an Odia poem in it (Dash and Pattanaik 2019). It was during this period that Odisha experienced the rise and growth of nationalism and its language moved from 'literization to literarization' (Pollock 2007).[14] Dash and Pattanaik rightly point out:

> This kind of political atmosphere not only consolidated a language and caste-based Odia identity, it also precipitated the process of literarization of Odia culture. There was a proliferation of literary activity which resulted in the production of several texts of lyric poetry, imaginative Kavyas and Kavyas based both on tales from puranas and folk tales.[15]

Literary works of this period, such as the *Bichitra Ramayana*, the *Mahabharata* and the *Chandi Purana* justify the statement given above; they provide the evidence as to how the language of the people, a basic language in many ways, could so successfully contain and deal with the great themes of Indian mythology.

The *Bichitra Ramayana* was written in Dandi *brutta* (rhyme scale) that had existed in Sanskrit and Prakrit before being introduced into Odia poetry in the fifteenth century. It continued to be used as a popular form for writing the Puranas in the next two centuries. It contained rhyming couplets, with lines of equal length, and in which, the long and short vowels were articulated differently. In Odia, the number of letters varied from one line to another, and the vowels, long and

[14] Sheldon Pollock, *The Language of Gods in the World of Men*, Permanent Black, Delhi, 2007.

[15] Saji Mathew, 'From Regional to Pan-Indian: Towards a Heterographic Praxis for Postcolonial Translation', in Paul St-Pierre and Prafulla C. Kar (eds.), *In Translation*, Amsterdam, John Benjamins Publishing Company, 2007.

short, were articulated with the same breath. On the lexical side, the text contained plenty of words from Magadhi Prakrit. A short list of words may serve as an example:[16]

Sanskrit	*Prakrit*	*Bichitra*
Byanjana	Menjana	Menjana
Nirbana	Nirmana	Nirmana
Binati	Minati	Minati
Ramayana	Rabayana	Rabayena
Bhumi	Bhubi	Bhubi
Achamana	Achobana	Achobana

There are some names which are spelt and pronounced differently. For example, Maruchi for Maricha, Supernekhi for Subarnarekha, Naukesha for Nikasha, Kapilas for Kailash, etc. 'Palace' is substituted by 'house', and 'throne' by 'seat'. The word 'Mahatmani', used as feminine gender of Mahatma, is a new coinage by Siddheswar which is not found anywhere in Odia literature except the works of Sarala Das.

Bichitra is adorned with richly-coloured images; those related to the description of body parts were invariably and extensively used by the epic writers of the medieval age. In *Bichitra*, there is the description of the beauty of one woman only, that of Bedamati who was born from the vibration created by Brahma's reading of the Vedas, and who was later raped by Ravana while meditating on Vishnu on the north bank of the holy river, Bhagirathi. Here is a graphic picture of her beauty as narrated by the poet:

Her face was like the moon on the full moon
Day of Autumn, lips as red as jaba
And nose as sharp as Garuda's.
Curls of hair flopping over her forehead

[16] Harish Trivedi, 'Translating Culture vs. Cultural Translation', in Paul St-Pierre and Prafulla C. Kar (eds.), *In Translation*, Amsterdam, John Benjamins Publishing Company, 2007.

Looked like bumble-bees swarming around
Her lotus-face. She had long ears,
A waist as slender as the middle
Of the *dambaru*, hips soft and round,
Belly like lotus-leaf, thighs like banana
Trees and arms like lotus-stems.
Her body shone like *champak* flower;
Lotus bloomed as she walked. Her
Fingers were like *champak* buds, teeth
Like *jui* flowers, breasts like a pair
Of golden pots and voice seemed
As sweet as that of a male cuckoo.

There are similes, too, that picturize the emotional state of a character. The simile given below reflects Lakshmana's state of mind when he leaves Sita, without her knowledge, in the forest:

x x x Buried in intense gloom,
He moved on, tears dropping from his eyes
Like pearls tumbling down
From a snapped necklace.

Or Sita's mental condition when she meets Valmiki at his hermitage after the wild beasts leave her there :

Then, she stood up, tears falling from
Her eyes like the fruits made of pearl.

Or Rama's condition after Sita's exile:

Buried in gloom day and night,
His feelings he could not let on to anyone
It was like a tree being burnt
By the fire spreading from the hollow
Of its trunk.

Similes are also used to express a situation. When Laba and Kusha are reading out the *Ramayana* to Rama:

x x x The listeners,
Like flies in the oil, fell silent.

'I' am narrating the *Ramayana* which a lay man can follow' (Laba and Kusha agree to sing together), says the poet. Keeping that in mind, he modulates the language in its most simplified form with no stylistic artificiality and conscious attempt to dramatize, romanticize or beautify it.

IV

Explaining the bilingual characteristic of the postcolonial translation scene in India, Saji Mathew, in his article 'From Regional into Pan-Indian'[17] observes that translators of *bhasa* texts have the source languages as their first language while the metropolitan English-educated Indians look down upon the *bhasas*. Mathew thinks that's why there are few *bhasa* translations of English texts compared to the enormous production of English translations of *bhasa* texts. He says, 'It could therefore be argued that translation in India aspires for an "upward" flow, that is from *bhasas* into English.'

Translating an ancient text such as the *Bichitra Ramayana* poses many aesthetic challenges. One of it is that we need to keep the distances of space and time and we cannot isolate it from the traditions that surround it. Second, it is a text in which language acts as the vehicle of a specific culture which makes the process of translation more complicated. Harish Trivedi[18] rightly points out that 'It becomes a transaction not between two languages, . . . but rather a more complex negotiation between two cultures'. Dash and Pattanaik go a step forward to add, '. . . it is not merely an exploration of the

[17] Mathew, 'From Regional to Pan-Indian', op. cit.
[18] Trivedi, 'Translating Culture vs. Cultural Translation', op. cit.

process through which texts are transferred from one culture to another, but uses the study of translation as an indication of the history of ideas in a particular culture'.[19] This has added a new dimension to the theory of translation which Susan Bassnett and Andre Lefevere describe as 'The Cultural Turn in Translation Studies' in the title of a chapter in their book *Translation, History and Culture.*[20] Since translation is not simply a linguistic affair, the need arises to liberate it from the bondage of linguistic tools and skills and to reconstruct a method so as to enable a cultural translation.

There is a difference between translating the Sanskrit *Ramayana* and translating its vernacular version into English. The difference lies in their individual nature, culture and language. Valmiki's text is brahmanical or *shastrik* in nature; it is designed as a holy text for the Hindus. To the contrary, Siddheswar's *Bichitra Ramayana* is not religious, though scriptural and it is secular in nature. As for culture, India is not only a multilingual nation, it is multicultural too. Again, each region has its own culture. Therefore, while retelling, the author of the vernacular text has to convert the cultural content of the master text into the local culture. Third, Sanskrit in those times was a self-sufficient and fully developed language, exhibiting its excellence in all branches of knowledge, where as Odia was at the primary stage of literarization, without a dictionary and recorded grammatical rules. The language used in it was borrowed straight from the mouths of the people who were mostly illiterate. In this context, the opinion of

[19] Debendra K. Dash and Dipti R. Pattanaik, 'Translating Medieval Odisha', *Translation Today*, vol. 3, nos. 1 and 2, 2006.

[20] Susan Bassnett and Andre Lefevere, 'The Cultural Turn in Translation Studies', *Translation, History and Culture*, 1990.

Arshia Sattar[21] who has translated *Tales from Kathasaritsagara* (1994) and *Ramayana by Valmiki* (1996) into English is worth mentioning. Besides speaking on the relevance of *Ramayana* in modern times, she reflects on the strategies she adopted for translating it. She suggests to the translators of the bhasa *Ramayanas* to go through the original to take note of the points of difference between the two. 'Each *Ramayan* is different, with a different agenda, a different politics and responds to a different historical and cultural milieu.' One should remember that all translations of *the Ramayana* become a part of the larger *Ramayana* tradition. Second, she argues that a translator should show the text as it is. Even though he finds some portions of it not upto the mark, he cannot afford to ignore them.

In translating the *Bichitra Ramayana* that belongs to *bhasa* literature, I have avoided too many notes and commentaries, but I have provided it with a glossary which I think will serve as an aid to the understanding of the names of persons and places that are exclusively found in Indian mythology. I have used a contemporary idiom to make the reading easy and not to allow the readers to feel alienated by space and time. I have restructured many sentences and interpreted the meaning as reasonably as I can. In most cases, I found the words have an implied meaning and words themselves are misleading. For example, after the fall of Lanka, Rama asked Sita to take a test by fire. Even though she stood the test, Rama was unwilling to accept her as he still thought she was not faithful. Here, the author writes: (I'm giving a prose translation of the couplet for an easy understanding).

[21] Arshia Sattar, 'You Shouldn't Translate a Text that You have no Feeling For', e-mail interview, *Ravenshaw Journal of Literary and Cultural Studies*, vol. VII, 2017.

Rama was still unwilling to accept her, but
the advice of his father changed his mind and his anger was pacified.

Rama's father had died long ago, on the day he left Ayodhya for the forest with Lakshmana and Sita. How could his father advise him, then? Here, the real meaning hides behind the words, which is *Remembering how his father loved Sita* . . . I have carefully tried to reconcile the expression and its meaning since the exact equivalent of many words and expressions are not available. I feel the translator should not be worried about the non-availability of English equivalents as his job is not to produce another original text. Paul St Pierre, Professor of Linguistics and Translation, Montreal University, in his Introduction to *In Translation: Reflections, Refractions, Transformations*, says, '. . . a translation must show itself to be a translation and, in so doing, will never be strictly equivalent to the original text'.[22]

V

The historical significance of the *Bichitra Ramayana* by Siddheswar Das is that it is not only the earliest epic in Odia literature dating back to the fifteenth century, but also the first bhasa *Ramayana* in the whole of India. Its literary significance is that it is written in a language which was at the primary stage of literarization. Culturally, it witnesses a shift from the national to the local, from an urban environment to a rural domain. Linguistically, it replaces God's language and its stylistic fireworks with the voice of man with no clothing or ornaments on it. The text, no doubt, gives a new, independent identity to the story of *Ramayana*, but more than that, it creates

[22] 'Introduction', *In Translation*, Paul St-Pierre and Prafulla C. Kar (eds.), Amsterdam, John Benjamins Publishing Company, 2007.

a separate identity for Odisha and its people. The author performs the crucial role of a cultural go-between so beautifully that it renders the original text invisible. Discarding the sound pattern, word order, the resonances and allusiveness of the original, he adds a new set of resonances and allusiveness that a native reader can easily understand. He prefers the natural to the rational, what people believe to what really happens. The reading of the text sounds like the murmer of a sequestered stream. It is simple, direct and expressive with a ramrod exactness. At the same time it is rebellious, uncompromising and unadorned.

It is an armful of wild flowers.

BASANT KUMAR TRIPATHY

BICHITRA RAMAYANA

1

Invocation

Glory to you, O Bighnaraj,
The Benevolent One!
Those whom you bless, succeed in life.
Glory to you, O Bighnaraj,
Remover of all barriers,
Redeemer of all sins, Yogi of yogis
And the source of eternal bliss.
Glory to Skanda, your elder brother.
Glory to you, O Gajanana,
Face daubed with vermilion,
Who protects His devotees from
Yama's wrath and pardons all their wrongs.
Praise be to Lord Sashankasekhar.
Praise be to Lambodara, the Virtuous.
Glory to you, O God, the Saviour.
Glory to you, O God, Gracious ever.
By listening to the *Bichitra Ramayana*,
The tale of Sita's exile, the greatest sins
In one's life are vanquished.

Glory to you, O Lord Gananath.
Siddheswar Das, the author,
Bows at your lotus-feet.

2

Prologue

Thus begins the story of Bichitra:
Srirama, the king of Raghu dynasty, heard
People talking about Sita's immorality.
Incensed, he held a meeting of sages
Such as Basistha, Jabali and Sumanta,
And addressed them thus:
'O great sages! It is hard to preserve
My dignity as long as Sita is here.
No more can I bear the subjects making
Fun of me. I am filled with anger when
I see Sita. As a descendant of the sacred clan
Of Sun, I can't let myself become
A laughing stock. Surely I shall banish Sita
From here and put an end to the scandal
Once and for all.' Basistha replied,
'You're the king and the mightiest of all.
You're free to do as you desire. If you turn out
Sita from the palace, you lose the chance
Of seeing her again. Janaka's daughter

Is highly resolute; she will never deign
To see your face.' Saying so, the sage
Stood up and left the place. Retiring
To the palace, Dasaratha's son finished
The rituals of evening worship.
The *kodanda*-bearer, then, sat for dinner.
But he could hardly eat anything
As he was feeling a surge of unease.

'Listen, O Yudhisthira,[1]
What happened to Sita next.'

Glory to Srihari, the Garuda-rider!
Remember Him, O Noble ones!
He will assuage all your sorrows.
One who thinks of Basudeva day and night,
Finds a place in heaven, honoured as a yogi.
How to explain Him who has no beginning,
Nor end? He is the Lord of the Universe
And the holiest of all. Chant His name
And all your sins are redeemed.
O Noble ones! Those who listen to
The story of Basudeva's life are purged
Of their sins. To remember Him is itself
A virtue. Siddheswar Das worships at
His lotus-feet.

Pandu's son, then, begged
Markanda benignly, his hands folded,

[1]This suggests that the story of *Ramayana* is retold by Sage Markanda to the Pandavas.

'O the greatest of all sages!
As you are born from Vishnu,
Your vision encompasses the past,
The present and the future. Tell me,
How Srirama sent Sita to the forest.
Let my curiosity be satisfied.'

3

Sita's Journey to the Forest

Markanda replied, 'Listen, O King!
May you put your anxiety to rest.
He who listens to the story of Sita's exile
Suffers not from sorrows in all his births.
After a sleepless night, as soon as it became
Morning, Srirama sent for Lakshmana.
Soon Lakshmana presented himself
And bowed at Srirama's feet.
Looking at him, Sita's consort commanded,
'Take Sita away from here and leave her
In the thick forest. Keep her amused,
By clever means. Leave her in the forest,
And let her not get a wind of our intent.'
Lakshmana pleaded, 'O King! I am scared
Of Sita's anger. She is your better half
And the queen of the kingdom. She was born
From the sacrificial fire and is considered
The jewel in the crown of Raghu dynasty.
I don't understand why you ask her

To leave the palace, but I know, she will
Surely curse me for my misdemeanour.'
Srirama explained, 'It is she who wants
To go to the forest. You don't know what
She is like. She is a slut, having relations
With other men and venturing outdoors often.
Virtuous women are steadfastly loyal to their
Husbands. Sita, instead, wants to go away
From me and live in the forest. When
My father sent me into exile, she accompanied
Me as a loyal wife would do.
If she was that loyal, why did she oblige
The sage when he asked for alms?
She scolded you, that day, as harshly
As she could. Why did she, regardless
Of your advice, crossed the lines you had
Drawn? The truth is, she left with Ravana
Wilfully. Now she is restless to go
To the forest. I tell you all this in confidence,
So that you know her character. One night
I was in bed with her. Leaving her,
I went out and had a walk around the palace
With the *kodanda* in hand. I heard
A woman speaking about Sita's
Base behaviour, quite unbecoming
Of a faithful wife. I hurried back,
But could not sleep. Seeing me awake,
Janaki asked, 'Why is my husband looking
So sad? Enhancing the glory of your family,
Let me tell you that I have conceived.'
When I wanted to give her some gift,
She didn't ask for wealth, but my consent

To send her into the forest. Why should she
Be angry with you? She would rather
Be happy and consider it an opportunity.
Leave her in some impenetrable part
Of the forest from where she can't return.
Let the wild animals devour her.
That will bring an end to my worry.
Now, watch her reaction. That will tell you
Whether I speak the truth or not.'
So saying, he sent for Janaka's daughter
Who reached there instantly. Addressing her,
Srirama said, 'As you desire, I am sending you
To the forest now, escorted by Lakshmana.
Stay there and live on fruits in plenty.'
Hearing this, Sita's joy knew no bounds;
Her face beamed with a smile.
'Let me inform my mother-in-law,'
So saying she hurried to Kausalya.
She called out to Kaikeyee, Sumitra
And many other respectable women
And told them, 'All of you are my
Mothers-in-law. The forest fascinates me for
My long association with it. I now wish
To go there.' Kausalya responded,
'It is not proper for a three months pregnant
Young woman to go outdoors. Even you can't
Sleep peacefully there.' Kaikeyee interrupted,
'Oh, it seems you don't know anything.
Don't think everyone is like you. Pregnant
Women love to stay away from home
And take food cooked by others.'
Those words filled Sita with immense pleasure.

Kausalya told her, 'If at all you are going,
Come back from the forest soon.'
Joyfully, Sita prostrated at their feet.
Queen Sumitra held her hand and said,
'O Vaidehi! We hope to see you soon.'
Then, she went to Srirama and paid her
Respect by taking dust from his feet
And touching it to her forehead.
Srirama, burning with anger inside,
Did not respond. He told Lakshmana,
Standing by his side, 'Remember my words.
Don't think, O Soumitri, that she will have
Any problem there. Come back after you
Accomplish the task.' Sita could not
Make out what those words meant.
She was ready to leave with the only
Clothes she had on her. Too innocent
To read into what Srirama meant to say,
She was only thinking of taking shelter
In the abode of Goddess Saraswati.

The journey started. The *kodanda* in hand,
Lakshmana led the way, Sita following him.[1]
Men and women thronged to see them.
'What an irony!' They said to each other,
'It is unbelievable to see Janaka's daughter
Walking on the street like this. She is the one
Whom the sun has never seen. How come,
Like a common woman she is left to the street?'
Seeing a crowd following them, Lakshmana

[1] In Valmiki's *Ramayana* Sita went to the forest in a chariot. Here she goes on foot.

Shouted out, 'How dare you follow the queen?
Have you no fear for your lives? Go back
To your houses or else face the consequence.'
On being warned, they stopped where they were.
Instead of going back, they kept standing
In groups of ten or twenty all along the street,
Watching the pathetic sight. But who could
Help it? All of them were awe-struck;
They only wailed and wept.

It was a Thursday, the fifth day
Of the bright fortnight of Baisakha,
With *Punarbasu* as the ruling star.
The morning was far spent.
In spite of her three months pregnancy,
Sita managed to walk along. She felt tired
When they were about to enter the forest,
The wild animals observing them agape.
They came across a parade
Of huge elephants, a string of white horses,
Herds of deer and boars as big as
Elephants. They also saw rhinoceros,
Bisons, horned deer and lions.
They were amused to notice
Parrots and cuckoos at play on the backs
Of buffaloes. There were porcupines
And crickets too. Sita was amused to see
The animals and birds of the forest.
The peacocks' scream and the cooing
Of cuckoos thrilled her. The heat of the sun
Was not to be felt as a gentle breeze

Blew across the place. Sumitra's son
Now entered the forest.

xxxx

She hurried to keep pace with Lakshmana,
Her face looking pale with beads of sweat.
Finding her extremely tired, Lakshmana said,
'It was your own choice to come here.
Could you tell me, why? Your body is too
Delicate to undertake a long journey.
Now hurry up. Let's scout the place
For somewhere to rest.' Hearing this,
She moved faster. They stopped at a pond
On a mountain top in which Srirama's queen
Washed her face. She drank some water too
As she was parched with thirst. To Sumitra's son,
It was a painful sight. He mused,
'What a pity! Everyday the cowherds
Would bring one thousand loads of water
From Ganga with which young women would
Bathe you. One thousand women would anoint
You with *kumkum* and wash your body
With water carried in golden pitchers,
And wipe your body with silken clothes.
The one who used to wash her face
With scented water from gem-studded
Jars, is now drinking water by collecting
It with her own hands. What a strange
Quirk of fate! How can I live
In peace, abandoning her in the forest?

Again, if I stay with her and do not
Return, Rama will take it amiss.'
Coming back from faraway thoughts,
Lakshmana consoled her, 'Let's proceed
Until we find a suitable place,
Rich with fruits, where we can rest.'

Hearing this, she left the pond
And hobbled over, her feet aching severely.
The moon-faced Sita said to herself,
'Why did God create a desire in me
To come to the forest? I could not
Foresee the dangers involved in it.
I insisted on my husband to send me
Here. Who shall I blame when I am
Responsible for it? O curse on me!'
She cried out. 'Lakshmana!
Help me! I can't move further.'

She had scraped her feet along the rocky
Ground. Besides, her belly pained
Due to her pregnancy. Filled with sorrow,
Lakshmana sat down under a tree,
Tears flowing from his eyes.
Rama's queen, resting on her thighs,
Perched there. The ground under
The *bahada* tree was neat and clean;
Mild breeze blowing there kept
The searing heat of the sun away.
It was early afternoon; she was feeling
Weary and sleepy. She spread a part
Of the clothing she wore on the ground,

And, tucking her hands beneath
Her head as a pillow, fell asleep there.
Lakshmana said to himself,
'It is the right time I must get going.
Once she wakes up, my deep sympathy
For her may not allow me to leave.
If I don't go back, Rama will be enraged.
He will accuse me of consorting
With his wife. His mind is now full of fury;
It has no room for good sense to prevail.
On the other hand, I shall incur
Sita's displeasure when she doesn't find
Me on waking up. A servant's life is
Wretched; he lives by doing errands
For his master. Making the five basic
Elements of creation, namely, water, fire,
Wind, earth and sky as witnesses,
Lakshmana drew an arrow
From the quiver and wrote a letter on
A leaf with it: Believe me, O the Virtuous One!
You are deceived by your husband.
You had been in Ravana's kingdom
For fourteen months. A rumour broke out
That you are unchaste. Affronted by
The growing criticism of your behaviour
He banished you to this forest. Don't return
To Ayodhya ever; spend the rest of your
Life at your father's house. O Vaidehi!
Don't misunderstand me.' Hanging the letter
From a branch of the tree under which
Sita was asleep, he returned. His feet
Hesitated to move; drops of perspiration

Speckled his face. He was looking back
At Sita's face, which was like the moon
On the full moon day of Aswina.
He feared soon she would be devoured
By the wild beasts. Buried in intense gloom,
He moved on, tears dropping from his eyes
Like pearls tumbling down
From a snapped necklace.

x x x x

Listen, O Pandu's son,
To the events that followed. By the time
Lakshmana left, it was afternoon.
The sun-god decided to remain
Unmoved in the sky. He thought,
'She is Janaka's innocent daughter
And the pride of my clan. Srirama
Punished her for no fault of hers.
If Lakshmana succeeds in prevailing on
Rama, he would send him again
To take her back to the palace,
If I disappear, she will be left in the dark.'
With this in mind, he stayed where he was.

Leaving Sita behind, Lakshmana reached
Ayodhya and met the king of Raghu dynasty,
Who was sitting with his head bent low.
Seeing Lakshmana, he felt as if
His life has flown away from his body.
In bewilderment, he was tearing the ground
With his toe-nails as Lakshmana took
His seat, his head downcast.

Moments later he asked, 'O Lakshmana!
Where did you leave Sita?' Lakshmana replied,
'In the dense forest near Ekadhara mountain
Where there is a *bahada* tree on the banks
Of a pond. We went so deep that I can't say
What exactly that place is called.
Tired of the journey, she soon fell asleep
Under that tree. Then, I left her and returned.
What you did, you should not have done.
No woman in the three worlds can claim
To be as honest and as chaste as Janaka's
Daughter is. You were mocked at by the people
Of your kingdom. Now the whole
World will laugh at you for what you
Have done. How will the sages take it?
Janaka will be shocked to death
When he hears of it. Heedless
To everyone's advice, you forsook
Her, how could such evil thought
Harbour in your mind?' Hearing
Patiently to all that Lakshmana said,
He banged his forehead with his hand
And let out a wail. The noise brought
The mothers, Bharata and Shatrughna
To the scene. The women of the palace
Soon joined them, crying bitterly,
Beating their chests. Hearing from
Others what was going on, the minister
And the courtiers were filled with grief.
Basistha, Sumanta and other sages
Arrived there. Seeing Basistha,
Sriramachandra bent his head down,

Tears dropping from his eyes like the
Dew drops falling on a lotus-leaf.
Basistha went near him and caressing
His back, said softly, 'We tried our best
To convince you. What did Sita do
Which enraged you so much that you
Had to banish her? Now that Lakshmana
Has left her in the forest, there is no
Hope of getting her back. She must
Have been devoured by beasts by now.
It is of no use crying for her. Now do
As I say. Let's send messengers to
Other kingdoms to find a bride.
Marry the princess you consider the best.
All religious works done by a king
Having no wife are fruitless.'
Srirama replied, 'O sage!
After marrying Sita, I had taken
A vow in the night of our wedding
Not to love, even to touch anyone else.
She was devoted to me all along. Alas!
Where is she and where am I now!
In obedience to my father's command,
When I left for the forest, she joined me.
She lived with me in a hut,
Living on sweet potatoes.

Seeing a two-headed deer, she begged me
For it. Leaving her in Lakshmana's care,
I followed it with the *kodanda*
In hand. Seeing me following it,
It ran farther and farther from me.
When I realized it can't be caught,

I shot an arrow at it which cut
Its heads off. Just then, a voice was heard
'O Lakshmana! Save me!' When Sita
Heard it, she sent Lakshmana to help me.
After he left the hut, there appeared Ravana,
Disguised as an ascetic, who enticed Sita
With sweet words. Pleased, Sita crossed
Over the lines, drawn by Lakshmana
And offered him alms. The Ten-headed
Ravana abducted her and flew away
In his flying chariot. He confined her to
The Ashoka forest and engaged demonesses
To keep guard over her. While returning
I found Lakshmana on the way.
Both of us returned to our hut.
Not finding Janaka's daughter there,
We combed the forest in vain. Jatayu
Informed us of her kidnapping, before
It succumbed to injuries.
Consigning it to the funeral pyre,
We proceeded to Pimpa Sarobara where
We found Hanumanta. We found Sugriba,
Jambabana and Satabali on Rishimukha
Mountain. We made friends with Sugriba
And killed Bali by means of trickery.
After Bali's death, we collected the army
Of monkeys and, with their help,
Built a bridge to Lanka. There we killed
Ravana in war. I took a test of Sita's
Chastity by fire. She succeeded in the test
And I returned to Ayodhya with her.
I ascended the throne ceremonially.
When I heard people calling Sita a fallen

Woman, I lost my cool and banished her
To the forest.' Basistha, with consolatory
Words, said, 'O King! We will have many
Idols of Sita made and deck them with
Enough jewellery. You will take her
Opinion in matters that concern you.'
When Srirama consented to it,
Basistha thought, 'Kausalya's son
Did not hear my advice. Now let him
Recount Sita's virtues by watching the idols.'

He had twenty-five idols
Made of solid gold by none other than
Brahma and clothed them in silk clothes.
He placed one of them on the ivory bed
In Srirama's bed chamber. While staring
At it, Srirama broke down in grief.
He could neither eat nor sleep.
Buried in gloom day and night,
His feelings he could not let on to anyone.
It was like a tree being burnt
By the fire spreading from the hollow
Of its trunk. This way, three days passed.
On the fourth, Rama called Shatrughna
And told him, 'Dear brother! Proceed
To Madhubana now and rule
The subjects well there. This is why
I called you here. Sita is not with me now.'

Carrying out Srirama's command,
Shatrughna left for Madhubanapura.
Then, he sent Bharata to Subahu bana
To rule there. He kept only Lakshmana

With him. He made Hanumanta
The ruler of the Kadali bana. He thought,
'Had Hanumanta been in Ayodhya earlier,
The unfortunate situation such as
Sending Sita away would not have occurred.
The wishes of God, however, must prevail.'

'O Pandu's son!
Listen to the *Bichitra Ramayana*.'

Glory to Sridhara, Sriya's consort!
Happily I meditate on Him, whose
Abode is Anantapura. Those who are
Devoted to Him are liberated from
The bondage of the mundane world.
He is enemy to demons and merciful
To his devotees. prays at His feet Siddheswar Das

x x x x

Learning the story
Of Sita's exile, Draupadi
The daughter of the King of Panchala said,
'O great sage! You say Srirama is godly.
He abandoned Sita for no fault of hers,
How to say that men are just, when
The king of Raghu dynasty acted on
The saying of others? Janaka's daughter
Was young and pregnant. What was
Her fault? I am upset to find her
Thus betrayed. I am eager to hear
More about her.' To which Yudhisthira
Added, 'O sage! Tell me about Sita
Elaborately. I would like to hear

The *Ramayana* from your mouth.
That will make me feel blessed.'

Mukanda's son replied,
'O King Yudhisthira! O Noble ones!
Listen to the story of the *Ramayana*
Carefully. It will redeem all your sorrows.
You will be born in a noble family
In your next birth. You will have
The mercy of Lakshmi, the daughter of the Sea.
A woman who hears it will be awarded
With divine blessings and all her
Misfortunes will disappear.
O Draupadi! Now that you are listening to
The Ramayana, your next eighty-six
Generations will be saved from
The power of evil. You will have all
That you want, and those who think
Ill of you shall be punished.'
Draupadi replied, 'May your words
Come true. I wish to see the one hundred
Sons of the blind king perished.
May Gandhari Devi's brother die.
May the wicked be destroyed. That will
Restore my lost dignity. This is all
I pray for and nothing else.'
Markanda told her, 'Now listen!
By the time Lakshmana left Sita
In the forest, it was late afternoon.
There, in Ayodhya, Srirama had
Many idols of Sita made.

x x x x

Tired of travelling long,
Janaki was long asleep. Waking up,
She wiped her eyes and looked around.
Not finding Lakshmana anywhere,
She was surprised. 'Did he go to fetch water?'
She wondered. Then, she called aloud,
'O Lakshmana! Where did you go, leaving
A young woman alone? Have you gone
Deep inside the forest to collect sweet potatoes?
Come here immediately. I am scared.'
Receiving no response, she stared
In all directions anxiously. She said
To herself, 'If alive, he might have gone
After some woman, forgetting me.'
But the place is bleak and desolate;
Not a soul is to be found here.
O Lakshmana! Have you become a prey
To the wild animals? You are as handsome
As Madana. None of the kshatriyas
In the three worlds can match your valour.
Your face is like the full moon,
Eyes like *olaka* leaves, eyebrow like
A flower-bow and nose as sharp as
Garuda's. Your earrings shine bright,
Your lips look like ripe *bimba* fruit
And teeth like pieces of pearl that dazzle
Like Diamond, creating heavenly beauty.
You have lovely cheeks and beautiful
Curly hair that excite honeybees to move
Around it. Both of your arms look like
Lotus-stems without thorns, fingers like
Champak buds, the soles of your feet

Like red water-lilies, toes like *jai* buds
And thighs like inverted banana trees.
You look like a bow made of flowers.
O curse on me! It is for me you lost
Your life. Why did I sleep so long
That I could not know how you died?
How can a woman like me, so forlon,
Fight my way to Ayodhya through this
Impassable forest? If at all I get there,
Your mother will ask me about you.
Kaikeyee and Kausalya will be distraught.
My silence will provoke the ire
Of everyone. What shall I say to them?
How can I look at their faces?
How will my mothers-in-law take it?
Three of my sisters will be greatly shocked.
Urmila will be widowed.
How shall I face my innocent sister?
All will launch a tirade of abuse
At me. Better to die than bear
The shame. Where did you go,
O Sumitra's son? You're one of the
Greatest warriors, unbeaten in war.
For fourteen years, you stayed with
My husband, serving him to his utmost
Satisfaction. During the period of our
Forest life, you abstained from sex,
Food and sleep. You killed Indrajita,
One of the fiercest demons. O, how many
Demons did you not kill in the Lankan war!
'O Lakshmana! Where are you?
Need I continue with this despicable life?'

She sat down under the tree, her eyes
Full of tears and sweat pouring off her.
The moon-faced one, bewildered, stared
In all directions. When her eyes alighted
On the letter hanging from a branch
Of the tree, she picked it and found it
To be written by Lakshmana. Anxious,
She looked at the pearl-like handwriting.
She went through the letter, now convinced
That Lakshmana will never return.
She mused, 'He has abandoned me.
I must reap what I have sown. Luckless
As I am, why should I blame him
When my husband is cruel to me?
I shall face the consequence of my own
Doings. Lakshmana's only fault is,
He did not tell me the truth before he left.
But what could he have done when
He had to carry out my husband's orders?
I was unnecessarily worried about him,
The letter clearly says he played a trick
On me. If I am chaste and faithful
To my husband and respectful to my
Elders, may Lakshmana reach Ayodhya
Safe and sound. May his journey
Be safe. Let him narrate to Srirama
All that happened; that will pacify him.
What shall I do now? I don't know
How to escape from here. The sun
Goes down; it is getting dark. Soon
There will be darkness everywhere.'

4

The Support of the Wild Animals[1]

Beset with fear, Sita continued to sit there.
Soon there gathered the beasts of the forest,
Such as monkeys, lions, rhinoceros,
Bisons, deer, pigs, porcupines, boars,
Kokadana, wild dogs, tigers and buffaloes.
Seeing them, she trembled in horror;
Her pulse quickened. Beating her head
In despair, she thought, 'They will surely
Eat me up today. No one is there
To come to my rescue, nor can I run away
For fear of life.' She stayed seated
There, her head bent down.
The wild animals felt a sudden change
Of heart. No doubt, they had gathered
There to feed on her, but when they saw

[1]This is a new chapter added by the author in which he contradicts Valmiki's text that Sita was rescued by the women of the hermitage.

Her face, they were mesmerised.
Coming closer, they asked her,
'What brings you here, O young woman?
How could you venture into the forest
All alone? Or you lost your way,
O *Mahatmani*? Your face illumines
Like the autumn moon. Whose
Daughter are you? Whose wife?
How will your husband bear with
Your absence? Your appearance suggests
You must be the deity of the forest.
Have no fear. Tell us all about you.
We no more require to take your life.'
Sita replied, 'O forest-dwellers!
I am the daughter of Maharsi Janaka
And wife to Sriramachandra, the great
Kshatriya and the eldest son of Dasaratha,
The king of Raghu dynasty, who was
Known for his valour and piety.
I'm known as Sita in the three worlds.
We were living happily as king
And queen of Ayodhya. Hearing
The scandal spread by the subjects
Against me, my husband banished me
To the forest, without letting me know
About it. He sent me here with Lakshmana,
His younger brother. Tired of walking,
We took rest under this tree. As
I was feeling tired and drowsy,
I fell asleep, while Lakshmana sat beside
Me. When I awoke, he was not there.
At first, I guessed he might have been

A prey to the wild animals. But soon
I discovered the truth from his letter
Hanging from a branch of the tree,
Under which I was asleep. Then, I stopped
Worrying about him. He has left
The place without my knowledge. That stupid man
Has betrayed me. What is the point, then,
To cry for him? Now, in this night,
Where shall I go, when I am a stranger
To this place? If I go somewhere, oblivious
Of a woman's dignity, the world will
Look down upon me. O shame on me!
What is the use of this life? Now, come,
Anyone of you, and eat me up.'

Hearing her words, the beasts
Began to tremble like banana leaves
When the wind blew. They whispered
To each other, 'Know that she is Sita,
Srirama's wife and Janaka's daughter
She is the most respectable and the most
Virtuous of all women. The sight of her face
Liberated us from the bondage of beastly life.
Srirama has sent her here for
Our redemption. Let's serve her by putting
Her up in some hermitage.' All of them
Bowed to her and, with folded hands,
Said, 'Why do you speak such cruel words?
Have no fear. Stay here; we will keep guard
Day and night. We'll lead the way
To a hermitage.' Being assured, she gave up
Fear and spent the night sitting there.

5

Sita in Valmiki's Hermitage

As the sun rose,
Sita started her journey,
Flanked by the beasts of the forest.
Janaka's daughter had the graceful gait
Of a swan, covering two *kos* each day.
She could hardly walk more in the hot
Summer. While walking she had injuries
That left her feet bleeding. The summer
Ended and the rains came. In the rainy
Month of Sravana, she had to take
Shelter under the trees. This way,
The travel went on for four months
Until she reached Maharsi Valmiki's
Hermitage. When Valmiki recognised her,
She bowed down and held his feet
In respect. She took the dust from his feet
And touched it to her forehead.
Then, she stood up, tears falling from
Her eyes like fruits made of pearl.

To assuage her grief, the sage caressed
Her head and blessed her. Offering
His *kamandalu* to her, he said,
'O Janaka's daughter! Wash your face
With the water from it. Tell me,
What made you suffer thus. I am sorry
For you, you may stay here in this hut.
Be assured, I love you as my daughter
And more than what Janaka does.'
Hearing those words of consolation,
She held back her tears. She washed
Her feet, wiped it with the end of her saree
And entered the hut, her heart
Still filled with anxiety. She ate
The sweet potatoes the sage offered
To her. Addressing the wild animals,
The sage said, 'You may go back
To your respective places now.
For your service to Srirama's wife,
You're liberated from your sins.
Indra will rule, as usual, heaven
In all four Ages. You will be born
As human beings in your next birth,
And, by doing noble works, you will be
Conveyed to heaven.' Thus assured,
The beasts went back to the forest.
Then, he called Sita and asked, 'Tell me,
What brought you to the forest.
Why don't you have any companions?
You come here like a common woman,
In one set of clothes and with no ornaments
On you. I don't see any justification

To what you experienced, especially during
The period of your pregnancy.'
Sita replied, 'O sage! Words fail me
To express my distress. You are wise,
Omniscient and the Saviour of mankind.
My conscience says I have not done
Anything wrong. I don't know why
My husband sent me to the forest.
I implore you to tell me the cause.'
Sage Valmiki sat in meditation.
The whole universe flashed before his eyes.
He found Brahma working towards the end
Of the Age that was continuing. He could see
Srirama and Sita in Ayodhya enjoying
The blessings of Lakshmi and the goodwill
Of the subjects. To work out Brahma's plan,
The gods sent Saraswati to poison
Srirama's mind. As a result, the situation
Began to change. The subjects turned
Hostile to Sita, charging her of adultery.
The scandal infuriated Srirama who
Banished Sita from the palace and lost
His glory in the process.' The sage
Broke his meditation and told Sita,
'One who doesn't keep the promise
To pardon ten mistakes of one's wife,
Is deprived of Lakshmi's mercy.
Don't think yourself a stranger. Stay
Here as my daughter without worry.
Sita pleaded, 'I am seven months pregnant
And I don't feel well. You asked me
About my clothes. How could I ask for them

When I am leaving for the forest?
O what a fool I am! When he wanted to know
My wish I told him about my desire
To go to the forest, in all innocence,
Which suited to his plan to turn me out.
He called Lakshmana and sent me
With him forthwith. If a young woman
Had any such wish, would her husband
Be unkind as to push her out of the house?
Keeping all my clothes and ornaments
With him, he turned me out of the palace.
If I knew his mind, why would I have
Said so? It is my stupidity that brought about
My misfortunes. O sage! There are no women
Here to look after me.[1] Besides, you devote
All your time to *yogic* practices.
If I stay here, you'll be disturbed.
Better, send me to my father's house.
The beasts were to take me there.
I could have gone there on my own,
Only if I knew the way.
Please take me to my father's house.'
Valmiki assured her,
'Don't worry. Have some more rest here.
I shall take you there as soon as
You feel comfortable.' Satisfied,
She stayed there for ten days, thinking
Of Rama day and night, without sleep.

[1] In Valmiki's *Ramayana* the women of the hermitage looked after Sita.

6

Sita's Journey to Bideha

When ten days passed by,
Sita prayed to Valmiki benignly,
'Now let's go to my father's house,
You may come back leaving me there'
The sage got ready to go. He took with him
His *kamandalu*, staff, a knife and some
Holy ash. He wore a garland of *rudraksha*,
Another of wooden beads around
His neck, and a piece of tiger skin
Around his loin. He had copper rings
On his ears and matted hair on his head.

The journey started, the sage walking
Along the forest path and Janaka's daughter
Following him. The forest was thick and wild,
Huge *sal* trees spreading their branches
Overhead. After bath each morning,
The sage would purify Sita sprinkling
Some holy water on her. She had left Ayodhya

In only one piece of cloth, now torn due to
Frequent use. So she cut it into half
And used each piece alternately. Once
Their morning chores completed, their
Journey would begin. When she would not
Walk any further, inconvenienced by
The increased weight of her body,
They would rest for sometime, eating
Fruits to remove the pangs of hunger.

The Autumn passed and the winter set in.
Eighty days had passed in the meantime.
Of a total of sixty-seven *yojanas*, only
One *kos* now remained to complete
The journey to the kingdom of Janaka.
After a day's walk through the *sal* trees
Which seemed to touch the sky,
She sat down, exhausted. Maharshi
Valmiki stopped and looked back.

7

The Birth of Laba and Kusha[1]

Seeing that Sita was wincing in pain,
The sage rushed to her, and, putting
His *kamandalu* and staff aside,
Started fanning her with peacock feathers.
'Alas! What a strange twist of fate!'
He sighed. In labour pains, Sita cried out,
'Oh! It is all too much to take in.
What shall I do? The world seems dark
To me.' Valmiki consoled her, saying,
'Look, my daughter! Your father's kingdom
Is very near. Let's walk slowly. A few
More steps and we reach our destination.'
Collecting herself, she stood up,
But as she started to walk, she lost her
Balance and slumped onto the ground,
Unconscious. She came round when
Valmiki sprinkled some water on her face.
Unable to sit steady, she heaved and groaned.

[1] In the author's opinion, Laba and Kusha were born in the forest.

Chanting Rama's name, she cried out,
'O Lord! Why did you let me down
So badly, being provoked by a malicious
Rumour? How could a man of faith
And integrity, as you are, banish me
Into the forest? Having a mother-in-law,
So good and so affectionate, I was allowed
To suffer thus! Alas! Being your wife,
I am wandering in the forest now!'
Saying so, she wept bitterly and passed out
Now and then. Valmiki comforted her,
Saying, 'Listen, my dear! It's no time
To weep. One should not lose patience
In times of crisis; that's how one can
Avert one's sorrow. Who will hear you here
Even if you cry your eyes out?
Noble men survive their misfortunes
By keeping faith in God. Don't shed tears,
O Janaka's daughter, as you're going
To give birth to your child.' Sita replied,
'But I don't know how to do it. Who'll
Hold me during my pains?' The sage
Advised her to hold onto the *siali* creeper
For support. She held the creeper tightly
With both of her hands, waiting for
The fateful moment.

It was a Thursday, the fifth day
Of the bright fortnight of Baishakha.
The presiding star of the day was *Rohini*.
It was late in the morning, the most auspicious
Time when Sita gave birth to a baby.

The sight of the new-born, like
The rising sun, filled her heart with joy.
As the baby touched the ground with a cry,
She felt another bout of labour pains.
'Why so?' she asked the sage, 'Tell me
What to do. I feel like dying.'
The sage gave her two rings of holy grass,
Purified with *mantras* and asked her
To move them over her belly, assuring her
That it would relieve her of her pains.
He was the one who possessed the highest
Yogic skills and shared Brahma's
Creative power, the one to write the *Ramayana*
And pluck the *slokas of Sama Veda* from
Obscurity, through recitation and propagation.
As she touched the grass-rings to her belly,
Another baby was born. This baby had
The radiance of Indra, his face shining
Brighter than a hundred moons.
The beauty of the children delighted her.
To the sage, they looked like Hari and Hara.
They were the glory of the Raghu dynasty
And the kings of Ayodhya in future.
'In exchange of your intense suffering
In the forest', the sage told Sita, 'you have
Gifted Rama with his descendants.
Now it's time you cut their umbilical cords,
And feed them with the milk from
Your breast'. 'But how can I? I don't
Have any. Having none to assist me,
You are doing the duties of my mother.
How can I go on if I am shy of telling you

What I feel?' The sage took some water
From his *kamandalu* and, reciting
Some *mantras*, sprinkled it on her.
Now her breasts became full of milk,
With which she fed her babies, cradling
Them in her lap. Then Valmiki gave her
A sharp blade of *bena* grass to cut
The umbilical cords. When done, she bathed
Her babies with water from the *kamandalu*.
When Sita complained of shortage of clothes
To make bed for them, the sage regretted,
'My loin-cloth, a piece of tiger skin,
Can't be used as it is never washed.'
He, however, brought some young *sal* leaves,
And made them into a bed for the babies.
With a sigh, the sage told Sita,
'What a pity! Had you been in your
Father's house, you wouldn't have faced
Such difficulties. Don't grumble for
Your suffering; accept them as providential.'

Spreading out the end of her saree,
She went to sleep, folding her arm around
Her babies, her face downward.
She slept to the west of the tree while
The sage sat to the east.
The consort of Chhaya was blazing hot;
The sage sweltered in the sun
Striking at his back.

8

Sita at her Father's House

'Did you hear, O Draupadi,
Under what pitiable circumstance
Sita gave birth to a couple of sons?'
The queen of the Pandavas was saddened,
Her eyes awash with emotion.
With folded hands, she lamented,
'O Sage! What sufferings she had to endure!
Tell me, how she managed to arrive at her
Father's house and how Valmiki helped her.
That'll put my anxiety to rest.'

Addressing Draupadi and the five Pandavas,
Markanda replied, 'Now hear carefully,
All of you! By hearing it, all your wishes
Will be fulfilled. All your enemies will concede
Defeat in war'. Sita fell asleep after giving birth
To her babies, leaving Valmiki worrying about
How he would take Sita to her father's place,
Carrying two babies in his lap.

Besides, there was no way to inform
Janaka about all that had happened.
Meanwhile, he saw a *sabara* passing by.
On being asked his whereabouts,
The *sabara* replied respectfully, 'I'm
Surekha from Bidehapur where Janaka
Is the king. It is for his pleasure,
I come to the forest everyday to collect
Sweet potatoes.' Glad to hear this,
The sage told him, 'Now hurry to your king
And tell him that sage Valmiki wants
To see you immediately. While on his way
To your palace, he felt exhausted,
And, not able to move further, he is sitting
In the forest, waiting for you. The woman
You see sleeping here, is none other than
His daughter, but don't reveal it to him.
He is Rajarsi, enjoying the trust and respect
Of hundreds of sages. If he comes to know
That his daughter is lying here, it will be
Too much for him to bear.
I shall explain to him the situation
When he comes and, leave for his place
With Sita's sons.'

Surekha left the place in haste
And reached Janaka, the sweat pouring off
His body. 'Where had you been so long,
Surekha?' Janaka asked, 'Why do you
Look so flustered? Why do you sweat?
What about the sweet potatoes?'
Surekha replied, 'O King! I saw Valmiki

In the forest, perched under a *sal* tree.
He was coming here, but stopped midway
As he was too tired to walk. He sent me back
To tell you to meet him as soon as possible,
Leaving all your works aside. I came
Running all the way without bringing
Sweet potatoes. That's why I am breathless,
Let's move now.' Delighted, Janaka called
Fourteen of his most faithful disciples,
Such as Somakeshi, Rabidasi, Parisimuni, Sura,
Binayi, Subhanga, Soma, Chandra, Mangala,
Supriti, Suratha, Dinajaya, Dhanajaya
And Akhila. Janaka and his disciples started
Their journey into the forest, led by Surekha.
There, in the forest, Valmiki was in deep
Thought : When Janaka finds Sita sleeping
In a hut made up of twigs and leaves,
He will surely drop dead then and there.

Soon Janaka arrived there with his disciples,
All of whom paid their obeisance to Valmiki.
Expressing his gratitude, Janaka said,
'O Brahma's son! O the Omniscient!
A look at you makes me sinless.
Let's now proceed to my place.'
Setting his eyes on him, Valmiki said,
'You may feel bad if I tell you why
I called you here.' When Janaka asked
Him to go on without hesitation, the sage
Explained, 'Know that Srirama has banished
Sita, your daughter, who was left alone
In this forest by Lakshmana.

While wandering in the forest, led by
Wild beasts, looking for your house,
They reached my hermitage. Finding her
Pregnant and in need of help, I gave her
Shelter. Today we started for your house,
But, due to severe labour pains, she sat down
Under this tree and gave birth to two sons.'
Janaka was dumbstruck to hear this,
His eyes swam with tears
And throat was clogged with emotion.
Taking him by hand, Valmiki entered
The hut where Sita lay with her sons
On a bed of leaves. Unable to stand the sight,
Janaka slumped onto the ground, unconscious.
The sage splashed some water on his face
And brought him round. Those present
There raised a loud cry. Janaka was
Speechless, his eyes looking as red as
Red lilies and tears flowing from his eyes.

Disturbed by the noise,
Sita woke up. Seeing her father standing
Before her, she burst into tears.
The moon-faced one, her head bent low,
Cried out, 'Father! See with your own eyes
How your daughter is doing. Alas!
Being your daughter, I had to rot like this!
The kind of torture I experience does not
Happen in anyone's fate. How shall I tell
You how much I endured! For four months
I wandered through the forest with wild beasts
To find our house. It was my good luck

That sage Valmiki provided shelter for me.
Today, while we were on our way to your
House, I gave birth to two sons under
This tree. How shameless I am!
Why didn't I die?' So saying, she cried.
Seeing his daughter in tears, Janaka struck
His head in despair, saying, 'O God!
Why did you punish us thus? How can
I see my daughter's suffering
With my own eyes! May be, it is the result
Of my misdeeds in the previous birth.
My life is of no use after I see all this.
I married you into a noble clan,
To the most righteous and the greatest
Warrior of Raghu dynasty, who was
Dasaratha's son. He was the one who
Killed Tadaki and broke Shiva's bow
Effortlessly in my court. Greatly
Impressed by his valour, I married
Four of my daughters to the four brothers.
When Srirama has treated you this way,
I am worried about my other three daughters'
Wellbeing. What was your fault
For which he turned you out? Tell me
Frankly what you did; that will relieve
Me of my sorrow.' Valmiki interrupted,
'She is not in a condition to reply to your
Questions. She was delivered of the babies
In the most wretched situation, with
None to assist her. First, take her
To your palace and take care of her children.
Let her first see her mother;

Then ask her what you want.'
Janaka and Valmiki held one child each
In their arms and moved on, Sita and others
Following them. It was the time of sunset
When they reached home.

Seeing Sita, the women of Bidehapur
Gathered around her, stunned to see
Janaka's daughter, the wife of Dasaratha's
Son, Srirama, come walking on her own.
Some of them ran to Janaka's queen
And informed her that her daughter,
Was arriving there all alone.
Taken aback, Janaka's queen left her
Chamber, and, with three of her maids,
Reached the gates. Just then, sage Janaka
Was entering the palace with Sita
And her sons. Seeing Sita, her mother
Passed out. When she came round,
She wailed and wept. Valmiki consoled
Her, 'Why do you weep? Now Srirama's
Queen has come to your house.
Look after her and her children.
It is your responsibility to groom her
Children properly, so that they become
Persons of name and fame. If you weep,
Sita will break down with grief.
She has suffered enough.' Hearing the words
Of the sage, all stopped weeping.

9

Birth Rituals of Laba and Kusha

Sita's mother took the babies into her lap;
They looked as bright as the sun and the moon.
She raised a fire with sandalwood sticks
To keep them warm. It was a time
Of great rejoicing in Janaka's palace, women
Welcoming the babies with lamps
And ululation. The palace was decorated
All around with canopies and buntings,
While lamps of gem stone were lit inside.
Nurses and maids were busy looking after
The babies. Rituals started on the fifth day,
With the babies made to drink milk. On the
Sixth, the men and the women of the palace
Remained awake all night. In the night
Of the twentieth day Janaka told Valmiki,
'Let's lay the babies on the swing and give
A name to each of them.' Valmiki replied,
'They were born in pathetic circumstances.

Sita delivered the first one clasping a *lata*;
So, let's name him Laba. When she had
Labour pains for the second time, I gave her
Kusha-rings to move over her belly,
That's how the second one was born.
So, he should be named Kusha.' Satisfied,
Janaka set swings of silk, hanging
With ropes made of gem. The young women
Of the palace ululated cheerfully and strewed
Holy grass and turmeric-mixed rice
From a golden plate on the babies.
It was followed by holding of lamps
Before them to light their faces. The sages
Recited from the Vedas, Valmiki blessing
The new-born. The palace throbbed with
Joy and the noise thus created was as
Deafening as that of the sea. Indra,
The brahmacharis, Devarsis, Rajarsis,
Sages, chaste women, cows, all the gods –
The whole universe rejoiced at the news.
On Indra's instruction, Puspasena strewed
Flowers on the babies. Thus the celebration
Came to an end, everybody returning
To their homes gleefully.

The children grew up as days crawled by.
Sita spent her days merrily in their company.

10

Sita's Trial by Fire

Six months elapsed.
One day sage Janaka told Valmiki,
'I'm anxious to know why Srirama turned
My daughter out whom he had married.
How will the sages and the people
Of my kingdom take it? They will surely
Laugh at me.' 'Tell me, why it happened?
What brought about such a disaster?'
'Why don't you go and ask your daughter?'
Valmiki said. So, Janaka called Sita
And, with soothing words, told her,
'Oh dear! You are the eldest of my daughters.
I married you to Rama, the pride of the clan
Of Sun, who broke Shiva's bow, which was
A necessary condition for marriage.
My other three daughters were also married
To three of his brothers. When you suffer
Such humiliation as this, it worries me
How my other daughters are doing.

Why didn't you bring all your ornaments
When you knew bad times are ahead?
You came to the forest with just one set
Of clothes on you. Why was Rama so unkind
To you if you had no fault? Tell me
The truth, or else I can't live in peace.
You are the jewel among my daughters.
Tell me, what prompted Rama to forsake you.'

Sita replied, 'Listen, father!
On the eve of my husband's coronation,
Kaikeyee, Bharata's mother, persuaded
The king to take an oath of making Bharata
The king and sending Rama to the forest.
Shocked, but helpless, the king told Rama
To leave the kingdom and go into exile.
In obedience to his wishes, Rama left for
The forest, and Lakshmana, Sumitra's son,
Accompanied him with a desire to serve him.
I, too, joined them in spite of my mother-in-law's
Unwillingness. We, threesome, stayed
In the dense forest, sleeping under the trees
And living on sweet potatoes. While in
Dandakaranya, I saw a herd of deer,
And captivated by their charm, I begged
Rama for catching one of them for me.
Bow and arrows in his hands, Rama went out.
But the quicker he chased the deer, the faster
It ran. Seeing it slipping away, Rama
Shot at it and severed both of its heads.
In fact, it was not a deer, but Tadaki's son
In disguise. While its heads were falling off,

It gave out a frightening call, imitating
Srirama'a voice, 'Lakshmana! Help me!'
When I heard it, I sent Lakshmana to help him.
Once he left, there appeared Ravana,
In the guise of an ascetic, begging for alms.
As I came out of the hut with sweet potatoes
To offer him, he caught hold of me
And took me away in his chariot. On their
Return, both the brothers looked for me
In the hut, and, not finding me there,
They combed the forest in utmost despair.
They came across Jatayu who told them
All that had happened to me. Rama, then,
Made friends with Sugriba and killed Bali
Cunningly. Forming an army of monkeys,
He built a bridge on the sea with their help.
Crossing the bridge, he reached Lanka where
He killed the demons and the Ten-headed one.
He made Bibhisana the King of Lanka,
Who married Ravana's wife, Mandodari.
To test my chastity, he put me in fire
For seven days. When I came out unhurt,
All his doubts were put to rest. Riding
The Pushpak chariot we returned to Ayodhya,
Where Rama's coronation took place,
Followed by many religious rites. We went
To Kashi on a pilgrimage and, returning,
We settled in Ayodhya, spending our days
In peace and happiness. One day, hearing
From me that I was three months pregnant,
Rama asked my wish, which he promised
To grant. As if under the spell of an evil power,

I told him to send me to the forest. Soon
He called Lakshmana and sent me
To the forest with him. How can I know that
It was a trick to get rid of me?
Why should I carry more clothes or ornaments
While on a journey to the forest?
On reaching there, too tired, I fell asleep.
When I woke up, Lakshmana was not there.
I cried, presuming that he was killed by
Wild beasts. Disappointed, when I looked around,
My eyes alighted on a letter, written on a leaf,
Hanging from a branch of the tree,
Under which I had fallen asleep. It said
That I must not return to Ayodhya
And that I spend the rest of my life in my
Father's house. It was only then that
I came to know that I had been abandoned.
The whole night I stayed there, among
The wild animals who guarded me. It is they
Who led me to Valmiki's hermitage.
With the sage I was coming to your place,
When, on the way, I gave birth to my sons.
Father! I have no idea how my sisters are.
I haven't seen them for thirteen months.'

Hearing this,
Janaka was speechless and sweat broke out all over him.
Looking at her, he said, 'To be sure that
You're innocent, you've to take a test by fire.
It will silence the public who ridicule me,
And the sages who raise a finger of suspicion
At you.' To which Sita consented. Then,

The sage commanded his disciples to make
Arrangements. The disciples piled branches
Of sandalwood and *deodar* trees, poured ghee
On it and set it ablaze. Janaka's daughter
Took a bath and stepped towards the raging fire.
Seeing her mother, Somakanti, crying,
Sita told her, 'Why do you weep, mother?
I am cursed, born in an inauspicious moment,
All your troubles will come to an end
If I die. Don't be sad. Why will the fire
Destroy me if I have not done any wrong?
Let the men and women of the kingdom see
How Janaka places his daughter on
Trial by fire to test her character.'
So saying, she held a coconut in her hands
And thinking on Rama, she invoked the fire,
'Let the gods who rule the ten directions
Be my witnesses. O Fire! You know
My virtues and vices as nothing hides
From your view. If I have done any wrong,
Knowingly or unknowingly, destroy me.
You're the best judge of one's conduct.
You've saved me from my husband's wrath
Before. Here is my humble submission:
A father protects his daughter in childhood
And a husband in her youth.
He may kill her or save her.
But have you ever seen a father deciding
The fate of his married daughter?
I am unfortunate; I have done nothing
Good in my previous birth. That's why
I incurred the displeasure of my husband

And am forced to take shelter in my
Father's house. My father did not trust me
And he accused me of causing disgrace
To his clan. If I am unchaste, destroy me.'
Saying so, she entered the flames.
The women present there wailed,
'How do you leave your sons behind?
Who'll look after them? Why did sage Janaka
Do this? Why didn't Valmiki stop him?'
Men, women and sages stood mute
Witnesses to the pathetic scene taking place.
It was a Thursday, the tenth day
Of the bright fortnight of the month of Jyestha.
Pusya was the star ruling the day
And the time was a little before the noon.
After three days and three nights,
Janaka ordered his men to douse the fire
And check how Sita was. When the fire
Was put out, they found Sita quite fine,
Her body shining like molten gold.
Janaka and Valmiki were greatly pleased,
While the others greeted her with loud applause.
Going near her, Janaka called out,
'Come out of fire now. It is a matter
Of honour that you've proved your innocence.
Your fame will spread through the three worlds.'
Sita's mother and the sages' wives welcomed
Her with praises and led her into the palace.
There, she continued to live without fear
And embarrassment, enjoying the lovable
Company of her children.

'Did you hear, O Yudhisthira,
How Laba and Kusha were born?
One who listens to it, becomes free of sins.'

Glory to Madhusudana, Lakshmi's consort,
Who holds conch, wheel, mace and lotus
In His four hands. Dressed in yellow finery,
He wears a crown and earrings that shine
Like the full moon. His eyes look like
White lotus, pupils like bumblebees
Kissing the lotus. He has one hundred
Necklaces around His neck and garlands
Of lotus covering His chest. The appearance
Of Madhusudana is complete in all respects.
Thinking on Him, one's soul is liberated.
Siddheswar Das prays at His feet.

11

Early Education of Laba and Kusha

King Yudhisthira was happy
To hear the words of Markanda.
The Pandava brothers and Draupadi
Bowed at the feet of Mukunda's son,
Who blessed them, saying, 'May your wishes
Be fulfilled. May you overcome the obstacles
In your lives. May you come out victorious
In war.' Obliged, Yudhisthira said, 'O sage!
You told us the glorious tale of the *Ramayana*.
The sad story of Sita's life in the forest
Burnt me all over, as the fire in the hollow
Of a tree burns it. But when you narrated
Her stay in her father's house and her
Winning of the test of her innocence by fire,
I was cooled down. Tell me, what
Rama's queen did next.' Markanda, in reply,
Said, *Bichitra Ramayana* is the holiest
Of the holy. Those who listen to it with devotion,

Are conveyed to heaven. Now I am telling
You what happened thereafter.

Sita stayed in her father's house with her
Children. Whenever her eyes fell on them,
The thought of Rama flashed through her mind.
They looked the same as Rama, in nature
And appearance. She pined for Rama, musing,
'Why did you become so unkind to me? I know,
My absence for a day bears heavily on you.
You can never dote on any women except me.'
Too shy to let on her feelings to anyone,
She kept it to herself. When a year elapsed,
Valmiki told Janaka, 'Now let me take leave
Of you. Take care of the babies with all your
Heart. They're the future of the Raghu dynasty.
They're so nice and so good! Educate
Them properly when they grow up.'

Janaka replied, 'Why do you say all this?
You're the greatest of all teachers. Since
You're here, I wish to utilise your services
Fully. I feel sad when I see Sita; it is your
Presence that provides me some relief.
Don't leave my house, I beg of you. Remain
Here and chant Rama's name day and night.
See, how Sita's sons take after their father!
You're well-versed in all the *shastras*;
You can teach and guide those children properly.
Considering my devotion to you, kindly
Keep my request and stay in my palace.'

Listen, O Pandu's son!

Sita's sons grew up as time passed by.
When they were seven, Janaka told the sage,
'Now it's time the children learnt alphabets.'
In response, Valmiki selected a day,
Which was a Thursday in the bright fortnight
Of the month of Magha, *Rohini* being
The star of the day. After the worship
Of Lord Ganesh and Goddess Saraswati,
The lessons started. In the span of a year
The boys could master hundreds of *shastras*.
At eight, the sage taught them archery,
Sword fighting, wrestling and politics.
Whatever the sage told them for once, they
Remembered it forever. By the time
They were ten, they had become proficient
In all branches of knowledge.

One day Kusha told Laba, 'Brother!
Let's ask mother where our father is.
We know our mother; now we are anxious
To see our father. Being the elder brother,
This question seems not to bother you.'
They decided to ask their mother at night.
The night came; Sita led her sons to bed.
Instead of narrating to her all that
They studied during the day, as they
Want to do every night, Laba, with folded
Hands, asked, 'We know you're our mother,
But where is our father? We are anxious
To see him. Tell us, mother, where to find him.'
Hearing this, Sita felt like dying, her heart
Went cold and pulse quickened. Overcome

With grief, she began to wail. Moments later,
Holding back her tears, she replied,
'How shall I help you see your father
When I, myself, don't know whether he is
Dead or alive. He turned me out of the house
For no fault of mine. He abandoned me
At a time when you were in my womb.
Had he been alive why would have I suffered
In the forest? If he is alive, why am I put up
In my father's house? You belong to the clan
Of Sun; I am fortunate to have borne you
In me. How can you see your father
Unless it is written in your fate?'
Hearing this, her sons fell silent.
Laba told his brother, 'See, how our question
Hurt our mother. We won't talk about
Our father any more. Let's concentrate on
Our studies only.' So saying,
They fell asleep. When it became morning,
Sita woke up, chanting Rama's name.

O Pandu's son!
Laba and Kusha learnt the *Ramayana*,
From beginning to end, from the sage,
Getting each of its lines by heart. Thereafter
The sage instructed them, 'Now that you've
Mastered the study of music, go out
Singing from door to door and collect alms.
A portion of the alms we will offer to gods
And guests, the rest we keep for ourselves.'
The boys went to their mother and begged
For her permission. Learning from her sons

What the sage said, she exclaimed, 'Why
Did he ask you to beg from door to door?
How can you, at this tender age, carry out
His command without exhausting yourself?'
Her sons replied, 'If we don't obey his words,
The guru will be greatly displeased, and would
Stop teaching us further. He'll feel hurt
And embarrassed.' The mother, grief-stricken,
Told them, 'But how shall I stay here, sending
You away? How tiresome it will be for you
To beg for alms, singing from door to door!
If you don't want to displease your guru,
Do as I say. Go to the neighbourhood
Only and always remain together. I shall be
Waiting for you at the door and won't go inside,
Nor take food until you return. Fetch as much
Rice as possible. If Maharsi wants more rice,
I shall give you enough from the palace.'

The young women of the palace smeared
The boys with turmeric and put collyrium on
Their eyes. They took off their ornaments as
They had to travel through the forest.
In white clothes and an almanac tucked
Under their arm, they walked out with slow steps.
They went from door to door, enticing people
With their song. People, leaving their works aside,
Thronged to listen to the *Ramayana*, which was
As melodious as the voice of cuckoos in spring.
At the end of the day they returned
Home with the alms. Their mother would take
Them to Valmiki. Putting the rice before him,

They would bow at his feet. Happy to see the alms,
The sage would tell her, 'Your sons are brilliant.
They were born in an auspicious moment.
I shall offer a portion of the alms
To the gods, and the rest we'll cook for
Ourselves.' Then she would go back with her
Children, take a bath and have her meal.
She thought, if God be kind, she would have
The luck to hear the *Ramayana* from
Her sons one day.

12

Laba and Kusha Collect Alms Outside Bideha

Delighted to hear the story of Laba and Kusha,
Kunti's eldest son told Markanda,
'O sage! The recitation of the *Ramayana*
Makes us feel like imbibing nectar.
O son of Sudeva!
Please tell us more about them.'
Markanda replied, 'The *Bichitra Ramayana*,
A sublimely sacred text, is the one that
Sita's sons sing to others. The alms collected
Daily are offered to Valmiki. Recitation
Sessions also continued in the palace,
Attended by the king, the queen, all the inmates
Of the palace and the sages. After a year,
Valmiki told the boys, 'Look! You've been
Moving around this place all these days.
Let me tell you a secret. The people here,
To whom you've sung, have been sufficiently
Benefitted by it. Now it's time you went

To other places that lie beyond your kingdom
And enlighten the householders there with
The story of the *Ramayana* from beginning
To end.' Valmiki instructed them,
'I would like you to go to Hariharapur,
A place inhabited by vaisnavas, brahmins,
Learned men, kshatriyas, vaisyas
And traders. Accept gladly whatever
They offer towards your service.
For their generosity their wealth will
Increase one thousand times.'
The boys asked curiously, 'If you say,
Reading of the *Ramayana* promises
A golden future, why should we beg for
Alms, then?' With a smile, Valmiki replied,
'Those who offer money towards listening to
The *shastras*, do it for their own benefit.
God of the three worlds fulfil their wishes.
Srihari is the witness to the acts of charity;
He will increase their wealth three-fold'.
Taking leave of the guru, Laba and Kusha
Met their mother and told her, 'You had told
Us not to go far. Now the guru asks us
To go to far-off places.
But don't worry. Don't wait for us
If we are late. Take your meal on time.'
'How can I take food until you return?'
The mother sighed. 'Do as your guru says,
But try not to be late for return.'

In the morning, after breakfast,
An almanac tucked under their arm,

Laba and Kusha left home smilingly.
Sita walked a distance with them,
And, then, coming back, sat at the doorstep,
Praying to God for her sons' safe return.
On reaching Hariharapur, the boys went
From door to door, singing the *Ramayana*
And collecting alms. After returning home,
They offered to the sage the rice they had
Collected, which he gladly received.
This went on for six months.

13

The Gods Plan for the End of Tretaya Yuga

In a meeting held in heaven,
Brahma and all the gods spoke of
How Rama and Sita, after being separated
From each other, were in doldrums.
To eliminate Ravana, the most virtuous
Goddess of heaven had to descend to the earth
As Janaka's daughter, Sita. Rama was born
To Dasaratha after a *yajna* performed by Gyadhi.
By breaking Shiva's bow, Rama married
Sita and brought her to Ayodhya.
Jealous of Rama's proposed coronation,
Kaikyee, Rama's step mother, prevailed on
Dasaratha to make Bharata the king.
Rama had to leave for the forest with Sita.
While in Panchubati forest, Ravana took away
Sita with him by fraud and guile.
With the help of an army of monkeys, Rama
Built a bridge on the sea to Lanka.

Reaching there, he killed the demons
And the Ten-headed one. Before his return
To Ayodhya, Sita had to face a trial
By fire. Hearing the people of his kingdom
Talking of Sita's infidelity, he sent her
To the forest again. Once she was gone,
Basistha had many golden idols of Sita
Made and placed inside the palace.
The more Rama saw them, the sadder
He became. Pining for her day and night,
He gave up food and sleep. Staying
Seated at one place, his head downcast,
He felt like having an epileptic fit.
Sita's condition was no less worse;
Her husband's memory haunted her
Whenever she saw her children.

How to bring Rama and Sita together
Was the key issue that Brahma had to explain,
'If, ever, he chanced upon his sons,
He will come to know that Sita is alive.
That will induce him to go to Sita
To bring her back. Infuriated by Rama's
Presence, she will sink into the netherworld
And disappear forever. Finding Rama
Returning alone and hearing from
Him that Sita is now no more,
His mothers will scold him
Bitterly and immolate themselves.
For a year Rama will stay in Ayodhya
And perform the rites of their death
Anniversary. He will get his sons married

And make Laba the king of Ayodhya,
While Kusha will rule Madhubana.
All this done, he will go on a pilgrimage
With his brothers and friends.
This is the overall scheme of things,
I propose, to bring an end to the Age of *Tretaya*
And to usher in a new Age, *Dwapara*.'

When Brahma ended, all the gods said
In chorus, 'O Father! The sooner your plan
Is worked out, the better. Sita's suffering
Bears heavily on us. She has been living
Miserably in her father's house while
Rama has been going through hell since
Their separation.' Brahma, then, instructed
Saraswati, 'Go to Janaka's house and prevail on
Laba and Kusha to visit Ayodhya.
O Mother! See that they unite with Rama soon.'
Then, to the Wind he commanded, 'Carry Laba
And Kusha to Ayodhya as swiftly as you can.
They needn't have to travel
Eighty-four *yojanas* to reach there.'

Glory to Madhava, the Lord of Vaikuntha,
The one having no beginning nor end.
Remember Him while on journey;
He will remove all the obstacles on your way.
He is the Master of heaven, the earth
And the netherworld. I pray to Him
To keep me away from sin. O Madhava!
Keep my mind calm and steady.
I narrated the story of Laba and Kusha,

As told by Markanda to the Pandavas.
Those who hear the *Bichitra Ramayana* become
Immortal. Thus says Siddheswar Das,
Meditating on Madhava's feet.

14

Laba's Journey to Ayodhya

'Listen, O King! At Brahma's command,
Saraswati inhabited Laba and Kusha.
One day, while passing through the forest,
Both the brothers fell out with each other.
Kusha complained, 'O brother! You don't sing
In tune as I do. That's why the quantity of alms
Has dropped. Seeing that, the guru asked us
To go to distant places. Now let's separate
And work each other alone. Let's see
Who fetches more!' Laba replied,
'When mother comes to know of it,
She will be annoyed and will blame me.
It'll displease King Janaka, and if
Valmiki knows it, we'll surely get
The cane.' But Kusha was firm. He said,
'I'll never accompany you nor sing
With you.' So saying, he went eastwards.
Shocked, Laba thought: why cajole him,
When, being my younger brother,

He could be so harsh to me? I shall find
My own destination and return home
Early with alms. He stood there, thinking
For a moment, and took the path running
Southwards. The wind drifted him away
And landed him in Ayodhya, crossing
The hilly terrain of eight-four *yojanas*.
Spread over thirty-two *yojanas*, Ayodhya
Was a city with clusters of decorated
Gates, platforms, exquisite buildings,
The residences of royal employees,
Houses of merchants and hermitages
Of sages. The inhabitants of the land looked
Like divinities. The whole place resonated
With hymns to Gananath, Saraswati, Sun
And Narayana. Overwhelmed by the sight
Of the place, Laba, praying to Brahma's
Daughter, began singing the episodes from
The *Ramayana*, in which the birth of
Risyashrunga and the curse on an *apsara* were
Described. He went on narrating how
Lomapada, the king of Anga, was cursed by
A brahmin, how he made friends with Dasaratha
And took Dasaratha's daughter, Shanta
With him. It was followed by the story
Of how Parsurama's bow was broken.
Enchanted by Laba's rich melodious voice,
The people of Ayodhya soon gathered there,
Each asking the other, 'How could this little boy
Know so much about what had happened
Long ago? He seems not to belong to this place.
Whoever he may be, see how beautifully

He sings! It's no time to ask his whereabouts,
It's time only to relish what he sings about.'

Laba's rendition continued :
Seeing Parsurama arriving, all the kings
Fled in fear. It was Basistha who pacified
Him and sent him back to his hermitage.
The messengers who had gone in search of
Risyashrunga found him in the Bipul
Mountain. Being reported by them,
The king was worried about how to bring
Bibhandaka's son to his place. After some
Days Lomapada arrived at Dasaratha's palace,
And both the friends talked about the misfortune
That had befallen them. Lomapada grieved
To say, 'My kingdom has turned to a desert
As there has been no rain for years.'
Dasaratha said, 'See, how cursed we are!
Both of us have no children.
It's better we leave our kingdoms
Than to live unhappily here.' Moved by
Their conversation, Basistha told
Lomapada, 'O King! The words of the Vedas
And Puranas can never be wrong.
There will be rain in your kingdom once
Risyashrunga visits it. You can appease
Him by marrying him to Shanta. In return,
He will bless you and Dasaratha with sons.'
Pleased to hear it, Lomapada returned
To his place with Shanta.

Deeply moved by
Laba's rendition of the *Ramayana*,

The listeners[1] surrounding him forgot
Themselves. In frenzy, a woman stood
Holding the hands of her husband's
Elder brother. Unmindful of their children
And their duties at home, the women followed
Laba wherever he went. At last, he stopped
At Dasaratha's palace. It was the day
Of Dasaratha's death anniversary, King Rama
Performing the rites, assisted by Bharata.
Basistha, surrounded by many priests,
Was conducting it in the presence of
Courtiers and Kausalya Devi. A golden
Idol of Sita was placed next to Rama,
The sight of which filled him with sorrow.
Lakshmana was handing over
Each *puja* material to Rama after touching
Them to Sita's idol. All of a sudden,
Laba's voice reached Rama's ears which
Seemed to him like the voice of a cuckoo
In Spring. He asked Lakshmana, 'Who sings
At the Lion Gates? Ask him to wait there
Until we are free.' Going out, Lakshmana
Found a cloud-complexioned boy singing,
Surrounded by a huge crowd. His face
Looked like the autumn moon
And chest like a lion's, as if Kama,
Leaving heaven, had arrived there.
Looking at his face, Lakshmana told him,
'Wait here until we finish the rites

[1]Unlike Valmiki's *Ramayana*, here the listeners are active participants in the story.

Of our father. We would like to hear
Your song, then. Since we are observing
Our father's death anniversary now,
We are forbidden to salute anyone,
Visit temples, clean our teeth, take food,
Quarrel with others and listen to music.
If we don't obey these rules, our ancestors
Will be displeased.' Hearing his words,
Sita's son fell silent and sat down
There in lotus-posture. Returning to Rama,
Lakshmana told him that the singer was a boy
Of tender age with handsome features
And that he had been asked to wait.
Pleased, Rama finished the rites quickly
By giving away donations to the priests
And brahmins to their utmost satisfaction.

15

Rama Listens to the *Ramayana*

The king of Raghu dynasty stepped towards
The throne, the *kodanda* in his left hand
And a sharp arrow in the right.
Basistha was seated at the front
And courtiers such as Sumanta and Gunanidhi
Stood close by. Bharata and Lakashmana
Positioned themselves behind the throne,
Made of crystal and studded with gems,
That rested on posts of gold. Settling onto
The seat, Ramachandra ordered the boy
To be brought before him. At this,
Lakshmana went out and told Laba,
'O babu! Come inside. You must be the son
Of a worthy mother. The one, whom the three
Worlds admire, wishes to hear your song.'
Following him, Laba walked into the hall
Like a mighty lion and occupied a seat,
Not waiting for anyone's permission.

Greatly impressed by his gait and manners,
Basistha thought as if Madana had arrived
There. He sat in meditation and knew
That he was Srirama's eldest son,
The heir to the throne of Ayodhya. Deciding
To keep it a secret, he mused,
'If I tell him he is your son, instead of
Listening to the *Ramayana*, Kausalya's son
Will engage himself in revelries.
If so, how will his sins be redeemed?
He must know what Valmiki says
In the scripture, that is how he will make,
Atonement for the wrongs he has committed.'

Marvelling at the heavenly beauty of the boy,
Dasaratha's son wondered: How lovely
He looks! His face shines like the sun,
His ears like betel leaves, eye like lotus
With a bumblebee, nose straight and sharp,
Lips like newly-sprung buds, teeth like
Pearls, arms like lotus stems, fingers like
Champak buds, belly like that of a lion,
Navel deeply set and chest wide.
Glory to the father who has such a son!
Praise be to the mother who bore him in her!

Jolted out of his trance,
The Jewel of Raghu dynasty made him sit
Near him. He asked him fondly which
Scripture he used to sing. Laba replied,
'O Mahatma! It is the *Ramayana* which

My guru taught me. I was narrating
How Dasaratha's daughter took shelter
At Lomapada's palace.' Srirama said,
'I would like to listen to the whole text;
That will wash my sins away. Now, start
From the beginning.' Then, he turned to
Basistha and said, 'O sage! How fortunate
I am to listen to the *Ramayana*!'
Basistha cautioned him, 'You've to follow
Certain rules before you listen to any
Scripture. Get an earthen pot filled with
Water, put a coconut on it and decorate
It with a piece of cloth, gold, flowers
And sandalwood paste. Place it before you
And declare the name of your place,
The astrological details of the day and your
Lineage. Then, perform the ritual of ordination,
Hiring someone to read out the scripture.
Take vegetarian diet. Don't be distracted
By anything until the reading of the scripture
Is finished. Keep your mind calm
And steady while listening to it.'

At the king's order, things were arranged
Accordingly. Basistha smeared some
Sandalwood paste on Laba's head.
He put a mark of gold on his forehead
And a garland around his neck.
He placed the scripture on a piece of
Fine cloth and worshipped it by
Lighting a lamp, burning incense
And offering food.

Now it was time to start reading
The scripture. The courtiers, Bharata,
Lakshmana and others sat down calmly
To hear it. Laba thus began:

'Being cursed, Risyashrunga was born
To a doe. Enticed by the beauty of a tribal
Woman, sage Bibhandaka lost control
Over himself. Impelled by a strong
Sexual desire he ejaculated his semen
In the water nearby. A doe, mad with thirst,
Drank the water. It was the semen
Of a sage who did not have intercourse
For eight *yugas*. The doe became pregnant
And gave birth to Risyashrunga.'

Hearing the detailed account
Of Risyashrunga's birth, sage Basistha,
Srirama and all others were delighted.

16

Calamity in Lomapada's Kingdom

Lomapada, the king of Anga,
Had no issue, for which he was unhappy.
Every day he used to donate money,
Clothes and food to brahmins and vaisnavas.
One day when Jadu, a brahmin boy
Begged for a cow, the king mocked a him
With harsh words. This enraged
The whole brahmin community who
Cursed him, 'Let calamity befall your land.'
Since then, there had been no rain in Anga.
The subjects suffered severely
Which upset the king.

Then Laba read out how Lomapada
Made friends with Dasaratha,
The famous king of the clan of Sun.
Hearing from the messenger that Dasaratha
Had no sons, Lomapada sent his minister
To him as a gesture of friendship.

Srirama interrupted, 'Tell us, why
Dasaratha had no sons and how he was
Blessed with them later. I am eager
To know that.' Laba continued:

Dasaratha was the undisputed monarch
Of the seven islands, who had three queens
And twenty-one hundred young women
In the palace to attend him. Failing to show
Respect to Suravi, the cow-goddess
Of heaven, during his visit to heaven,
He was cursed by her: You'll have no sons.

Dasaratha held a *swayambara* for Shanta,
His only child. Parsurama, aggrieved for
Not being invited, suddenly appeared there.
Seeing him, all the kings fled away.
Parsurama accused Dasaratha of having
Forgotton good manners.

Seeing the sorry state of his kingdom,
Devastated by continuous drought,
Lomapada broke down with grief. Holding
Himself responsible for the loss of
So many lives, he thought of expiating his sin
By going on a pilgrimage. He left for
Ayodhya to consult Dasaratha,
His friend. Expressing his agony, he said,
'My kingdom is in ruins. I want to leave
It as I have failed in my duty.' Dasaratha
Told him, ' What shall I speak about myself?
I have no sons. My grown up daughter

Is sitting at home, unmarried. Noone
Is willing to marry her
For fear of Parsurama.'
Responding to their conversation,
Basistha, with consolatory words, said
To Lomapada, 'Do as I say; all your worries
Will come to an end. While going back,
Take Shanta with you and keep her in your
Palace. Bring Bibhandaka's son to your
Kingdom by any means. I say, it is bound
To happen. You and Dasaratha will be
Blessed with sons at the same time.'
Lomapada went back to his kingdom,
Accompanied by Shanta. He kept
Her in the palace, instructing the maids
To look after her. He kept on thinking
How to implement Basistha's advice.

17

Preparations to Fetch Risyashrunga

The king announced that whoever brings
Risyshrunga to his kingdom will get
Plenty of gold. But as no one came forward,
He was extremely worried.
One night, while moving around aimlessly,
He reached the hamlet where prostitutes lived.
There, he saw Jaratakosa, a prostitute
Of immense beauty, in conversation with
Ten or twenty of her friends. She was saying
Boastfully, 'The king is ignorant.
He doesn't know my skills. Why doesn't
He send me to fetch Bibhandaka's son?
His announcement will never work.
Just allow me to have a word with the sage,
And you'll see he readily agrees to come
With me.' Hearing this, king Lomapada
Took off his pearl necklace and hurled it
At the roof her house. Next morning,
He ordered his messenger, 'Rush to the hamlet

Of the prostitutes. Bring the woman
To me on whose roof you find my pearl
Necklace.' The messenger hurried
To the hamlet and found the necklace
On the roof of Jaratakosa. When she learnt
About the king's order, she shook in fear.
'For what fault of mine the king has summoned
Me?' She was asking herself. As she reached
The palace, the king welcomed her respectfully,
Offering her enough wealth. Bowing at
The king's feet, the young woman asked
Politely, 'What can I do for you, O King?
Does a fallen woman as I am deserve
So much respect?' The king replied,
'Last night I heard you say you can bring
Risyashrunga here. Tell me, can you
Do it? There will be no rain until he comes.
You'll do a great service to your land
If you keep your words. As a mother
Protects her children from all troubles,
You can save the subjects from the calamity.'
'O King!' Jarata said, 'What you heard
Is right. How can I lie to you? But I have
No idea of the whereabouts of the sage.'
Lomapada replied, 'Some brahmins
Of Ayodhya have recently found him out.
If you agree, I'll invite them to accompany
You.' Jarata consented, 'Well! I shall take
Their help to meet the sage. I'll try my best
To carry out your orders, even if I have
To face the anger of the sage.' Satisfied,
Lomapada sent a messenger to Dasaratha

With a letter requesting him to send
The brahmins. He wrote, 'There is a prostitute
Called Jarata in my kingdom who is willing
To approach Risyashrunga. They'll show
Her the way to where the sage lives.'
Dasaratha sent four brahmins whom
Lomapada welcomed most respectfully,
Offering them a lot of wealth. They told
Jarata, 'The journey to Bipul mountain
Is most hazardous as the route passes
Through hills and jungles. If you can
Persuade the king to dig a canal, ten
Yojanas long, to Krishnabeni, we can go
By boat and reach our destination
Easily. Journey by land is extremely difficult.
A delicate woman as you are,
You can't walk such a long distance.'

Jarata went to the king and told him,
'It is dangerous to walk through the forest,
Teeming with wild beasts. Could you
Dig a canal from here to Krishnabeni,
So that we can go by boat and reach the place
Without difficulty?' Pleased, Lomapada
Ordered his subjects to construct a canal
And connect it to a river. After three
Years of hard labour the canal to Krishnabeni
Was complete. Jarata arranged one hundred
Boats which she stuffed with things
Needed for use during the journey.
She also took with her one thousand
Young women as helping hands. The brahmins

And Jarata boarded a boat. The boatmen
Sailed northwards and anchored
At a ghat near Bipul forest. Leaving
The boat, Jarata and the brahmins
Proceeded towards the Bipul mountain.

Laba's soulful song
Filled Srirama's heart
With immense pleasure.

18

Risyashrunga Seduced by the Prostitutes

Looking at the boy, Srirama asked,
'How did the prostitutes seduce
Risyashrunga? How could the sage,
Unfamiliar to romantic feelings,
Be prevailed upon to accompany
The young women? Tell us, how could
That happen? We are anxious to hear
About Risyashrunga's journey to Anga.'
Laba resumed singing in *Basanta Baradi*
Raga, in a voice that seemed as sweet as
That of a cuckoo in spring. Silence
Prevailed over the whole place; people
Stopped talking between themselves,
Paying attention only to the recitation.
Laba began:

On reaching the Bipul mountain,
Jarata and her companions came across

Sage Bibhandaka's hermitage. A little farther
To the south, they built a tent with sarees.
They installed a *linga* made of sand inside
And worshipped it with great devotion.
Next morning, when Bibhandaka left for
Meditation, they burst into song so nicely
That it excited Risyashrunga's attention.
Leaving the hermitage, he walked down
To the tent and moved around it to see
What went on there. A sweet smell of flowers
And sandalwood, coming from inside the tent,
Excited his senses. While plucking flowers,
He could see a bevy of young women
Casting sidelong glances on him, which
Scared him. He returned to the hermitage,
Affected by an erotic stimulation.
Hit by Madana's arrows, he lost control
Over himself. He felt like floating
In the air. In his dream he saw the tent
Of sarees. Startled, he woke up, but it
Flashed through his mind again and again.
The smell of flowers drove him crazy.

When it became morning,
Bibhandaka left for his bath, as usual.
Seeing him gone, Jarata told her companions,
'Now that he came to our place on his own,
Why should we fear him any longer?'
They dressed themselves seductively
And went to him, singing sweet songs.
Seeing them, Bibhandaka's son asked,
'O Wise women! Where do you come from?

What brings you here?' The women replied,
'O sage! Hearing from others that
You're a man of great learning, we came
To see you, fighting our way through
Hills and forests. We reached here early
As we came by boat. We hope you will
Enlighten us with the spiritual knowledge
You possess, and we, in return, will tell
You what we've in store for you.'
Glad to hear it, Bibhandaka's son said,
'Since you're my guests, I'll feed you
With what I have.' He made them sit
On the deer-skin and fetched from inside
Some sweet potatoes, skinned *mung*
And *harida* fruits. He brought his *kamandalu*,
Filling it with spring water. He told them,
'Please eat these and be happy.'Jarata smiled
And said, 'We always aspire for the best.
We only eat those which are the tastiest.
Being a sage of such eminence, how do you
Live on this kind of food? Accepting food from
You will not be nice, if we don't give you
Some food in return. Well, it's between
You and us. Now you've to eat what we offer.'
Risyashrunga replied, 'Since I love you,
I'll accept what you offer. It's my
Good fortune to have you here.'
Filled with joy, they served him with
Cow-milk, cream, sugarcane, sweets,
Coconut and banana. They offered him
Water mixed with musk and camphor
To drink. They put a garland around

His neck, smeared his body with turmeric,
Dressed him in fine clothes, tucked flowers
To his hair, put a mark of musk on
His forehead and, then, showed him
A mirror to have a look at himself.
Seeing his own image in the mirror,
He was completely overwhelmed.
He asked Jarata, 'I wonder at your
Spiritual feats. Where did you get
This thing from? How do I see myself
In it? Tell me, what makes it possible.'

Jarata replied, 'It's very much available
In the place we live. If you wish,
You can have things more wonderful
Than this.' Risyshrunga, delighted, drank
Some of the milk. How could he go against
What God ordained him to do?
He had already submitted himself
To the wishes of the young women.
When it became sunset, they told him,
'Your father is one of the greatest sages.
He is jealous and violent in nature.
If he finds us here, he'll take it amiss.
Our presence may cause a conflict
Between you and him. Let's go back
Now. We'll see you again in the morning.'
Risyashrunga replied, 'Do come when
My father is away. I would like to share
All that you've learnt.' Thereafter,
Jarata and her companions left the place.

Bibhandaka returned when it became evening.
As he entered the hermitage, he caught
A whiff of perfume that took him by surprise.
'Where does the smell of perfume, which
The prostitutes use, come from?' he yelled
At his son. Risyashrunga replied,
'A group of holy men, old and wise,
Came here today who had smeared
Their bodies with sweet-smelling holy ash.
They had long matted hair with marks
Of sandalwood paste on their foreheads.
They offered me sweet potatoes that
Tasted like nectar.' Bibhandaka warned
Him, 'Listen, son! Demons disguised as
Holy men wander in the forest whose intent
Is to harm us. Indra, the King of the gods
Sends young women to seduce us, in order to
Destroy our spiritual powers.' This annoyed
Risyashrunga who retorted, 'Those
Holy men said that you are wicked.
What for you choose to live in the forest alone?
Why can't you tolerate when others are being
Praised?' Bibhandaka was taken aback.
The father and the son spent the night
Without speaking to each other.

It became morning. Soon after the sage
Left the hermitage, Jarata and her friends
Reached there. Seeing them, Risyashrunga
Said, 'My father was displeased with me
Last night when he found an aromatic smell
In the hermitage. I didn't reply, nor did I

Press his legs as I used to do every night.'
Putting their hands against their ears,
They said regretfully, 'Better we don't stay
Here too long. Your father is an angry man.
If he finds us here, he may take us for
Demonesses.' Saying so, they got out
Of the hermitage and walked towards the tent.
Seeing them leaving, Risyashrunga ran after
Them, saying, 'Why are you angry with me?
Why do you punish me for what
My father did? You must teach me
The *shastras* you've mastered. I'll follow
You wherever you go.' The women took
Him to their tent and made him sit on a bed,
Studded with gems. They washed his feet
And wiped it with the end of their sarees
Sitting close to him, Jarata caressed his body,
Which thrilled him. Intoxicated with
The passion of love, he forgot modesty
And held her in deep embrace. They made
Jokes at each other's expense and had
A lot of fun. When he began to sweat,
They washed his body with scented water.
Some of them fanned him and offered
Coconut juice and betel. Decking him
In ornaments, they made him stand
Before a mirror. Seeing his image in it,
His joy knew no bounds. He asked
Jarata, 'Where is your home? Take me
There and teach me *Ratishastra*.'
Jarata replied, 'We live in a sacred place
To the north of this mountain.' When

The young sage insisted on going with
Her, she said, 'Your father is full of fire.
When he would not find you in the hermitage,
He will be angry and destroy all of us.
Everyone is scared of him. Only if
You obtain his permission, then we will
Take you with us. Now go back
And persuade him to allow you to join us.
Remember, we are leaving next morning.
We have spent the whole month of Magha
Here, visiting places of spiritual importance.
He who visits the gods after bath in
Magha, the holiest of all months, leads
A happy family life with a devoted husband.'
Risyashrunga's heart began to palpitate;
He heaved deep sighs and proceeded
Towards the hermitage, though his legs
Were unwilling to move. Chanda's
Grandson was turning back and looking
At Jarata again and again. He was
Fully overcome by the power of lust.

The way Risyashrunga behaved
Made Srirama laugh. Basistha
And others were captivated by
The charm of Laba's narration.

19

Risyashrunga Arrives in Anga

Looking at Basistha, Srirama said,
'How come, never had I heard such things!
A child as he is, how nicely he narrates
All that! He must be a worthy son
Of worthy parents!' Basistha replied,
'He is the son of venerable man.
You may ask about his parents later.'
He, then, turned to Laba and asked,
'How did Risyashrunga persuade
Bibhandaka? We'll be obliged to hear
The episode in detail from your mouth.'
Laba started singing in *Bhopalapriya*
Raga that sounded like the song
Of a cuckoo in the spring time:

Leaving the women, Risyashrunga returned,
His face pale and his manliness obscured.
At nightfall, Bibhandaka came back
To the hermitage after meditation.

Surprised to find no one there, he looked
Around. Just then, Risyashrunga came in.
Seeing him, the great sage asked in anger,
'Where had you been so long? There are
No water and flowers in the hermitage.
Why did you put out the fire? Today
You haven't taken the cow out to graze;
Her calf is unfed. Why is your moon-like
Face looking so gloomy?' With a smile
On his face, Risyashrunga replied,
'Father! You spend all your time
In meditation only. Glory to those holy men
I saw today. What a hermitage they have!
It's as beautiful as a lotus-forest.
Father! I want to join them. I'll learn
Many things and visit many places.
Don't deny me this opportunity.'
Infuriated, the sage said, 'You were born
In an evil moment. Children born of
Human parents are obedient to their fathers.
Lured by the beauty of a tribal woman
I ejaculated; a doe who swallowed my semen
Gave birth to you. Why would you like
To stay in my hermitage? Because of
Your actions you will wander from one place
To another.' Shocked at his father's revelation
He wept bitterly and fell down. Bibhandaka,
Puzzled, raised him to his feet. To explore
The cause of his son's misdemeanour,
The sage sat in meditation. He came to know
That Lomapada, troubled by the absence
Of rain in his land, has sent prostitutes

To fetch his son. He told Risyashrunga,
'Those whom you call holy men and hold
In high esteem, are merely prostitutes.
One who falls in love with them loses one's
Son, wife, daughter-in-law, wealth and life.
You made love to the prostitutes
And accepted them as your mentors.
You preferred their company to mine
To satisfy your carnal desire. I warn you:
Stay away from those women
And don't quit the hermitage.'

Suddenly a voice from above was heard:
Why do you stop your son from going away?
Risyashrunga's presence is highly needed
In Lomapada's kingdom which has been
Suffering from aridity for years.
Risyashrunga's arrival there is the only
Way to bring rain. King Dasaratha of
The clan of Sun will be blessed with sons
If Risyashrunga performs a *yajna* for him.
As the result of the *yajna*, Rama,
The incarnation of Vishnu will be born.
It is he who will kill the Ten-headed demon
And bring relief to the earth.

Moved by the voice of Providence,
Bibhandaka, with soothing words, told
His son, 'You're free to go with
The young women. As you are going
To Lomapada's kingdom, leaving me, I expect
You'll fulfil the wishes of those who suffer.'

Next morning, after Bibhandaka went out,
Risyashrunga joined the prostitutes who,
Keeping the young sage in their middle,
Proceeded northwards. Reaching the ferry ghat
In two days, they boarded the boats which
Sailed at the speed of the wind. The sage sat
In his boat, lost in lustful thoughts,
Surrounded by some women singing and playing
Veena. As soon as they reached the banks
Of river Beni, the messenger deployed there,
Informed Lomapada, 'O King! Jarata has come
With Risyashrunga in her company.'
Delighted, the king proceeded to the river bank
On foot to greet the sage. He bowed at his
Feet most respectfully, when the sage asked
Jarata, 'Why does this Mahatma pay me
So much respect? What does he want from me?
Who is he?' Jarata replied, 'He is Lomapada,
The King of Anga, on whose orders, I went to
Your place to bring you here. I lured you
Guilefully and prevailed upon you to come
With me with your father's permission.
Please have mercy on him.' Satisfied,
He blessed the king, putting his hand on
His head. Lomapada took him to his palace
And offered him banana, sugarcane,
Sweets, coconut juice and betel with camphor.
The sage ate them and expressed
A look of satisfaction. After sometime
He felt his body hot, and, for relief,
Asked the king for some water. To which
The king replied, 'Mine is an arid kingdom.

For consecutively twelve years
There had been no rain here. I pray to you
To save my country from such misfortune.'

Moved by his words, the sage invoked Indra,
'O King of the gods! O consort of Sachi!
Send rain to the kingdom of Anga immediately.'
At this, Indra, the Thousand-eyed one, called
Rain and commanded, 'Sage Risyashrunga has
Already arrived in Lomapada's land.
Go and pour down there now.'
As he finished, the sky was swept
With clouds, with cracks of thunder
And flashes of lightning, followed by
Rain that continued throughout the night,
Until grass began to sprout. Seeing all this,
Lomapada's joy knew no bounds.
He gave away presents to the prostitutes
Who returned to their houses happily.
Risyashrunga continued to stay
In Lomapada's palace merrily.

Laba's musical presentation
Filled Rama with immense pleasure.

20

Laba's Return to Bideha

The scripture-reading continued
Till the afternoon when Lakshmana reminded
Rama, 'In any religious work you do,
Your duty towards your father comes first.
It's time we offered a meal of cooked rice
To the departed soul. Next we have to feed
Our relatives and friends. I suggest,
Give the reading session a rest now
And resume it after you take your meal.'
Finding Basistha consenting to it,
Srirama told Laba, 'Let's put it off
For sometime. We'll take our meals together
And start reading the *Ramayana* again.'
To which Laba replied, 'It's time for me
To leave. My mother will be waiting for me.
My brother and I left home for begging,
But, on the way, we fell out with each other.
When he left me and chose to beg separately,
I came here. If he returns home with alms

Before I do, the guru will punish me.
You're asking me to eat with you,
But I don't know your caste and clan.
Why should I waste my time here?
I've to hurry up.' Seeing Srirama annoyed,
Basistha said, 'Those who come from
Noble families stick to their principles,
Even in times of adversity. He comes from
An aristocratic family which you'll know
After the reading of the scripture is finished.
Now send him off with alms and attend
To your duties in hand.'

On Rama's instructions,
Sumitra's son brought rice, vegetables
And many other gifts which Rama packed
With his own hands and gave to Laba.
'Come tomorrow and read out the *Ramayana*
To me. It gives me the peace of mind.
I am unhappy as my wife is not with me.
Your pious words will relieve me of agony.'
Laba replied, 'I am bound to come as you've
Ordained me the scripture-reader. It'll be
A sin if I don't turn up.' So saying, he left.

After he was gone,
Sita's husband fed his friends and relatives.
Then, he took his meal and went to bed,
Recapitulating the episodes
Laba narrated that day.

21

Kusha's Delay in Return Makes Sita Angry

Listen, O Pandu's son,
The amazing story of Srirama.
Laba returned home, blown over by the wind
Over the terrain, at a speed that
He could not know when he reached
Janaka's house. Sita, sitting at the door, was
Anxiously waiting for her children's return.
Seeing Laba, she felt like a blind man
Getting back his eyesight or a poor man
Coming across a heap of gold. Getting up,
She kissed her son and asked about Kusha.
Laba told her, 'He insulted me and boasted
He could sing better than I did. He, too,
Claimed he would fetch more alms
If he sang separately. He refused
To accompany me and promised to prove
That he would collect more alms than I did.
I said to him that mother would scold me

When she knew of it, that Valmiki would be
Angry and Janaka would be displeased.
Paying no heed to my words, he left me
And went in another direction.'
Plunged into despair, Sita said, 'You took
Him with you when you left home.
Where did you leave my dear son?
How to find him now? You came back,
But he didn't.' Laba replied, 'Listen,
Mother! After he left me, I crossed
The forest and reached a place where
Everything was spectacular. I went on
Singing from door to door until I reached
The house of a kshatriya. That Mahatma
Was engaged in the rituals of his
Dead father. When my song reached
His ears, he asked me to wait until
The rituals were over. When it was finished,
He gave me a warm welcome and ordained
Me a priest for reading out the *Ramayana*,
Which I did. He invited me to eat
In his house. When I refused, he gave me
Rice and vegetables. Hoping that
Kusha must have returned home,
I came here in a hurry.' Sita broke down
With grief and said, 'Both of you used to go
Together. Which evil force tricked you
Into keeping yourself apart from him?
Why did you take your younger brother's
Words amiss? I was free from worry
To see you going together. Why did such
Evil thought come to your mind?'

She began to weep bitterly, which made
Laba also cry. With consolatory words,
He told her, 'Don't weep, mother! I'll follow
The path he took and get him back
To you.' Still not convinced, she cried out,
'I've lost one of my sons already.
How can I let you go again? As you're
Depressed, you're likely to lose your way
In the dense forest. Let both of us go
And look for him, even if we've to go
Far into the forest. If I don't find Kusha
Today, I'll immolate myself.' Both the mother
And the son started their journey. After
Walking some distance, Laba stopped where
His brother had parted with him. He said,
'Mother! Your son went eastwords from here.'
There stood a huge banyan tree under
Which Sita sat down, while Laba, climbing
To the top of the tree, called out to Kusha
At the top of his voice. Kusha's reply was heard
From a distance. Soon, he was found running
Towards the tree. Seeing his mother, he bowed
At her feet. She cradled her son in her arms,
Caressed his head and kissed him. She said,
'Why do you make me cry, O Kusha?
You were born when I was passing through
The worst period of my life. Why did you
Leave each other today? May all your
Misfortunes befall me. You were my only
Companions during my sorrowful days.
How many times I told you to remain together!
Driven by self pride and wickedness,

You ignored my advice and paid for it.
Your father has made me suffer a lot;
Now you are adding to what he did.
They say a widow's son is unruly.
O God! Why are you so unkind to me?'
Saying so, she held her sons and let out
A wail. Seeing their mother in tears,
Both the sons began to cry. Janaka's daughter
Took them in her arms with love.

22

Laba and Kusha Agree to Sing Together

Listen, O Pandu's son!
Not finding Sita in the palace,
Janaka called out to the maids
And asked them, 'Sita was sitting
At the door. Do anyone of you know
Where she has gone?
Where are Laba and Kusha?'
The maids replied, 'O sage! Both
Of her sons had gone for singing.
Only Laba returned and Kusha did not.
Not seeing Kusha, she, in a rage, scolded
Laba.Then, both the mother and the son went
Out to look for him.' Hearing this,
Janaka was worried. When he informed
Valmiki about it, the sage picked his stick
And went in search of Sita, followed by
Janaka, some other sages and their wives,
Maids and attendants. Reaching

The banyan tree in the forest, they found
Sita sitting under it with her sons.
Feeling happy, Janaka asked her,
'Why did you venture into this impassable
Forest? You could have ordered others
To do it.' Sita replied, 'Father! Small
And innocent as my children are,
They used to travel together everyday.
But today they left each other, each
Going in a different direction. Seeing
Laba returning alone, and not knowing
Where Kusha is, I was so upset that
I came here looking for him.'

Janaka took Kusha into his arms
And Valmiki held Laba by the wrist,
And all of them returned to the palace.
The maids fed Laba and Kusha with dainty
Dishes. Thereafter, Sita went for bath.
By the time she sat down to eat, it was
Midnight already. After she finished,
Janaka ate some sweet potatoes as his
Supper. After dinner, Sita washed her
Hands and sat on her bed with her sons
In her lap. All around there were lamps,
Studded with gems. Laba told Kusha,
'You left me and went away on your own.
But mother did not blame you, rather
She scolded me in anger. She usually
Took her meal after we returned
And were fed. Then, sage Janaka and others
Would eat. You quarrelled with me,

Saying that you would fetch more alms
Without me. Now let our mother see
With her own eyes who, between us,
Has brought more. Let Janaka and Valmiki
Also know it.' At this, Kusha fetched
His bundle and opened it. It contained
Three measures of rice of many kinds
Mixed together. With a smile,
Laba remarked, 'Your claims are proved
False. My rice looks as white as milk
Or jasmine flowers.' Kusha interrupted,
'It's a lie. Let mother see what you've
Brought.' When Laba opened his bundle,
They found in it twelve measures of rice,
Of the best quality. Kusha asked in surprise,
'Where did you get so much from? Did you
Break into someone's house and make
Off with all this? Who'll give you so much
For your song? It's unbelievable.'
Laba explained, 'After you left me,
I went southwards and reached a city
Where each house had a golden urn
On its top. The most prosperous house
There belonged to a pious kshatriya
Who made me pledge to read out
The scripture to him. That Mahatma gave
Me all this. I'll go to him tomorrow again
And recite the *Ramayana* in his house.'
Kusha, curiously, begged, 'We will go
Together. You'll show me the beautiful
City.' To which Laba agreed. The mother,
Happy to hear them, said,

'You're the sons of a destitute.
Never leave each other in the forest which is
Full of wild beasts who prey on the passer-by,
Finding him alone. Don't go for singing
Tomorrow. I'll arrange alms for you from
My father's house.' Laba objected, 'How can
You say that? The sage will not appreciate it.'
The mother replied, 'Well, if you go, be together.'
When they consented, the maids made the bed
And left. The boys fell fast asleep as
They were tired. But a surge of uneasiness
Seized her for which she had no sleep.

Glory to Narayana, Lakshmi's consort!
I bow at your feet. Indra, Yama, Agni,
Nairuta, Kubera and all sages worship
Him. His name is as sweet as nectar.
Chanting His name, all diseases are cured.
He is Brahman, the Redeemer of all souls.
Thinking on Him, I'm narrating the *Ramayana*
Which a layman can follow. A sudra
By caste, I'm not able to keep my mind steady.
It is the blessing of Narayana that works
Behind the writing of the scripture.
I take refuge at Narayana's feet.
Thus says Siddheswar Das.

23

Laba and Kusha Leave for Ayodhya

King Yudhisthira of the clan of Moon
Told Markanda, 'O sage! Listening to
The *Ramayana* from you makes me forget
All my sorrows. The amazing story of Laba
And Kusha relieved me of my worries.
You had stopped where Sita went to bed
With her sons. Tell me what happened next.'

Markanda said, 'Listen!
As the sun rose, Udayagiri simmered with
Light; bumblebees swarmed around lotuses;
Cocks crowed; crows cawed, brahmins
And sages went for bath. Sita woke her
Sons up. After they washed their faces with
Scented water, the maids came and smeared
Their bodies with *kumkum*. They adorned
Their foreheads with marks of musk
And sandalwood paste. They dressed

Them in fine silk clothes, combed and braided
Their hair and put collyrium on their eyes.
They put around their necks necklaces
Of wooden beads, pendants hanging from them.
Now their faces shone like the moon on
The fullmoon day. Taking them into her lap,
Sita advised them to come back early.
She mused, 'Kausalya's son has not yet seen
His sons. Nor my sons know who their
Father is. I'm too upset with him to declare
His name to my sons. What'll be their future
If they continue to live among the sages?
Their real place is in Ayodhya.
Had their father known it, would he have
Ever allowed them to be here? He even
Doesn't know that I'm still alive.
Lakshmana left me in the forest; I'm
Least bothered to know what he told
Rama when he returned home.'

Tears poured down from her eyes which
She wiped with the end of her saree.
Curious to know what happened to her,
Her sons asked, 'What makes you cry, mother?
We can't bear to see your sad face.
It makes us feel like dying. Tell us,
What pains you so much.' Sita replied,
'My son! Last night I told you
How miserable I felt to hear you keeping
Apart from each other. When I remembered
It now, tears came to my eyes. Laba!
Don't do it again. If Kusha doesn't obey

You, come and tell me. I'll break his bones.
If you don't do as I say, I'll inform
Your guru about it.' Frightened, Laba
Told her, 'Take care of your son, first.
He begins the row and then, forsakes me.'
Kusha said apologetically, 'I won't do
Anything of that sort again. I'll follow
My brother wherever he goes.' 'I won't
Believe you', the mother said, 'Unless
You swear, by touching my body.'
When he did so, she was relieved
Of anxiety. She fed them with milk, curd,
Sweets and banana, and, then, offered
Them betel to chew. She caressed
Laba's face and told him to go to nearby
Places and come back home early after
Singing. Before leaving, they bowed at
Their mother's feet; she kissed on their
Lips and bade them goodbye. As her sons
Left, a palm-leaf manuscript tucked
Under their arms, she kept watching them,
And they, too, turned back from time
To time to look at their mother. When they
Completely disappeared from her sight,
Then only she entered the palace.'

Hearing this, Drupada's daughter said,
'I don't understand why she sends her sons
Away from home for singing. She is
Forsaken by her husband. She ought to be
In the company of her children, the only
Source of her happiness. Instead, those

Innocent children are sent to the forest,
Which is fraught with danger. Why doesn't
Janaka stop them? O sage! Tell me, why don't
They do it?' Markanda replied, 'God's will
Must prevail. Saraswati inhabits every soul;
Behind each word a man speaks, there is
The unseen hand of Saraswati.'
Joy and sorrow are the products of a man's
Action, which is determined by the three
Eternal qualities: *Satwa*, *Raja* and *Tama*.
Rama will come to know about Sita only
When he is united with his sons. With them,
He will come to Janaka's palace
To bring Sita back. Seeing him, Sita will
Fly into a rage and sink into the netherworld.
This is God's scheme of things
Which none can alter.

Listen, O Panchali! O Pandavas!
May your enemies be wiped out.
Leaving Sita, Laba and Kusha walked through
The forest, when Laba said, 'Let's go
To some nearby place,' Kusha asked,
'Did you forget what you said yesterday?
You agreed to show me the place where
You read out the *Ramayana* to a kshatriya.
I'm anxious to see that Mahatma.'
Laba, then, turned southwards. The wind
Drifted them away and, in a short time,
Landed both of them in Ayodhya.
Enchanted by their uncommon beauty,
The women of Ayodhya entered their

Neighbours' houses and called out,
'O uncles! O aunts! O elders! O friends!
Come and see. The boy who was reading
The *Ramayana* yesterday has brought
Another boy with him. Both of them look
Alike. How lovely they look!'

Laba and Kusha walked along the street,
As a crowd gathered on both sides.
The old women with thin grey hair
And frail bodies flocked to the street
To have a look at them. Children,
Leaving their play, followed them.
A cloud of dust rose as the crowd moved,
Flanking the two boys. Some of them were
Asking them to stop for a while and sing
From the *Ramayana* to them. Laba replied,
'How can we stop here? I've given
A pledge that I'll sing at the kshatriya's
House. That's why I've brought my brother
With me.' 'Let's go to Srirama's house,
Then,' they said and followed the boys.
Some of them, while walking on the street,
Stumbled and fell down; nevertheless,
They could not take their eyes off them.

24

Singing by Laba and Kusha

Listen, O Pandu's son!
Next morning Rama bathed early,
And, after finishing the daily worship,
He sent for Basistha. He asked Sumanta
And the courtiers to remain with him.
Bharata and Lakshmana were there already.
The sages, the learned men and the vaisnavas
Had assembled in the hall. After
Everyone took their seats, the king
Of Raghu dynasty occupied the throne.
Turning to Basistha, Rama asked,
'O sage! Where is the boy who sang to us
Yesterday? As he has given a pledge,
I think, he'll arrive soon. It's not too late.'
Basistha replied, 'O King! I have no doubt
About it. He may arrive any moment
From now.' Seeing the king too
Impatient at the delay, Basistha told him,
'Only he who is well prepared can dare

Read out the *Ramayana*. He who reads
And those who listen to it, both find
A place for themselves in the abode
Of Vishnu.' Lakshmana, being asked
To see if the boy was coming,
Found Laba and another boy among
The men and women of Ayodhya.
Sumitra's son took Laba into arms,
Caressed him and kissed him.
Pointing at the other boy, he asked,
'Whose son have you brought with you?'
'He is my younger brother,' Laba replied.
Holding both of them by the arm,
Lakshmana went to Rama who was
Surprised to see both the boys looking
The same in appearance and age.

Both of them wore their hair in braids
And the dots of sandalwood on their foreheads
Shone as bright as stars. Their faces
Looked like the moon on the full moon day,
Eyes like the waves of the sea, noses like
Garuda's beak and teeth like small pieces
Of pearl. Their hanging ears touched
The shoulders; chests were fairly wide
And attractive and loins were like that of
A young lion. Their arms were extended
To their knees, fingers like *champak* buds,
Thighs like inverted plantain tree
And feet as soft and as lovely as leaves.
In age and appearance they looked alike.
Srirama, holding Laba by the hand,

Made him sit near him and asked,
'What is your relationship with this boy?
How is it that you look the same?'
Laba answered, 'We're twins. I'm
The elder one, but he is senior to me
In singing. I was ordained to read out
The scripture. To make thing easier
For me, I've brought him with me.'
Feeling happy, the *kodanda*-bearer
Praised his parents for having been
Blessed with such sons. He, then, asked
Kusha to take his seat. Before the reading
Could start, Laba and Kusha bowed
At Basistha's feet who blessed them,
Saying, 'May you be kings in future!
May your wishes be fulfilled!
May you do noble things in your life!
May you enjoy peace and happiness!
O sons! You respect me as I'm
A brahmin. It's desirable on your part
To show respect to your king who
Is the representative of Vishnu and who
Commands the respect of all.
Laba and Kusha went to the king
And, with folded hands, paid respect
To him. Rama blessed them and asked
Laba to start reading out the *Ramayana*.
He reminded him, 'Last day you stopped
At Risyashrunga's arrival in Lomapada's
Kingdom and Indra blessing the land
With showers of rain. Now, tell us
What Risyashrunga did next.'

25

Shanta's Marriage

As desired by Srirama,
Laba began singing in a low voice,
Which gradually rose as Kusha joined him.
The listeners heard it delightfully;
It appeared to them like the sweet notes
Of a cuckoo in autumn. All of them,
Like flies in the oil, fell silent.
If someone tried to speak something,
Another stopped his mouth with his hand.
Laba began with prayers to Durga, Ganesh,
Saraswati, Hari, Hara, Sun and the ten *dikpalas*.
Then, he read out the lines from
The *Bichitra Ramayana* for Kusha
To explain its meaning.

Risyashrunga stayed at Lomapada's
Palace, the king serving him with great devotion.
Time passed. One day the king called
His wives and Shanta. He told Shanta,

'Your father sent you here with a purpose.
I had to devise many a way to fetch
Risyashrunga to my kingdom. As soon as
He reached here, he blessed my land
With rain. Now go and meet him. Let's
Watch the effect of your meeting on
Bibhandaka's son. My queens will be with
You. Show him respect with all humility.'
The king's words made her happy.

Reaching the sage, the queens paid respect
To him and drew aside. Shanta, offering
Coconut and flowers at his feet,
Bowed to him with greatest respect.
The sage blessed the queens, 'May fortune
Smile on you!' Enamoured of Shanta's
Beauty, he felt a surge of passion in him.
He asked Lomapada, standing a little away,
'Which of your queens is her mother?
When Lomapada said she was the daughter
Of King Dasaratha, the sage remarked,
'No matter whether she is your daughter
Or someone else's, I wonder how such a
Grown up girl is still kept unmarried.
In spite of being chaste and modest,
She'll be subject to public ridicule.
A wise king as you're,
You must explain this to me.'
With folded hands, Lomapada replied,
'King Dasaratha is my friend. He has
No sons, nor do I have any. We consider
This girl our daughter, the only source

Of our happiness.' 'Which kingdom
And clan does he belong to?' The sage asked.
Lomapada said, 'He is the King of Ayodhya,
Belonging to clan of the Sun. He is as
Pious as he is mighty. As no king was
Found suitable, his daughter is still
Unmarried.' Convinced, the sage remarked,
'The clan of Sun is a sacred clan.
Well! I'll marry this girl. Send a messenger
To Dasaratha and bring him here.'

Lomapada ordered two of his courtiers,
Kausika and Bhagadatta, 'Carry my letter
To Ayodhya. Tell the king Risyashrunga
Has arrived and he wants to meet him.'
The courtiers left in haste, in a chariot
That took twenty days to reach Ayodhya.
They stopped at the Lion Gates. Soon
They were taken to the king, where
Basistha, Sumanta and his courtiers were
Present. Handing over the letter to the king,
They stood apart, their hands folded.
Sumanta read out the letter to others:
'Risyashrunga has arrived in Anga,
And, as he commanded, it started raining
There. He wishes to marry Shanta.
Come immediately, my friend! Consider
This to be the will of God.' Dasaratha
Looked at his courtiers when Bhagadatta
Said, 'The will of God must prevail.
Let's go now.' Finding the king in a dilemma,
Basistha told him, 'Now that Bibhandaka's

Son has arrived in Anga, be assured
That all your worries are over. Rush
To Anga this moment and prepare
For the marriage.' With a lot of gems,
Diamonds, bridal robes, horses
And elephants he set out in a chariot
For Anga. After ten days of journey
He reached there.

With great joy, Lomapada welcomed him,
He told him, 'Risyashrunga has brought
An end to all my sorrows. He brought
Rain to my land and relief to my people.
Now let's go and meet the great sage.'
Saying so, he held Dasaratha's hand
And led him the way to the sage.
When Dasaratha bowed to him,
The sage asked Lomapada, 'Who is this
Old man? Why has he come to me?'
Lomapada introduced him to the sage,
Who, with a smile, asked him to get up.
When he expressed his desire to marry
Shanta, Dasaratha said, 'You are asking for
My daughter's hand, to which I agree,
I'll also give you enough dowry.
Now let's know each other's lineage
And zodiac sign.' It was revealed
That Risyashrunga belongs to
Bhargava's family and his zodiac
Sign is Pisces and star *Rebati*
Santa comes from Ikshaku's family
And Taurus is her zodiac sign,

Star *Mrugasira*. On a Monday
In the dark fortnight of Baisakha,
When the star was *Sravana* and lagna
Makara, the marriage between
The sage and Shanta took place.
The brahmins recited *mantras* from
The Vedas, and Dasaratha, taking
Water in a conch, took a vow
Of offering his daughter to the sage.
As dowry, he gave Kanayakosa gem stones,
Silk clothes, a pot studded with nine
Gems, cows with gold-plated horns
And their calves. The couple looked
As charming as Kama and Rati.
Lomapada offered one hundred
Gold coins as dowry. Dasaratha said,
'By marrying my daughter to the sage,
All the sins of my forefathers are
Redeemed. I don't have sons. O sage!
My daughter has no one except you
On whom she can depend. Please
Pardon her for her mistakes.
If she does anything wrong, don't
Blame her; I take the blame on my
Shoulders. Please have mercy on her.'

x x x x

After the seventh generation of the kings
Of the clan of Sun, Sagara ascended
The throne, whose fame spread across
The land. Of his two wives, Sabya,

His eldest queen, gave birth to a mass
Of flesh, of the size of a gourd.
They put it in a pot of ghee, from
Which sixty thousand sons were born,
All handsome, smart and intelligent.
Baidharvi, his second wife had a son,
More handsome than Ananga. Formerly
Baidharvi's mother, Madanika was
An *apsara* who used to dance in Indra's
Court. Once while dancing, Indra found
Her tottering, which enraged him.
He cursed her, 'O proud *apsara*!
Go to the earth and let Bidyu,
The demon ravish you.' Falling at
Indra's feet, she asked benignly,
'How long shall I be the demon's wife?
When shall I come back to heaven?'
Indra replied, 'You'll come back
When you give birth to a daughter.'
Thus she came to the earth and Bidyu,
The demon forcibly took her away.
Bidyu killed Saranga bird, the grandson
Of Binata. Saranga's elder brother, Kanka,
Who was a witness to the murder, took
Revenge on Bidyu by killing him.
Thereafter, Madanika took shelter in
Kanka's house; she was two months
Pregnant by then. When a girl
Was born to her, the period of her curse
Ended and she flew back to heaven.
Kanka named her as Baidharvi
And he looked after her until she became

A grown up woman. One day, King Sagara,
While on hunting, saw her and took her
From Kanka. He made her his second queen.

Baidharvi gave birth to a son, whose
Cry was as terrible as a demon's.
When the King asked sage Bhargava about
It, he explained, 'Enchanted by her beauty
You married her. She was born to a demon
And brought up by a bird. Her child
Inherits the behaviour of a demon
And a bird. As he cries like a demon,
Name him as Aswaja.' The child was
As handsome as he was mighty.
At eight, Aswaja roamed across the city
And wherever he saw his half brothers,
He threw them into the well or tied their
Necks with ropes or thrashed them or tore
Their hair or hit them with a sword.
Greatly dissatisfied, the king sent him
Many mountains away with
One thousand wrestlers. He commanded
Them, 'See that he never comes back here.
Seize him by the arm always and don't
Let him break free from you.'
When he was twelve, Aswja asked
The wrestlers, 'Why do you hold my arm?'
They replied, 'It's the king's order.
We're instructed to hold you back
In case you try to escape.' With a jerk
Of his hands, Aswaja threw the wrestlers
Ten to twenty *yojanas* away. He told

The messenger, 'I'll not disobey
My father's order. One who does that
Goes to hell. A son, obedient to his
Father earns name and fame.'
The messenger went back to the king
And conveyed his son's message to him,
Filled with joy, Sagara sent a messenger
To King Harasasen, asking his daughter's
Hand for Aswaja. For fear of Sagara,
Harasasan married his daughter,
Harasamati, to Aswaja. The couple
Looked like the moon and the *Rohini* star
Placed side by side. As time passed by,
Harasamati gave birth to a son.
Hearing the news, the king brought
His grandson to the palace
And named him as Aswavanta.

One day a sage arrived at the palace.
When the king introduced Aswavanta
To him, he said, 'You're lucky to have
A grandson. Now it is time for you
To leave the palace and go on a pilgrimage.'
To which Sagara replied, 'I'll perform
A *yajna*, for which my sons have arranged
A white horse. I'll give away donations
To the brahmins; that will redeem my sins.'
The sage warned him, 'Why do you need
A *yajna*? Know that the virtues of holding
The *yajna* will go to your grandson.'
Paying no heed to the sage's words,
He made arrangements to start the *yajna*.

Aspiring to rise to the position of Brahma,
Sage Kapil was in deep meditation
At the eastern coast of the sea.
In order to foil his ambition, Narada
Took away the white horse and tethered
It behind the seat of the sage.
Not finding the horse where it was,
Sagara's sons searched for it everywhere.
They went on digging the earth, suspecting
It might be under the ground.
Narada stopped them, saying, 'Sage Kapil
Has stolen away the horse.' Informing
Their father about it, Sagara's sons
Went to the sage and found the horse
Near him. As the sage did not respond,
They let loose a stream of abuse at him,
Threw dust at him and pulled his beard.
In anger. As the sage opened his eyes.
The sixty thousand sons
Of Sagar a began to burn by fire.
Hearing the news from Narada,
Sagara was worried. Seeing
His grandfather in despair,
Aswavanta begged his permission
To go to Kapil and get back the horse
From him. Sagara told him,
'Well! You may go. Pray to him
To save my sons' lives. Let not people
Say that those belonging to the clan,
Of Sun misbehaved with a brahmin.'
Thereafter, Aswavanta set out for

The place where the sage
Was meditating. He bowed
At his feet, as humbly as he could,
And said, 'My uncles are not at fault.
To foil your attempt to become Brahma,
Narada has played a trick on you.
You're a great sage; you're omniscient.
How couldn't you know who was guilty?'
The sage sat in meditation and came
To know about Narada's mischief.
Looking at Aswavanta, he said,
'I appreciate your fearlessness. You're
A child of five. At this tender age,
You've the courage to come to me. It gives
Me great pleasure to grant you a boon.
Tell me your wish.' With folded
Hands, Aswavanta said, 'If you're
So kind, save my uncles from burning.'
The sage blessed him, saying, 'They'll
Be saved by your grandson who will
Bring Ganga to them.'

Aswavanta returned to the king
And told him all that happened.
Sagara ordained him the king
And left for the forest where he died
In sorrow. In course of time Aswavanta
Was blessed with a son, Dilip by name.
Dilip's son was Bhagiratha who brought
Ganga from heaven and rescued
Sagara's sons from fire. Bhagiratha's
Son was Raghu and Raghu's son was Aja.

Dasaratha told Risyashrunga,
'I'm Aja's son. Unfortunately
I don't have sons. My ancestors had
One son each, who continued the clan
So far. The girl you married is my
Only daughter.' The sage consoled him,
'Don't worry. I'll perform a *yajna* to give
You a son.' Dasaratha felt joy like
A blind man getting back eyesight
Or a poor man possessing a lot of wealth.

The rituals of marriage came to an end.
Risyashrunga and Shanta spent
The night of their wedding joyfully.
When their thirst was satisfied,
They became calm and quiet.

x x x x

When it became morning,
Dasaratha met Risyashrunga and told him,
'O young sage! I've given you, as dowry,
A golden water-pot, one lakh cows,
Silk clothes, finery and many other
Valuable goods. What'll you do with
All these? No other sage is as great as
You're. May I tell you that it is not proper
To leave the gifts unused.' Risyashrunga
Replied, 'Listen, O King! Send the cows
To my father who must be anxiously
Waiting for my return. I've left him
Alone. Seeing the cows he'll be relieved
Of agony.' In obedience to his words,

Dasaratha called the cowherds, and offering
Them many gifts, commanded, 'Take
These cows to the Bipul mountain
And hand them over to Bibhandaka.'
The cowherds loaded the boats with
The wealth and riches, cows and calves
And sailed along until they reached
The Uttaranga ghat. Leaving the boats,
With the cows and the calves, they entered
The Bipul mountain. Leaving the cows
To graze on the grassy surface,
They collected many kinds of fruits
And ate them. They drank the water
They found on the mountain. Then, they sat
Under the trees and began playing their
Flutes with melodious notes. The sound
Of the flute reached the ears of Bibhandaka
Who was relaxing in his hermitage.
Chanda's son wondered: where the sound
Comes from? In anger, he came out
Of his hermitage and found the cowherds
Singing and dancing and a herd of cows
Grazing near them. Infuriated, he ran
Towards the cowherds, brandishing
His trident, and shouting, 'Why do you
Disturb the peace of the forest?' He tried
To beat them, but the cowherds saved
Themselves with the help of their sticks.
One of them held him by the neck
And pushed him back. On second attempt,
The sage stumbled and fell down.
The cowherds said, 'O sage! Have you

Taken leave of your senses?
Why do you beat us unnecessarily?
As a great sage, you're not attached
To anything. Why do you create trouble,
Not realising the consequence? Why
Did you beat us? Have you no fear?
Do you think we'll let you get away?'
Saying so, they burst into laughter
And clapped. The way he was treated
Filled the sage with anger. Generally
Brahmins are ill-tempered by nature.
Bibhandaka asked them, 'Whose cows
Are these? Why did you bring them
Here and damage my forest?
In addition, you've beaten me up.
I'll bring it to the notice of the owner
And you'll be duly punished.' The cowherds
Replied, 'They're the cows of a great sage
Who lives far away. We're looking for
Risyashrunga's father. Risyashrunga
Is the owner, whom you perhaps know.
He had left this place with a group of women.
He has married Dasaratha's daughter
And got the cows and many valuable
Articles as dowry. Lomapada gave all
These things in our hands and ordered
Us to deliver them to Risyashrunga's father.
In return for our services we were
Beaten by you.' Hearing this, Bibhandaka
Was filled with pleasure. Tears of joy
Rolled down from his eyes. Embracing
The cowherds and kissing them, he said,

'I'm Risyashrunga's father whom
You've have been looking for. He has been
Away for two months. Without him,
The world seems dark to me. Listening
To your words, I feel as if I'm drinking
Nectar. What a crazy boy my son is!'

The beauty of Laba's narration made
Srirama laugh. Basistha and others
Enjoyed it thoroughly. Looking at
Basistha, Srirama said, 'Can anyone
Sing as Laba does? What a virtuous
Mother he must have! One who sees
His father's face will be redeemed of his
Sins.' Basistha replied, 'Have patience.
Wait till the reading of the scripture
Is finished. Then only you may ask him
About his parents.' At this, Rama fell silent
And the singing resumed. Laba sang
The lines from the scripture in a melodious
Voice while Kusha did the paraphrasing.

Inviting the cowherds to the hermitage,
Bibhandaka offered them sweet potatoes
To eat. He arranged their stay there
And brought the wealth and the riches
From the boat to the hermitage. Then
He told the cowherds, 'Stay here and look after
The cows until I return. Now I'll take
The boat and go to my son. After
Giving him a piece of advice I'll come back.'
So saying, he boarded a boat and sailed
For Anga at the speed of the wind.

Reaching Anga after ten days,
He went straight to Risyashrunga.
Seeing his father before him,
Risyashrunga left his seat and bowed
At his feet. He took the dust from
His feet and smeared it on his forehead.
He asked benignly, 'Why did you take
So much pain to come here, leaving
The hermitage?' Bibhandaka replied,
'My son! In your absence, the world
Seemed a void to me. You married
Dasaratha's daughter and sent me
All the wealth you got as dowry.
Receiving the news from the cowherds,
I came here to see you. By accepting
A young woman as your wife, you've
Taken a great burden on yourself.
Now you should oblige Dasaratha by
Blessing him with a son. Lomapada
Had arranged the girl for you, so
Have mercy on him. Hold a *yajna* in
The palace so that he can have a son.
Do as I say. Let the world praise you
For your noble deed. When your work
Comes to an end, return to the hermitage.'
So saying, Bibhandaka left him.
He came by boat and reached the Bipul
Mountain. To the cowherds he said,
'You will go back after my son returns.'
Happy to hear it, the cowherds lived
With the sage, spending their days merrily.

x x x x

Laba continued:

Bibhandaka came and left without
The knowledge of Dasaratha and Lomapada.
After his departure, Risyashrunga
Called Lomapada and told him,
'You don't have any issue. Now I'll
Perform a *yajna* by which you'll be
Blessed with sons. By taking the *charu*,
Your wives will bear children.
I'll show you my spiritual powers now.'
Filled with joy, Lomapada arranged
A *yajna* in the palace. Reciting *mantras*,
The young sage worshipped the God
Of Fire by offering ghee. After
Propitiating the *dikpalas*,
He chanted *mantras* and brought out
The *charu* from the sacrificial pit.
He asked Lomapada to call his queens,
And when they came, the sage gave them
The *charu* to eat, chanting Narayana.
No sooner did the four queens, such as
Sriya, Panchali, Mruda and Ratnabali
Eat it than they conceived. Ratnabali
Had eaten the *charu* two times, so she
Gave birth to two sons. They had five
Sons in all, each of them looked as
Radiant as fire. Soon celebrations
Started all over Lomapada's kingdom.

x x x x

Seeing Lomapada blessed with sons,
Dasaratha was happy, but impatient.
He asked Risyashrunga, 'When will
You have mercy on me? If I get
A son, your name and fame will live
Forever.' Risyashrunga replied,
'Since you're old, you'll have to observe
A *brata* for a year. Tell your queens
To do the same with austerity. After
A year, I'll perform a *yajna* and offer
Ghee to the God of Fire. I'll pray to
All the gods to bless you. Only those
Of your queens who observe the *brata*
With devotion will be given the *charu*
To beget sons. Like all others, they'll
Experience ten months of pregnancy.'
With folded hands, Dasaratha said,
'Let's go to my kingdom. You'll explain
To my queens the rules of the *brata*.
They'll be happy to see their son-in-law
And daughter.' The sage consented,
And when they arrived in Ayodhya,
The queens gave them a warm welcome.
The women of Ayodhya thronged
To the palace to see them; they strewed
Young leaves of grass on the sage's
Head as a sign of love and respect.
They said the groom and the bride were
A wonderful match.

While Laba and Kusha were narrating it,
The women whispered to each other:

How could the boys know all this?
We've never heard of such things
From anyone before. Who are they?
How beautifully they are singing!
When the whisper rose to a loud noise,
Laba and Kusha fell silent.
After a while Laba started singing
Again and when Kusha joined him,
All became as silent as flies in the oil.

x x x x

Laba sang in *Gundarikari* raga:

Bibandaka's son laid down
A set of rules connected to the *brata*.
Dasaratha conveyed those rules
To his twenty-one hundred queens:
'For a year you've to follow an austere
Way of life. Give up oil, flowers
And non-vegetarian meals. Take bath
Early in the morning everyday. Pray
To the sun when it rises and sets.
Cook your food on time and take your
Meal only once in the evening silently.
Only those who obey the rules strictly,
Will be blessed with sons. These are
The sage's instructions.' All the queens
Promised to follow the rules.
There were celebrations everywhere.
To propitiate Lokeswari, the presiding
Deity of Ayodhya, the king offered
Sacrifices of goats and buffaloes.

Singing and dancing went on around
The palace. The sound of trumpets
Filled the air. Hearing the sound,
Jamadagni's son, who was meditating
In Kapila *tirtha*, came to Ayodhya,
Burning with anger. Seeing him,
Dasaratha lay prostrate before him.
Parsurama asked, 'What is this noise
About, which brought me here?'
Dasaratha explained, 'O Parsurama!
I've brought Risyashrunga to my palace.
As he married my daughter, Shanta,
He wants to oblige me by performing
A *yajna*, which will give me a son.
People are rejoicing at the good news.'
Convinced, Parsurama told him in
Confidence, 'Don't have the *yajna* here.
Go to Krishnabeni, the most sacred place
In the world, where Vishnu lies on
A snake-bed. By holding the *yajna* there.
You can have a son. Name your
Eldest son after me. Beware, there are
Twenty-four witches in Ayodhya
Who eat the infants while in the womb.
They're undergoing a period of curse
Pronounced by Indra; they will be
Liberated when they go to Krishnabeni.'
So saying, he left for his hermitage.

Returning to Risyashrunga,
Dasaratha told the sage all that Parsurama
Had instructed. Risyashrunga said,

'Jamadagni's son is Vishnu himself.
Who dare defy him? Any disregard for
His advice will incur his displeasure.
O King! Now go and ask your queens
If they've observed the *brata* as
They were told. What's the point in taking
Those who have failed to do it? We'll
Leave for Krishnabeni and arrange
The *yajna* there.' Dasaratha went inside,
Called his queens and asked them,
'Have all of you done the *brata* properly?
Tell me the truth. If you lie, the sage will
Curse you.' The queens stood silently
With their heads down. Only three of
His queens, Kaikeyee, Kausalya
And Sumitra said with folded hands,
'We've obeyed all your instructions.'

Going back to the sage, Dasaratha informed,
Only three of my queens confessed
Having performed the *brata* rightly.'
'Whatever is God's wish!' the sage said,
'Get your soldiers ready. We'll move now.'
With the queens and a huge quantity of gold,
Dasaratha and Risyashrunga set out
For Krishnabeni. They reached there
After a journey of thirty days. Basistha,
Who accompanied them decided the
Day on which the *yajna* should commence.

Dasaratha made friends with Nishad,
The ruler of Krishnabeni and the head

Of a tribe. A devotee of Risyashrunga,
Nishad asked the sage, 'How shall I
Get a child?' The sage told him,
'Remain at the entrance of the *yajna* site.
Your wife will suck in the smoke coming
From the holy pit and conceive.
Soon the *yajna* started.
To propitiate the *grahas*, the sage offered
Red paddy grains. To appease the *dikpalas*,
He offered sacred wood, holy grass, flowers
Of different colours and ghee into
The sacrificial pit. Nisad remained
At the entrance while his wife sucked
In the smoke. She became pregnant
And later, gave birth to Sabari Narayana.
The twenty-four witches who had gone
There from Ayodhya with the soldiers,
Had lost their strength considerably.
For fear of Nisad, they perched on
The roof that covered the pit. Consuming
Smoke, they also conceived and gave birth to
Monkeys. Bimbu, one of them was delivered
Of two babies. In all, twenty-five monkeys
Were born. Now that the period of their
Curse ended, they went back to heaven.
The newly-born monkeys stayed in
The mountain, and later, fought for Rama.
Those bears who used to live in the forest,
Also became pregnant by inhaling
The smoke and gave birth to many bears,
Who became Ramachandra's followers.

Hearing this,
Srirama said to Basistha, 'O sage!
These brothers are telling the truth. Surely,
The monkeys were born earlier to me.
That's why they started the battle before
I did.' Basistha stopped him, saying,
'Be quiet! It's not good to discuss other
Things while the scripture is being read.
Laba is reading out the *Bichitra Ramayana*
So sweetly. Listen to him carefully.'

The *yajna* started on a Monday,
The thirteenth day of the bright fortnight
Of Asadha, *Sravana* star. The place
Resonated with Vedic *mantras*. Vishnu,
Leaving his snake-bed, appeared there.
Seeing Narayana arriving on Garuda,
Risyashrunga lay prostrate before him.
He said, 'Why did you come here, O Lord?
I was born to an animal. I'm frightened
To see you.' Srihari told him, 'Don't fear.
I'll incarnate as Dasaratha's son.
He has been praying to me for a long time
To have me as his son.' Risyashrunga
Asked, 'O Mace-bearer! Why do you take
Pains to shelter in a human womb,
O Wheel-bearer!' Srikrishna stated,
'My suffering will bring an end
To Ravana's life. He has enslaved
Thirty-three crores of gods. Such power
Was granted to him by Uma's consort.
I'll incarnate to kill Ravana. Sita is to be

Born in Janaka's house. I'll marry Sita
And stay in the forest with her.
The Ten-headed demon will abduct her
From there. For that reason, I'll wipe out
His whole clan.' Risyashrunga said,
'You'll hold bow in your hands. Born as
A man you'll lose your power of omniscience.
If you've four hands, the sinners will be
Liberated easily, by seeing you. For this,
The gods will put the blame on me.
O Vishnu! How shall I believe in your words?'
At this, Vishnu jumped into the sacrificial
Fire. Bibhandaka's son, reciting *mantras*,
Offered ghee to the fire. On the tenth day
Of the bright fortnight of Aswina,
The *yajna* came to an end. Risyashrunga,
With all austerity, made the last offering
To the fire, chanting the name of Vishnu.

It was a Thursday, Star *Anuradha*,
On which the sage collected the *charu* from
The sacrificial pit. God, appearing from
The *charu*, said, 'Listen, Risyashrunga!
Don't destroy the *charu*. One who eats it
Will have a son instantly.' The sage
Forbade him to do so. He said,
'Three of Dasaratha's queens have been
Crying for sons since long. It's for them.
But I want them to follow the process
Of physical union with their husbands as
Other human beings do.' God consented
And, then, disappeared. The sage handed over

The *charu* to Dasaratha and instructed him,
'Give it to your queens. They'll soon conceive.'
Dasaratha's joy knew no bounds. When
He called the queens, Kaikeyee was the first
To come, followed by Kausalya. After
It was distributed to them, Sumitra arrived.
Looking at the king, Kausalya said,
'Aren't you doing injustice to Sumitra,
By giving all the *charu* to us? She was
One of us who took part in the *brata*.
Why are you so unkind to her?'
Dasaratha replied apologetically,
'Out of joy, I forgot to think about her.
All of you are born to the same parents.
All of you have sacrificed a lot for the *brata*.
Now divide the *charu* into three parts
And take a part each. Don't mind my words.'
But Sumitra declined. She told her sisters,
With folded hands, 'Why divide it into
Three? It will not be fair. I'm the youngest
One, the third wife of your husband.
I deserve to be counted among maids.
One who takes a share from her
Elder sister, loses all her virtues.
Since my husband gave the *charu* only
To you two, why should I share it?
Better, both of you eat your share
Of *charu* and give me whatever is left
Over.' So saying, Sumitra divided it
Into halves and gave it to them.
The portion in her right hand she gave
To Kausalya and the left one to Kaikeyee.

Kausalya ate it chanting Vishnu's name,
Kaikeyee dedicated it to Indra. Sumitra
Ate the left over *charu* chanting Narayana.

To conclude the affairs of the *yajna*,
Risyashrunga asked Dasaratha to pay
To the priests, sages, brahmins and
Vaisnavas, in accordance of their positions.
Dasaratha paid to them to their utmost
Satisfaction. Thereafter, he returned
To Ayodhya with his queens. Celebrations
Went on everywhere. As the queens were
Old in age, they had lost their sexual
Appetite. The *charu* brought back
Their lost instinct. Dasaratha, too, felt
A desire for sex. He decided the days
On which he'll be in bed with his queens.

On the thirteenth day of the bright fortnight
Of Kartik, he slept with Kausalya,
On the twelfth day of the dark fortnight
Of Margasira with Kaikeyee and on
A Thursday, the third day of the month,
Star *Pusya* with Sumitra. All the three
Queens conceived and were looked after
By the maids of the palace day and night.
Dasaratha also did not leave their side,
Not even for a moment. They were given
Cool food to eat. The maids decked them
In fine clothes and flowers, and some
Of them fanned them from time to time.

x x x x

Ten months passed,
Kausalya went into labour.
In the midnight of the eleventh day
Of the bright fortnight of Bhadraba,[1]
She gave birth to a son. In joy, the women
Ululated. When its sound reached heaven.
Indra asked Brihaspati what it was
All about. Brihaspati replied,
'Vishnu is born in Ayodhya. Now
Peace and order will be restored to the earth.'
As ordered by Indra, Kusumasen strewed
Flowers on Ayodhya. The men and women
Of Ayodhya rejoiced at the news.
The maids cut the umbilical cord
Of the baby with a golden knife.
They washed the baby with scented water,
Spread silk clothes to make the bed
And lit a fire to keep them warm.
In the night of the full moon day of Bhadraba,
Kaikeyee was delivered of a son.
In the late hours of the same night,
Sumitra gave birth to two sons.

The maids took the three sons and made
Them lie with the eldest one, on a beautiful
Bed, a canopy hanging over it
And with bars on all sides. To keep
Them warm, they raised a fire with
Sandalwood sticks. Basistha, Sumanta,
Madhukeshi and all the courtiers gathered

[1] In all other versions of *Ramayana* Rama was born on the ninth day of Chaitra.

There to see the king's sons. Basistha told
The king, 'Send messengers to Gruhamedha,
The brother to your three wives. Let him
Have the pleasure of seeing the children.'
The king's messenger, after a journey
Of ten days, reached Gruhamedha's
Palace. They informed him, 'King Dasaratha
Is blessed with sons. Your sisters have
Become mothers.' Extremely happy,
Gruhamedha offered them valuable gifts.
With his seven sons, he arrived in Ayodhya
In three days. He found Dasaratha sitting
On the throne with sage Basistha near him.
After paying respect to them, he went
To meet his sisters. Expressing his
Good wishes to them, he kept one lakh
Gems on the bed where the sons lay.
He took them into his lap; he could see
Vishnu's image in them. He felt happy
That the world, at last, will be relieved
Of oppression and injustice.

Hearing the news of Sridhar Narayana
Taking birth in Ayodhya, sages from
Far and wide thronged there, reciting
Vedic *mantras*. With folded hands,
Dasaratha told them, 'O sages! I feel blessed
To see you. Your pious presence will bring
Salvation to my eighty-six generations.'
The sages replied, 'You're the mightiest
King of the clan of Sun. You've greatest
Respect for the gods and brahmins.
So we came here. We heard you're blessed

With sons. We would like to see them.
It will be a divine blessing for us.'

Dasaratha asked the nurses to fetch
The babies. Srirama's nurse was
Mochina, Bharata's Chandala kanya,
Lakshmana's Chinta and Shatrughna's
Ubasa Sundari. The four nurses soon
Presented the sons before the sages.
Leaving their seats, they got up to have
A clear view of the babies. They whispered
Among themselves, 'The eldest one will
Bring an end to the misery of the people.
The wicked demon, the Ten-headed
One who is the enemy of the gods will
Abduct his wife. He'll kill the demon,
The King of Lanka. Our stay in the forest
Will be much safer. We can freely
Visit various places of pilgrimage
And enhance our spiritual knowledge.'

Turning to Dasaratha, they said, 'Listen!
For the timebeing we'll remain in
Your palace. In the night of the twentieth
Day, we'll put the babies on the swing,
And, after naming them, we'll leave.'
The king arranged their stay in the palace
And fed them with sugarcane juice,
Banana and many kinds of fruits.
In the night of the twentieth day,
The rituals began. Swings
Made of silk ropes and studded

With gems, garlands and strewn with
Camphor dust, were hung. The babies
Were put on the swings, among the sound
Of ululation and recitation of Vedic
Mantras. Sages such as Basistha, Bharadwaja,
Pulah, Paulasti, Jaba Ankur, Jay,
Pareswar, Kapila, Chyaban, Bedabrata,
Gyadhi and Astabakra chanted *slokas*
In a melodious voice. Before the naming
Ceremony, Dasaratha said, 'O sages!
Parsurama had told me to name my
Eldest son after him.' So Kausalya's
Son was named as Rama. Next,
They named Kaikeyee's son as Bharata
And Sumitra's as Lakshmana and Shatrughna.
When it was over, the sages left for
Their hermitage. Gruhamedha returned
To his kingdom and Lomapada to Anga.
Risyashrunga told Dasaratha, ' Look after
Your sons. It's time for me to leave for
The Bipul mountain where my father
Has been waiting for me. Dasaratha
Sent his daughter and son-in-law
To Anga by palanquin. From there
The couple sailed for the Bipul mountain.
On reaching the hermitage they bowed
At Bibhandaka's feet. He blessed
His daughter-in-law, 'May you have
Seven sons.' The words of the sage
Never went in vain. Risyashrunga,
Therefore, was blessed with seven sons.

O Yudhisthira!
Rama was overwhelmed to listen to
The *Ramayana* as authored by Valmiki.
Tears of joy were rolling down from
His eyes. He was amazed to hear the story
Of his own birth. Basistha, Sumanta
And other were feeling as if they were
Drinking nectar. Who could alter
Valmiki's words? O Panchali, Drupada's
Daughter! Here the father is the listener
And the son, the narrator.

Glory to Srihari, the Lord of the Universe!
Chanting His name can bring salvation.
Hari removes the sorrows of those who
Think of Him everyday. He who
Narrates Hari's tale finds a place
In Hari's abode. Hari! Hari!
Hari! Sriranga Srihari! One who
Chants your name becomes immortal.
Think on Hari all the time, while you're
Sleeping or bathing. Listen to the story
Of His life with greatest devotion.
Siddheswar Das, humbly, prays at His feet.

x x x x

Holding Markanda's feet,
King Yudhisthira said, 'O sage! I'm happy
To learn about Srirama's birth, as
Narrated by Laba and Kusha.
What did Dasaratha do next? I've with
Me eighty-eight thousand brahmins,

Twelve thousand sages from many
Religious places, my friends, relatives
And people from far and wide who came
Here to listen to the *Ramayana* from your
Mouth. It's of great value to each of us.
Now I pray to you to resume telling
The story of the *Ramayana*.' Markanda said,
'Listen, O Pandu's son! May the obstacles
In your life be removed.'

Coming to know about his own birth,
Srirama was thrilled. He asked Basistha,
'How come, these boys, at this tender age,
Incline to spirituality?
How are they able to cast a spell on
The listeners through their song? Surely,
They don't belong to this place.
I'm surprised to see their command over
The scripture!' Basistha replied, 'It's only
Possible for someone coming of a noble
Family. It's beyond the reach of common
People. These boys belong to a noble family.
Ask them about their parentage after
The scripture is finished.' At this,
Srirama fell silent. He kissed the boys
And said to them, 'I'm happy to learn
About the birth of Dasaratha's sons.
Now I'm eager to know about Ravana,
For whom Vishnu, leaving his heavenly
Abode, took birth as a human being.
How was that Ten-headed Ravana,
The enemy of the three worlds, born

As a demon? How could he become so
Wicked when his father was a sage?
He garnered more power by Lord Shiva's
Boon. I'm anxious to know about him.'
As he finished, Laba began singing in
Dhanasree raga, jointly with Kusha.
There was absolute silence as
The reading of the scripture started.
Laba sang with gusto:

Once, when Brahma was meditating
In Lanka, five *apsaras*, led by Urvasi,
Got there. Finding the place absolutely
Lonely, they went on singing and dancing
Merrily. With a *linga* in front of him,
Brahma was sitting on the banks
Of river Manibati. When his eyes fell
On the *apsaras*, he felt a sensation.
He left his meditation, his eyes pinned
On them. Captivated by the *apsaras*,
Who were the beauties of heaven,
He went to them and begged for love,
Having no shame. The *apsaras* said
Mockingly, 'You're too old for us
To be sweet on you. O Mahatma! Find
A woman of your age and make love
To her.' The sage, unable to control
His temptation, held them by hand. But
The *apsaras* gave him the slip and flew back
To heaven. The sage had not had sex
For five *manus*; now his sexual urge was
Let loose and he discharged his semen
Into his loin-cloth.

At this, the listeners burst into laughter.
Basistha cautioned them, 'What makes you
Laugh? These are sacred words; try to
Preserve them in your heart.'
Now everyone fell silent. Laba resumed
Reading out the scripture. If anywhere
The listeners had a difficulty in
Understanding, Kusha would come forward
To explain the meaning to them.

The semen splashed from the loin-cloth
Onto the ground, giving birth to a son, looking
Exceedingly beautiful. Embarrassed,
The sage was trying to make a hasty retreat
To his heavenly abode, when his son,
Following him, called from behind, 'Father!
Where are you going leaving me here?
Why don't you take me with you? How shall
I survive without a mother in this disolate
Land?' The sage turned back and replied,
'If you're my son, stay where you're. Don't
Follow me.' He named him as Paulasti.
He instructed him, 'Go to Rudrakshabana
Where sage Bidu lives. Marry his daughter,
Priyabati. Tell him you're my son,
And he'll offer his daughter to you.'
Saying so, Brahma left him.

Paulasti went to Rudrakshabana
And met Bidu. When the sage asked him
His father's name, he said, 'I'm born into
A brahmin family. My father sent me
To you to learn the Vedas.' Accepting him

As a disciple, the sage taught him the *shastras*.
When he found him well-versed in them,
He married his daughter to him.
He told Paulasti, 'Look after her.
She'll serve you faithfully. She'll be
Blessed with a son. Now that you're
Married, find another hermitage
Where to live. Paulasti took his wife,
And settled in Bharadwaja's hermitage.
Soon Priyabati conceived.

x x x x

Priyabati gave birth to a beautiful son;
Bharadwaja named him as Bisraba.
Observing his excellence in learning
And his handsome appearance, Bharadwaja
Told Paulasti, 'I would like your son marry
My daughter, Saloka. That'll give me
The privilege of being one of Brahma's
Relatives.' Delighted at the proposal,
Paulasti chose an auspicious day on which
The marriage took place. In due course
Of time, Saloka gave birth to two sons,
Namely, Baisrabanas. For his unflinching
Devotion to Lord Shiva, one of them
Became Kubera. Jaba Ankura, Bharadwaja's
Son and Kubera were great friends.
They used to eat, sleep and play
Together. Once, while playing a game
Of sticks, Jaba Ankura's stick was steered
By Kubera into a dilapidated well.
'Why did you throw my stick

Into the well? Go and bring it back
If you want our friendship to continue.'
Jaba Ankura retorted in anger. Kubera replied,
'The well is very deep. After all, it's your
Stick. Why don't you fetch it?' Infuriated,
Jaba Ankura scolded him, 'You stay in our
Hermitage. Why don't your father
And you two go elsewhere? Since the day
Your father married, he has been staying
Here. You, two brothers, were born here.
You're living on the mercy of my father.
Had it not been so, I would have
Chopped your head off now and here.
To speak the truth, you're eating our food.
You, moron! How dare you direct me
To go into the well?' Not able to consume
The hurtful things he said, he began to burn
In anger, as the fire from the hollow
Of a tree burns it. Hanging his head
In shame, he ran to his mother with some
Playmates as witnesses. Saloka saw
Her son crying, tears rolling down from
His eyes. She wiped his face with the end
Of her saree. She said, 'May all
Your troubles befall me! With whom did
You quarrel, my son? Wasn't Jaba Ankura
With you? Baisrabana did not go to play
Today. Stop crying. Tell me the truth.
Who did you wrangle with?'
Kubera said, 'It's your younger brother
Who insulted me. Why do you think
I'm telling a lie? Ask your brother.'

When Saloka asked his playmates, they said,
'Jaba Ankura's stick fell into the well.
He asked your son to fetch it. When
Kubera refused, he scolded him with
Harsh words.' Hearing this, Saloka took
Her son by the hand and rushed to her
Mother in rage. She told her, 'Mother!
See, what your son has done! He scolded
Kubera bitterly and asked him to get out
Of here now.' Sukanti, Saloka's mother,
Tried to pacify her. She washed her
Grandson's face and said, 'Saloka!
Why are you so angry? Why do you mind
What your younger brother said?
I brought up your children by feeding
Them from my breast. I looked after them
At the cost of my own child. Now when
Kubera accuses Jaba Ankura, why are
You angry with him?' Satisfied,
She returned to her hut and consoled
Her son. But Kubera was unbending;
He went to his father, Bisraba, who was
In meditation. Bisraba saw his son
Crying bitterly. He asked, 'What happened?
Your face, as bright as the full moon,
Looks as pale as the moon by the day!'
But Kubera kept crying. Leaving his seat,
The sage took his son into his lap
And consoled him, saying, 'My son!
Jewel of my clan! Tell me, why do you cry.'
Kubera said, 'Father! Why have you been
Staying in your father-in-law's house

Since your marriage? It's like living
On alms. How did your conscience
Allow you to live among insults? Whatever
Your brother-in-law told me today was
Highly objectionable. While at play,
He scolded me harshly. He took my words
Amiss and crossed all limits. He said :
Your father is a low-born, without means.
You stay here only to get food for free.
You're shameless. You don't ever realise
That it is beneath one's dignity
To depend on others. He abused me
With these words which are unbearable.
We must find another hermitage
Where we can live in peace.
If you still think of staying here,
I'll kill myself.'Bisraba said, 'O son!
My father did not give me any place
To stay. Let's ask him. Fetch your mother
And Baisrabana here.' They met Paulasti
And bowed at his feet. Seeing his
Daughter-in-law and grandsons, he was
Delighted. He blessed them and wanted
To know why they have come to him.
Bisraba said, 'Father! My son had
A quarrel with his uncle. We came
To ask you where we should stay.'
Paulasti replied, 'I was not given
Any land by my father. After I was born,
He went away, leaving me behind.
What you ask for is justified. Let's go
And ask my father about it.'

All of them went to Brahma. Paulasti
Bowed at his feet and others followed suit.
When Brahma asked his son why he has
Come to him with his son, grandsons
And daughter-in-law, he said, 'Father!
You're the Creator of the universe. After
I was born, you left me alone. Now I've
A son and grandsons. Where will we stay?
We can't stay with our relatives and be
Humiliated. Where is our own place?'
Brahma replied, 'Sages can settle anywhere.
As your family has grown bigger,
I advise you to settle in Lanka.'

26

The Story of Lanka

Paulasti asked Brahma,
'Who owns the land of Lanka?
Give me more information about the place.
My son used to stay in his father-in-law's
House. Bharadwaja's son insulted
My grandson. One who lives on the mercy
Of others gets such treatment.'
Brahma said, 'Listen, then. Once the Meru
And the Wind fell out with each other.
One day, while the Meru's son, Madri
And his daughter, Marisa were playing
Outside, the Wind's sons Chandatila
And Prachanda saw them. Enchanted by
Marisa's beauty, Chandatila told Madri,
'I'll tell you something and you've to do
As I say.' When Madri asked him what
It was he asked for his sister's hand.
Madri replied, 'It's my father who will
Decide it, not I.' Chandatila warned

Him, 'Give her to me or I'll abduct her.'
It was too much for Madri to bear.
He flared up, 'You aren't as mighty as
You think. It's your self-indulgence
That makes you say so.' At this, Chanda
Dealt him a blow, which made him
Fall down, unconscious. Regaining
Consciousness after sometime, Madri,
Held them by the hair and delt them
With blows that sprawled them onto
The ground, unconscious.
When they recovered, they found Madri
And Marisa had left. Soon they met
Their father, their eyes swimming with tears.
The Wind asked them, 'Did you have
A quarrel with someone? Your bodies are
Covered with dust and blood coming out
Of your mouths.' Chandatila said,
'Madri, the Meru's son has done this.
When we asked for his sister's hand,
He beat us senseless. Then, they ran away.'
Enraged, the Wind said, 'I'll crush
The Meru into hundred pieces. I'll kill
Madri and bring Marisa. I'll marry
The girl to you.' So saying, he went
To the Meru and challenged him, 'Fight
With me, if you can. Your son, Madri,
Has beaten my sons. I come here seeking
Revenge. Leave this place. If you want
To remain here, marry your daughter
To my son.' Irritated, the Meru replied,
'How dare you speak like this! I know

Your might very well. Your actions
Are a proof of it. Your son is no
Match for a girl such as Marisa.
None in the three worlds can be her
Equal in beauty. Neither fifteen,
Nor seventeen, she is sixteen,
Who enchants the heart of everyone.'
Hearing these words, the Wind blew
Ferociously at its maximum speed,
But the fearless Meru stood unmoved.
Completely vanquished, the Wind left
The place, and hid himself
In some unknown quarters of heaven.

Thus Brahma said to Paulasti,
Which Laba narrated to Srirama,
Kusha explaining the meaning wherever
Necessary. Caressing and kissing them,
Srirama asked, 'What happened after
The Wind went into hiding?'
Elaborating on it, Laba sang:

The absence of the Wind worried the gods.
Brahma, Vishnu, Indra and others
Found out where he was. They asked him,
'Why are you hiding? Are you in a mind
To destroy the three worlds?'
The Wind replied, 'I think, my life is of no use.
Today I was completely embarrassed.
While fighting with the Meru, I was badly
Beaten.' The gods, then, met the Meru
And persuaded him, 'Don't be angry

With the Wind any longer. Now the lives
Of all created beings are at stake. You can save
them by parting with one of your peaks.'
When the Meru consented, they returned
And told the Wind, 'Now go and fight
With the Meru. We bestow all our powers
On you. Don't worry. We're with you.'
The Wind launched an attack on the Meru,
Battering violently against it. Unable
To resist the attack, its golden peak
Gave in and fell into the Milky sea,
Which, later, was known as Lanka.'

Brahma continued,
'To wipe out the clan of the demons,
Vishnu attacked them from time to time.
Apprehensive of the future, a demon
Called Sumali, who used to live in Lanka,
Escaped into the netherworld.
There are no demons in Lanka now.
You may live there with your son
And grandsons. I was there for five
Manus long until you were born.
Lanka, made up of gold is a very
Sacred place. Go and stay there.'

Following Brahma's advice,
Paulasti left for Lanka with his son
And grandsons. He asked Bisraba
To fetch the daughter-in-law there.
Then, he went on a pilgrimage.
Bisraba lived there, spending his time

In meditating on Lord Shiva. There
Baisrabana died of consumption.
The other son, for his unflinching devotion
To Shiva, was rewarded
By the Lord with the post of Kubera.
In addition, he was given a flying
Chariot called Pushpak. Lakshmi gave
Him a lot of riches. He commanded
The respect of all the celestial beings
And became close to the gods.
He used to fly in his chariot in
All directions, while the *dikpalas*
Watched him in admiration.
Lanka was a beautiful land where
Two hundred twenty-four rivers flowed.

Thus Laba narrated the story of Lanka
To Srirama. If anything was difficult
To follow, Kusha made it easy
By explaining its meaning.

x x x x

Bisraba's hermitage stood on the banks
Of river Manibati, that flowed in
The middle of Lanka. The sage spent
His time there in prayers and meditation,
While Kubera kept playing around him.

Who can go against God's will?
As time went by, Sumali, the demon, who
Lived in the nether regions of the earth,
Had married Pusyadanta's daughter,

Sadanika, and had three daughters
And a son named Jambomali.
At the time there were no demons there;
All of them had fled to the nether regions,
Accepting Sumali as their chief.
The change of place could not deter Sumali
From ruminating over his days in Lanka.
He thought of visiting Lanka for a day.
A spear tucked under his arm,
He was about to leave home for Lanka
When Naukesha,[1] his daughter, held him
By the hand, asking him where he was
Going. Sumali said, 'Listen, my dear!
I'm going on a visit to my former land.
I'm not taking you with me. Don't
Let on to anyone about my journey.
Go back, and enjoy yourself at home.'
Naukesha implored, 'Father! I would
Like to see your kingdom. Please
Don't say no to me.' While saying so,
She wept. Looking at his daughter's
Tearful eyes, he held her by the hand
And left for Lanka. Reaching
There, he looked around, trying to
Recognise the places he was familiar
With. He could see a vast stretch
Of land with no one around, only
The wild beasts raising loud cries.
After travelling fifty *yojanas*, much to
Their surprise, they found Kubera at play.

[1] In all other versions of *Ramayana* it is Nikasha.

Dressed in finery, he was adorned with
Earrings, rings and necklaces. He looked
Pretty with dots of sandalwood paste
And musk on his forehead. The presence
Of a demon, with a spear in hand,
Scared him. He sensed that Sumali
Has come back to Lanka. The demon
Asked him, 'O Mahatma! Where have
You come from? What are you doing
In my kingdom?' Kubera replied,
'We didn't know it is your kingdom.
Finding no one here we chose this place
To stay. It was Brahma who sent us
Here. Once, while he was meditating,
A son named Paulasti was born to him.
Paulasti's son, Bisraba is my father.
After seeing us settled here, Paulasti
Went on a pilgrimage. Now you may take
Your land back. We're leaving.'
Sumali told him, 'Since your father
Is here, it's not proper to talk to you.
I'm, however, pleased with your manners.
Take me to your father.' Kubera led
The way to his father's hermitage.
It was surrounded by plants blooming
With flowers and bumblebees swarming
Around them. They found Bisraba
In meditation in a grove of *bel* trees.

Sumali shouted at him, 'O sage!
How could you be so unjust? You've
Trespassed on my land.' As there was

No response, Sumali let out a roar
Of rage, so deafening that the sage
Fell down from his seat, unconscious.
Thanks to God that Kubera was there.
He sprinkled some water on his face
And fanned him. When he recovered,
He saw a demon standing before him
With a spear in his hand. Looking at
Bisraba, Sumali asked, 'Why have you
Tresspassed on my land? The right place
For you is the forest. Why do you ruin
My golden kingdom?' Bisraba thought:
He must be Sumali, formerly the Lord
Of Lanka. Now that he has come back,
We've to quit the place. He told Sumali,
'We were in the Jambu island.
I'm the son of sage Paulasti. Brahma
Advised us to settle here. You are
The title-holder of this land. If you
Let us stay here, we stay, or else we'll
Go away.' Sumali was pacified.
At the time Naukesha was struck by
The sudden thought: The sage belongs to
Brahma's family. How would it be
If I marry him? I'll have a lovely son
Like the one he has. If I've past virtues
My father will bring the proposal.
Just then, as if by divine bliss, her father
Asked her, 'would you like to marry the sage?
If yes, I'll make it happen today itself.
Your son will inherit all the wealth
I have.' Naukesha replied, 'If it is
Your wish, how can I go against it?'

Delighted at her reply,
Sumali said to Bisraba, 'I want you
To marry my daughter. She will be
Blessed with a nice and intelligent son.
This land will be yours. As you stay here,
You've to do as I say. I offer my daughter
To you.' The sage was worried; sweat
Poured off him. He mused: For staying
In the demon's kingdom, I'm now going
To lose my caste. One who marries a low-born
Is bound to go to hell. How shall
I worship God of Fire again?
Won't others laugh at me?'

Finding Bisraba plunged in thought,
Sumali spoke, 'O sage! Why are you silent?
You're not saying either yes or no. If you
Don't agree with me, I'll kill you
And your son now.' Having no other option,
The sage agreed to marry his daughter.
Sumali said, 'I've two more daughters.
You'll marry all three of them. My sole
Objective is to have a son. If one of them
Fails to conceive, there will be other two
To supplement it.' He asked the sage to take
A vow to that effect. Then the demon left for
His home and informed his wife about it.
He soon returned to Lanka with his daughter,
Naukesha, Puspautkata and Puspamaluni.
The marriage was solemnized, the demon
Vowing of offering his daughters to the sage,
Raising a conch filled with sesame seeds
And water, he offered the sage a lot of gems

And the ownership of Lanka as dowry.
After the marriage, the demon went back
To his home, while the sage lived in Lanka
With the three girls. Each of the girls
Was given a hermitage of her own.
Bisraba, as usual, spent his time
In prayers and meditation. Saloka,
Bharadwaja's daughter and Kubera's mother
Lived with her son and the three newly-weds.

x x x x

As time passed by,
Naukesha reached puberty, followed by
Puspautkata and Puspamaluni. They felt
The compulsions of adulthood in form
Of sexual urges that needed to be attended
To urgently. But what to do when the sage
Remained outdoors all the time? Anguished,
They spoke to each other, 'How can we ignore
Our physical desires? Our father, lacking
Foresight, married us to an old man.
We're made to pay for our past sins.
Now, what to do? Shall we hang ourselves
To death or jump into the river and kill
Ourselves?' Naukesha protested, 'It's a sin
To commit suicide. By that you lose
Your claim to be born as human beings
In your next birth.' Puspautkata asked,
'How will it be if we inform our father
About it? Or leave the place?' Puspamaluni
Said, 'What'll happen to the sage and his son,

If our father comes to know of it? It'll be
A betrayal to our husband, and, for that,
We'll live as widows in our next births.'
Naukesha proposed, 'Let's seduce him
By singing and dancing.' All of them
Went near him, and, clapping their hands,
Sang and danced salaciously to
Stimulate the passion of love in him.
But when their attempt failed,
They changed themselves into parrot
And myna and perched on the tree
Under which the sage was meditating.
One of them threw a leaf at another,
Who shouted out, 'Do you think you're
My equal? You're as stupid as
Sage Bisraba. His yogic practices
Are all false. He is not able to make out
Vice from virtue. It's foreboding
To see his face in the morning. Likewise,
One who sees your face will have to
Go without food for the day. You pretend
Yourself to be as pious as the sage does.
How dare you think yourself my equal?'
Hearing their conversation,
The sage looked above and said to the bird
Which was accusing him, 'For your
Past sins, you were born as bird.
How am I inferior to you? I worship
Shiva everyday after an early bath.
I chant *gayatri* and *Om* regularly.
As a brahmin, my sins are redeemed
As I worship God of Fire. You don't speak

Of my virtues, instead, you speak
Ill of me. Tell me, what sin I have committed,
Or else I'll pronounce a curse on you.'
The bird replied, 'O sage! You're righteous,
Wise and well-versed in *shastras*.
Don't be angry with me. Your only fault
Is that you're indifferent to your wives.
They've reached puberty and they pine for
Your company. But they're disappointed.
Have you no fear for Sumali? If they inform
Their father, do you imagine what'll happen
To you and your son? He offered his
Daughters to you with the hope of getting
A son. But you take no interest in them.
For not making love to them, all your
Virtues will be perish.'

Moved by the bird's words,
The sage picked his staff and *kamandalu*
And went straight to the hermitage.
As he left, the three sisters, disguised
As birds, returned to their former self
And went back to their respective places.
They bowed at the sage's feet. The sage
Blessed them, 'May you be blessed with
Sons.' His wives asked him, 'Why did you
Come here, leaving meditation?'
The sage replied, 'Since you've reached
Puberty, I feel it's time you bear children.
Tell me, each of you, on which day
Did you menstruate?' Naukesha said
Hers was ten days ago, Puspautkata

Said five and Puspamaluni three.
The sage blessed them, 'May Naukesha
Have ten sons, Puspautkata three sons
And a daughter and Puspamaluni a son
And a daughter.' Raising a protest,
Naukesha said, 'O sage! If I've ten sons,
Who'll look after them? You'll be away
For meditation. I just want one son whose
Fame will spread across the world,
And a daughter of immense beauty.'
The sage replied, 'What I've said can't be
Changed. But it may be substituted by
A son with ten heads and twenty hands.
That'll do justice to either of us. Let
The world be a witness to it.' The sage's
Words pleased all of them.

That night, the sage made love to Naukesha.
She conceived, and, after the completion
Of ten months, she gave birth to a son.
The baby was exactly as the sage had predicted;
He had one body, two feet, ten heads
And twenty hands. Disappointed by the sight
Of the baby, Naukesha asked her husband,
'How shall I bring him up? Which of his mouths
Shall I feed?' The sage advised her to feed
The one that cried. She, then, cut the umbilical
Cord and bathed him. He had four heads
On his left and five on the right. She fed
The middle one with the milk from her breast.
She was also blessed with a daughter who
Shone as bright as gold. Puspautkata

Became a mother of three sons
And a brown-eyed daughter. Puspamaluni
Had one son and one daughter
Looking as beautiful as a star.
Each of them looked after their own children.
They implored the sage to name the babies.
The sage said, 'Naukesha's son be called
Dasanana and her daughter Subarnarekha;
The sons of Puspautkata be named as
Kumbhakarna, Khara and Duhsana,
Her daughter, Pingali, and Puspamaluni's
Son be known as Bibhisana and daughter, Tara.

As days crawled by,
The children grew up. One day Bisraba told
Dasanana, 'I would like to give you
A piece of advice. Be righteous and keep
Discipline. Respect the gods and brahmins.
Don't disappoint your friends and relatives,
Don't take the wicked into confidence.'
Dasanana replied, 'My only concern is how
To please Gouri's consort. If you're kind
To me, tell me what to do to achieve it.
I can't afford to displease sages, cattle
And my subjects as I've to rule over them.'
Bisraba could guess what was going on
In his son's mind. It appeared to him
That he'll come out as the enemy of the gods.
He would torture those who are virtuous
And trust those who are wicked.
He advised Dasanana to chant a *mantra*
And said, 'If you can please Shiva,

You'll have everything in your life.
But you must pay me fees for my advice.'
When he consented, Bisraba told him,
'Listen, Dasanana! Kubera is your
Elder brother. The area of Lanka
Is one hundred *yojanas*. I divide it
Into two halves; you take the area
On the east and leave the other part
For Kubera. Don't be envious of him.
If you distrust him, your life will be
Shortened.' He, then, told Kubera
Confidentially, 'Don't trust Dasanana.
Don't leave Lanka. Grow relations
With the gods. I'm going on a pilgrimage
And I'll devote my life to the service of God.'
Leaving Lanka to his sons, he went
To the forest, looking for solitude.

The story of Dasanana's birth was
Narrated by Sita's sons,
To the enlightenment of Srirama
And enjoyment of the listeners in the hall,
Which was filled to capacity.

27

Ravana Blessed with a Boon

Addressing Laba and Kusha,
Srirama said, 'O dear! You're the first
To let me know about how the Ten-headed
Demon was born. Bisraba had named him
As Dasanana. How did he come to be known
As Ravana? Could you please explain it
To remove my doubts?' At this, Laba started
Singing in *Basanta Baradi* raga. As he missed
The tune, Kusha came to his help by setting it
Right. Absolute silence prevailed there;
Tears of joy were dropping down from
Every eye. Thus Laba began:

One day, while Naukesha's son was roaming
With his brothers, Kubera swished past him
In his Pushpak chariot. He returned home
Gloomily and walked into his room, shutting
The door from behind. He lay on his bed in
A mood of despair. Naukesha, puzzled,

Called him from outside, 'O son! Why do you
Sleep inside with doors shut? You're getting
Late for meal. Tell me what you want.
Nothing is impossible for you to get.'
Dasanana replied, 'Mother! I feel a pang
Of envy at Kubera's success. We're the sons
Of the same father. Why should he get
A preferential treatment, such as flying
Across the sky in a chariot? I'm green with
Jealousy to see him fly. I want that chariot
For myself. If I don't get it, I'll go without
Food and die.' His mother explained,
'He led a righteous life and pleased Shiva
By his devotion. The Lord blessed him to be
Immortal and gave him the chariot for
His personal use.' Dasanana reacted,
'Then, I'll worship Shiva and please him.
I'll ask for the chariot and get it.'
Naukesha consoled him, 'Dear son!
Don't be upset about your elder brother's
Achievement. I advise you to serve him.
This will go to your benefit.' Dasanana
Protested, 'Mother! What you say
Is not acceptable. I'll devote myself
To the service of Lord Trilochana.' Then,
He flung open the door and came out.

Clad in saffron clothes and adorned with
Necklaces of *rudraksha* and wooden beads,
Copper earrings, he smeared his body with
Holy ash and held a *kamandalu* in his hand.
He worshipped the *linga* that Brahma had

Used long ago. He poured on it water
From a golden pot and decorated it with
Many kinds of flowers. He chanted 'Shiva'
Day and night. He danced and clapped
While singing his name. He left taking
Food, stood on head for days together,
As a part of devotion. He blew ten conches
At a time in honour of Lord Shiva.
Pleased with his single-minded devotion,
Shiva appeared before him, riding a bull.
Addressing him as Bisraba's son, he offered
Him a boon. Dasanana begged him, 'O Lord!
Srihari has been killing the demons regularly.
If you're kind to me, give me the boon
That I'll defeat Srihari in war.' Annoyed,
Shiva told him, Srihari destroys those
Who are wicked. Son of a sage, as you are,
How dare you wish for the impossible?
I can't grant you such a boon.' When
Dasanana refused to change his mind,
The Lord disappeared. But Dasanana did not
Lose patience, he continued his worship,
Dancing with one leg for six months.
Impressed by his dedication, Shiva appeared
Before him again and told him, 'Ask for
Anything other than challenging Srihari's
Supremacy.' Dasanana was unbending.
He said, 'I've nothing else to ask for.
You may go now.' Enraged, Shiva left him.

With renewed vigour, he continued
The worship. He severed one of his heads,

And, circling the sacrificial fire three times,
He threw it into it. He, then, cut off another
Head and consigned it to the fire. This way,
He severed nine of his heads. Observing
His steadfast devotion, all the gods led by
Brahma and Indra, prayed to Shiva,
'Look! Dasanana has cut away nine
Of his heads. One more head gone and he'll
Occupy the position of Vishnu. Therefore,
Fulfil his wishes. His unflinching devotion
Scares us. He has completed six years
Of meditation, sacrificing nine
Of his heads in the end.' Shiva said
To them, 'He is asking for Srihari's defeat
In his hands. He'll make all of you
Serve at his feet. Don't blame me afterwards.'
Brahma replied, 'Considering his sacrifices,
He deserves to get what he demands.'
Keeping their request, Shiva went
To Dasanana. As he sprinkled some water
On him, his lost heads appeared again.
In the greater interest of the creation,
Brahma ordered Saraswati to inhabit
Dasanana and prevail on him to change
His demand.

When Shiva told him to ask for a boon,
Dasanana said, 'Give me the boon that
I'll rule for two hundred twenty-four Ages,
That all my sons, daughters and grand children
Act in obedience to me, that I wrest
The Pushpak chariot from Kubera and turn

Him out from Lanka, that Indra,
Yama, Kubera and the *dikpalas* serve
At my feet, that I'll be the monarch
Of the three worlds, that I'll bear
The *akshaya linga* in me so that
When my head is cut off, it will be replaced
Soon, that Brahma's weapon will not work
On me and that I'll be immortal and
The ruler of the three worlds forever.'
'Let it be so', Shiva blessed him.

Filled with joy, Dasanana returned home.
When he told his mother about the boon,
She said, 'That you'll be immortal is not true.
Bali, Benu, Janughanta – all of these were
The most powerful ones, yet none of them
Lived forever. Go back to Shiva
And ask him the secret of your death.'

Dasanana hurried to Shiva's abode.
Not finding him there, in anger, he severed
A head and a hand and plucked out
One of his eyes. He put it on the *linga*
And bathed it with blood. Shiva soon appeared
And told him, 'O Bisraba's son! Have you
Taken leave of your senses? I gave you
All that you asked for. What more do you want?'
'Tell me how I'll die,' Dasanana asked him.
Shiva held his hand and took him to the Kapilas,
On the walls of which pictures of the *Ramayana*
Were drawn. Showing them to him, he said,
'You'll abduct Sita and be killed by Rama.'

Scared, Paulasti's grandson told Shiva,
'O Lord of Beasts! I'll not go near Sita.
I'll write her name where I bathe, eat
And sit.' The Lord assured him, 'If you
Stick to your words, nothing will happen
To you and your fortunes will be doubled.'
He put a *rudraksha* necklace around
His neck and gave him a sword called
Chandrahasa and bade him farewell.

On his way back, he saw Nandi
And Bhrukuti at the gates, who told him,
'O Dasanana! Tell us how you got
The *rudraksha* necklace and the *chandrahasa*
Sword which Shiva did not give even
To his sons. Tell us which *mantra*
We should chant to please Lord Shiva.'
Dasanana flared up, 'Do you think
You're my equals? How dare you ask
Me such things? I'm the King of Lanka.
I'm Paulasti's grandson and a member
Of Brahma's family. You, monkey-faced
Gate-keepers! I'll ask Shiva
To hand you over to me. I'll post
You at the gates of Lanka.'
Unable to digest the insult, Nandi
And Bhrukuti retaliated, 'You, wicked fellow!
How dare you call us monkeys!
One day your kingdom will be ravaged
By a monkey. We are vaisnavas,
Serving Lord Shiva! Beware! One day
A vaisnava will get into Lanka and bring
An end to all your glory.'

Aggrieved, Dasanana went back to Shiva,
And, with folded hands, complained,
'Being envious of your favour to me,
Nandi and Bhrukuti cursed me. They say
I would meet my doom very soon
And that a vaisnava will take my life.'
Shiva said, 'Nandi and Bhrukuti are
Staunch vaisnavas. They are immortal.
It's unwise to displease them. Any way,
What is written in your fate is bound
To happen. Now return to Lanka
And forget the idea of abducting Sita.
No abduction, no death for you.'

On his way back,
He saw a beautiful woman sitting
In the Nandan forest. Enticed by her beauty,
He went near her and told her, 'O dear!
Come with me to my kingdom. I'm immortal
By the blessing of Lord Shiva. I'm the King
Of Lanka. Be my wife and enjoy your life
To the best of your wishes.' With a smile,
Himalaya's daughter replied,
'I'm Kamakshi, Shiva's consort. I've no
Attraction for anyone else. My body
Belongs to Shiva; if he says, I'll go with you.'
'Wait here', he said, 'Until I return.
I'll ask your husband to hand you over
To me. If he doesn't agree, I'll kill myself
Before him.' Parvati was worried.
She thought her husband, under duress,
Might grant his request. To avoid

Any untoward incident she left for
Her abode and hid herself there.

Dasanana met Shiva and told him,
'I saw Kamakshi Devi in the Nandan forest.
Her beauty enchanted me. You gave me
Kingship, wealth and riches. But you didn't
Say who will be my chief queen.
I wish to have Kamakshi as my wife.'
Shiva warned him, 'She's the mother
Of the world and my consort. How do you
Stoop so low? Well! If you find her
Where she was, take her with you.'
Dasanana came back, but did not find
Her where she was. He searched the whole
Forest, but she was nowhere to be seen.
He thought he had been deceived by
Shiva. He resolved to uproot the Kapilas
Mountain and carry it to Lanka.
Wishing to show the world what he could
Do, he uprooted the mountain and put
It on his head. Seeing this, the followers
Of Shiva pulled the mountain upwards.
Unable to hold it on his head, Dasanana
Let out a roar, blood flowing from his mouth.
He fell down and passed out.

Those who were listening to the scripture
Burst into laughter. Laba continued:

Hearing the roar,
Shiva asked his followers what it was.

They explained, 'Trying to take away
Kapilas with him, Dasanana uprooted it
And carried it on his head. As we pulled
It from above, he lost his balance and fell down
With a roar. In the process, he lost
His consciousness.' Trilochan felt sorry
For him and said, 'I find my boon is meeting
A disastrous end. Noone will know what
He did; they will put the blame on me.
Who will worship me, then?' Saying so,
He went to the spot where Dasanana lay.
He sprinkled some water on his face.
He gave him a slap and woke him up.
When he recovered, Shiva told him,
'You tried to take away my mountain.
How wicked you are! For the *raba* (roar)
You let out now, you'll be known as
Ravana henceforward.'

Srirama patted Laba on his back
And praised him. He acknowledged,
'I didn't know all this before. It's you
Who enlightened me with these.
Now continue. Throw light on what
Dasanana did thereafter.' Laba
And Kusha resumed reading the scripture:

Returning home, Dasanana informed
His mother that he was not going to die
Unless he abducted Sita. Naukesha said,
'My son! Do as Lord Shiva says.
And live happily everafter.'

x x x x

For their steadfast devotion to Brahma,
They were rewarded with boons:
Kumbhakarna asked for good sleep
While Bibhisana prayed for becoming
Vishnu's devotee. The wishes of both
Were granted by the Creator.

Elated by Ravana's fame, the demons
From everywhere, even Sumali's
Children and grand children, arrived at
Lanka and settled there. Their number was
Too large to be quoted. Ravana launched
An attack on Kubera, vanquished him,
And took away everything he had,
Including the Pushpak chariot.
Scared, Kubera hid in heaven.

Riding the chariot,
Ravana flew in all directions. He fetched
Mandodari from the Mandara mountain
And made her his chief queen. One day
He left for heaven. Seeing him, all the gods
Fled to Bindhyagiri, the abode
Of the Wind. The *dikpalas*, whom the gods
Had left out, revealed to Ravana where
The gods had sheltered. Ravana stormed
Into Bindhyagiri and captured the gods
And ninety-six crores of *apsaras*
And made them serve at his feet.
Deceitfully, he took the three worlds under
His sway. Heaven was swept by panic;
The *gandharvas* and the gods stood down
His throne, waiting for his orders.

The stairs leading to the throne were made
Of emerald, ruby and sapphire. Riding
The Pushpak he conquered fifty crore kings
And brought them with him. As punishment,
He did not kill them; he married them
To his daughters, grand daughters
And relatives. He appointed their sons
Kings at various places. Subarnarekha,
His sister, married the demon Trisira
And Kumbhakarna's sister to Trijata,
Trisira's brother. Tara, the one-breasted
Sister of Bibhisana devoted herself
To the worship of God of Fire. Subarnarekha
Gave birth to a son, who, from five years
Of age, went on chanting the name of God,
For which he was called Japasura.

It was midday, then. The song of Laba
And Kusha reverberated across
The seven seas and the seven islands.
No word passed the lips of the listeners.

Glory to Uma's consort, the Destroyer
Of the creation. You've sheltered
The white moon on your white matted
Hair. Your body looks white, smeared
With white holy ashes. A garland of heads
Covered your chest. You ride a white bull.
You play *dambaru* on holy occasions,
You've white Basuki cobra around
Your neck. You've white bracelets
And anklets on you. Your face is as
White as lotus and your three eyes

Are white. One who worships you with
A pious mind is conveyed
To the white Kapilas.[1] Your heart is all
Out for your devotees.
Siddheswar Das prays to the white
Linga with single-minded devotion.

x x x x

"Listen, O Pandu's son!
Looking at Laba, Srirama said thankfully,
'I'm happy to learn how Ravana was born.
Now I'm anxious to know about Sita,
The prime cause of Ravana's death.'
At this, Laba came up with *Bichitra Baisakha*
Raga that enthralled the listeners.
With ears raised and eyes open, they jostled
With each other to have a clear view
Of Sita's sons. Lakshmana pushed them
Back, appealing for calm. Soon there was
Absolute silence and Laba began:

Brahma composed the Vedas in *Satya yuga*.
Raising a sacrificial fire and offering
Ghee, oats and sesame seeds to it,
He began reciting the Vedas. It was
In the afternoon of a Thursday,
The fifth day of the bright fortnight
Of Magha, star *Punarbasu*. From
The rhythmical vibration of the recitation,
A beautiful woman was born,[2] as if

[1] Kailash.
[2] This is altogether a new story invented by the author.

Gold from mud. She was named Bedamati.
Her face was like the moon on the full moon
Day of Autumn, lips as red as *jaba*
And nose as sharp as Garuda's.
Curls of hair flopping over her forehead
Looked like bumblebees swarming around
Her lotus-face. She had long ears,
A waist as slender as the middle
Of the *dambaru*, hips soft and round,
Belly like lotus-leaf, thighs like banana
Trees and arms like lotus-stems.
Her body shone like *champak* flower;
Lotus bloomed as she walked. Her
Fingers were like *champak* buds, teeth
Like *jui* flowers, breasts like a pair
Of golden pots and voice seemed
As sweet as that of a male cuckoo.

Surprised at her striking beauty,
The sage mused, 'Where shall I find a groom
For her? How can I hand her over to someone
Who is no match for her?' Guessing what
Her father was worried about, Bedamati
Said, 'The Lord of the Universe, Lakshmi's
Consort is the one I wish for. He is the jewel
Among men. I need no other groom.'
On the north bank of the holy river,
Bhagirathi, she sat in meditation, praying
To Vishnu. Dressed in ochre clothes,
Smearing her forehead with holy ash
And putting on a *rudraksha* garland
Around her neck, she sat in deep
Meditation, thinking on Vishnu.

One day Ravana, the monarch of the three
Worlds was passing by that way in
His chariot, when his eyes fell on her.
Completely bewitched by her beauty,
He stopped his chariot there and came
To her. He asked her, 'Why you meditate?
I'm Ravana, Lord of the three worlds.
Come, sit in my chariot. I'll take you
To my kingdom. You'll be my wife. Many
Maids will be at your service.' Bedamati
Did not respond as her mind was focused
On Vishnu. In anger, the Ten-headed demon
Shouted at her, 'How dare you disrespect
Me, whom all the kshatriyas are mortally
Afraid of?' So saying, he pulled her
Towards him. He cut her long hair,
Undressed her and ravished her as
Cruelly as he could. Then, he sat in his
Chariot and flew away towards the north.

After he was gone, she became conscious
Of the tragedy that had befallen her.
She found blood flowing from her genitals
And splashing down onto her feet.
She burst into tears. She told herself,
'What's the use of this life, after being
Sexually abused by Dasanana?
How shall I show my face to my father?
Committing suicide will be a sin.
Alas! I'm a blight on my clan
And a laughing stock for others.'
Cursing Ravana for his misdemeanour,

She prepared a pyre and lit it.
Accepting the *dikpalas* as witnesses,
She said, 'Listen, O gods, to my prayer.
Wishing to have Vishnu as my husband
I was meditating while Dasanana came
And defiled my caste. O Srihari!
Bless me so that you'll be mine in my next
Birth. It's you who will kill Dasanana.'
Saying so, she jumped into the burning pyre.

The tale of Bedamati's sad demise
Brought tears to Srirama's eyes.
The misty-eyed listeners sat still,
Their mouths hung open.
When Srirama asked the boys to go on,
Laba and Kusha read out:

Returning from his northern tour,
Ravana stopped where he had met the girl.
He saw her body burning in the pyre.
Loading it in the chariot, he brought it
To the palace. Giving it in the hands
Of his wife, he told her, 'Cook it by
Yourself and don't let others touch it.
Serve me at my meal.' Horrified
By the incident, Indra sent Narada
To meet Mandodari. When Narada arrived,
Mandodari asked him, 'What bring you here,
O sage? You're Brahma's son who looks
Like Rudra. I feel myself blessed
By your presence.' Narada said,
'Indra has sent me to talk to you.

The purpose of your marriage with
Ravana is going to be materialised.
By bringing the dead body, Ravana
Has dug his own grave. It's the body
Of Bedamati whom Ravana had
Sexually exploited. The sage's daughter,
Unable to bear the insult, consigned
Herself into the sacrificial fire.
Save her body at any cost
And pave the way for Ravana's death.
Hide it somewhere secretly.' After
He was gone, she hid the dead body
In a golden pot. She fed Ravana with
The flesh of an animal and he ate
It to his heart's content.

Some days later, Narada appeared again.
He asked Mandodari to check what has
Happened to the dead body. To her surprise,
The dead body had turned to a beautiful
Girl. Her eyes looked like those of a doe,
Face like the moon on the full moon day
And arms like lotus-stem. She told
Narada, 'Your words have come true.
There is a beautiful girl in the pot.
The sage cautioned her, 'If Ravana
Sees her, he'll marry her instantly.
An elderly person cannot avoid
The temptation of sleeping with a girl.
It's unsafe to keep her in the palace.
So, put her in a box and float it
In the sea.' When it became night

Mandodari kept her in a box which
She floated in the sea.

The box floated on and on,
Until it got stuck to the shore
In Bideha kingdom, where King Janaka
Lived. He had four queens, but no issues.
In consultation with the sages,
He had decided to perform a *yajna*.
He chose the sandy shore for it,
And to sanctify the place, they sowed
Sesame seeds there. When the plants bore
Fruits on them, they allowed the cattle
To graze there. When the altar was under
Construction, Janaka saw an *apsara*
Flying above. Seeing her beauty, Janaka
Said, 'Can't I have a daughter, such as
She is, whom I'll marry to Vishnu?
Then only my sins will be expiated
And I'll find a berth for myself
In heaven.' Hearing his words, the *apsara*
Stopped the chariot and spoke out,
'O sage! The kind of daughter you're
Looking for is lying under the sand.
Take her home and marry her to Vishnu,
The saviour of the world.' They dug
Deeper and found a box which contained
A beautiful girl in it, who looked like
The incarnation of Lakshmi.
Janaka thought: Five generations ago,
One of my ancestors appeased Shiva
By his devotion and was rewarded with
The Lord's bow. Since then, we have been

Worshipping it in our house.' He vowed,
'One who breaks the bow shall marry
My daughter.' Just then, heaven resounded
With praises of God. People rejoiced at
The news, and Janaka's joy knew no bounds.
She was named Sita[3] and was looked after
By Somakanti, one of Janaka's wives.
The *yajna* was held ceremoniously
And by eating the *charu* collected from
The sacrificial fire, Janaka's queens
Gave birth to three daughters,
Alaka, Urmila and Tara.

To find a groom for Sita,
Janaka held a *swayambara*, to which
Kings from far and wide were invited.
None of them could lift the bow,
Let alone break it. 'Where do I find
A groom for Sita now? My other
Daughters are already grown-up!'
Janaka broke down with grief.

Listening to the tale of Sita's birth
Srirama told Laba, 'I never knew
All this before. Now I would like to know
How Sita was married; that'll give me
Eternal peace.' Laba started singing
In *Baradi* raga. As if under a spell,
All the listeners fell silent,
Their eyes locked on Laba.

x x x x

[3]The story of Sita's birth was the author's own invention.

Laba and Kusha continued:
When the sages of Mithila came to know
That Dasaratha was blessed with four sons,
They begged sage Biswamitra delightedly,
'O sage! Go to Ayodhya and get Rama,
Dasaratha's son here. We'll deploy him
At the entrance of the *yajna* site
And perform the rituals without fear.
As the supreme authority of Mithila,
It's your responsibility to bring Rama
Here. He is the incarnation of Vishnu.
Seeing him, our sins will be redeemed.'
In response to their request, Gyadhi's son
Arrived in Ayodhya. Conveying
His deep respect to Basistha, he occupied
The throne, on request.

Dasaratha bowed at the sage's feet.
With folded hands, he told the sage humbly,
'My kingdom feels blessed by your presence.
You've the rare distinction of carrying,
The titles of Rajarsi and Brahmarsi.'
Biswamitra told him, 'You're one of
The greatest kings of the clan of Sun,
Known for your heroic exploits.
In your old age, you became the father
Of four sons. Our lives in the forest
Are beset with the fear for the demons.
We're unable to observe the rituals
Uninterrupted, which is a sin.
The sages do their work under the protection
Of the king; therefore, the king shares

Half of the virtues. The king is duty-bound
To protect the righteous and destroy
The wicked. He is the saviour of the oppressed
Mass. Born to Bhagirath's family,
You're the greatest of all kings in Jambu
Island. Of your four sons, send
Rama and Lakshmana with me.
I'll teach them the methods of warfare
As well as scriptures. They'll be given
The responsibility of guarding
The *yajna* site.'

Dumbstruck, Dasaratha fainted. Basistha
And the courtiers took him inside
And brought him round. With consolatory
Words, Basistha told him, 'If you don't
Send your sons with him, leaving aside
Your emotional bondage, the Sun dynasty
Is sure to perish in the fathomless sea.
Haven't you heard of Biswamitra's power?
He'd killed my hundred sons.
His anger is as dangerous as fire.
So, without a second thought,
Hand over your sons to Biswamitra.'
Dasaratha said sorrowfully, 'My conscience
Doesn't approve of it. How can I send
My dearest son, Rama to the forest?'
Just then, Rama and Lakshmana, leaving
Their shooting practice, returned to their
Father, bow and arrow in hand.
Finding his father worried, Rama asked
Him the cause of his worry. Dasaratha

Replied, 'Son! Biswamitra has come
To take you to his hermitage. How can
I live here, leaving you in the forest?
Never shall I do it, even if it costs
My life.' Srirama consoled him, 'Father!
Why do you worry? Send for Bharata
And Shatrughna who are at our uncle's
House. We should consider ourselves
Fortunate enough to go with the sage
To the forest. Children as we're,
Will the sage do any harm to us?
Father! Allow us to go with the sage
Without any apprehension.'

Moved by his words, Dasaratha took
Rama and Lakshmana to Biswamitra.
He told him, 'I love my sons more than my life.
They'll follow you wherever you go.
How will they walk all the way through
Hills and deep forest? Let me arrange
A chariot.' Carrying out his order,
The charioteer presented himself before
Him with the chariot. Seeing it, the sage said,
'This is of no use to us. Listen, O King!
Your sons will have no problem. I'll make
Them proficient in scriptures and archery.
I'll bring them back to you in time.
Be assured, not a thorn will prick your sons.
They'll stay in my hermitage comfortably.'
Relaxed, Dasaratha bade them farewell.
Hearing the news of Rama's journey
To the forest, the queens and others

Wailed and wept. Brahma's son, however,
Consoled them. Bharata and Shatrughna
Reached the palace that day, and, hearing
The news, got themselves ready to go
With them. But Dasaratha forbade them to do so.

The details put forth by Laba
Took Rama by surprise. He told Basistha,
'How could they know what I had said to
My father?' Basistha cautioned him,
'Don't interrupt. Only listen to what they say.'
Then, turning to Laba and Kusha, he said,
'Gyadhi's son took away Rama and Lakshmana
With him. What did they do next?'
Laba continued:

Listen carefully. Led by Biswamitra,
Rama and Lakshmana reached the forest.
The sight of wild beasts such as lions,
Boars, elephants and bears,
And the melodious notes of forest birds
Thrilled them. Passing the range of mountains,
They entered the deep forest. Seeing Rama,
The dead warriors of Bali, lying there, were
Liberated from their earthly bondage.
After a bath in the Narmada, they visited
The shrine of Shiva. The Lord appeared
Before them and blessed them, saying,
'May you save the world from the wicked.
Wage war against the demons and destroy them.'
Saying so, he disappeared.

Giving them some tips on archery,
Biswamitra left the Narmada and led them
Along the shore. He told them,
'Beware of a demoness called Tadaki,
The widow of Tadaka, who eats those who
Pass by the way. We can reach Mithila
In three days if we take this way.
But as it is teemed with demons,
We've to take the longest route, along
The eastern bank to reach our destination
In six months.' Srirama suggested,
'We'll go by the shortest route. Let's see
How powerful the demoness is!' As
They were walking along, they saw Tadaki,
Her head touching the sky, suddenly
Appearing before them, followed by her
Two younger brothers. Frightened,
Biswamitra told Rama, 'Didn't I forbid
You to take this way? Now, chant the *mantra*
I had told you and shoot at them.'
Raising the bow, Rama took the aim.
He shot a *habada* arrow at her while
She was rushing forward to attack him.
It struck her face; she fell down on
The ground, unconscious. Soon she
Recovered and stood up. This time, Rama
Sent a *babal* arrow, which hit her
At the waist, and tore her body into half.
Seeing this, her sons, Subahu and Maruchi,
Disguised as bulls, ran towards Rama,
Seeking revenge. Rama shot at them
With *pabana* arrow. The arrow drifted

Maruchi to the seashore, where
He hid in a well. Subahu was carried
In the air to the other side of the sea.
With another *babal* arrow he chopped off
Balamochana's head, who was her brother.

Excited by Rama's heroic deed,
The listeners of Ayodhya showered
Praises on him. They chanted in chorus:
'Glory to you, O Kausalya's son!
As a child, you killed the great demoness.
Your fame has no bounds.
But why did you diminish your fame,
By banishing Janaki to the forest?'
Struck by grief, Srirama was quiet,
His head in his hands. Basistha instructed
Everyone to observe silence when
The scripture was being read out.
Soon there was silence all over the place.

x x x x

After killing Tadaki, Rama,
With Lakshmana and Biswamitra bathed
At Kapala Bimochana, a place of pilgrimage.
On their arrival in Mithila, the sages
There applauded Biswamitra, saying,
'You've done a great service to us.
It's for you that we could
See God with our own eyes. Now,
Let's arrange a *yajna* and deploy Rama
At the entrance. On the eleventh day
Of the bright fortnight of Margasira

The *yajna* was held, the entrance guarded
By Rama and Lakshmana. Hearing
The recitation of the Vedic *slokas*,
The demons flocked to the *yajna* site
And put out the holy fire. At this, Rama
Challenged them, and, except ten or
Twenty who escaped, he killed all of them.
The sage completed the fire-worship,
Uttering *Sri Bhagabate Basudevaya*.
Thereafter peace and order prevailed;
There the sages could move freely
Through the forest, without fear for demons.

Caressing Nandini, the wish-fulfilling cow,
Biswamitra prayed to her, 'Mother!
Feed Rama and Lakshmana to their
Heart's content.' She gave them cream,
Banana and many nice things to eat.
Thus, Dasaratha's sons spent their days
In Mithila quite comfortably.

When the news of Rama's arrival
In Mithila reached sage Goutama,
He sent Sadananda, one of his disciples
To Biswamitra to fetch them.
Sadananda reached Mithila and told
The sage, 'My guru asks you to come
To his hermitage with Rama and Lakshmana.'
Biswamitra told the boys, 'Look! Goutama,
Brahma's son, has sent for you.
Let's go to him with his messenger
And avail of ourselves the privilege

Of seeing the sage.'
While entering Goutama's cottage,
Rama's feet struck against a stone,
That instantly turned to a beautiful
Woman, who flew away into heaven.
Going inside, they bowed at Goutama's feet.

Laba and Kusha gave a detailed
Account of the conversation that went on
Between Rama and Goutama.
Hearing this, Rama asked Basistha,
'How could they know what Goutama said
To me? Even Lakshmana, being my brother,
Doesn't know it. We feel the taste
Of nectar when they read out the *Ramayana*!'
Basistha replied, 'Saraswati inhabits
Him who reads out the scripture.
Whatever happens in the three worlds
Never hides from his view, as Narayana
Speaks through him. The guru who taught
Him is a great sage. We'll know all that
Afterwards. But now, focus your mind
Only on the scripture.' When they stopped,
Laba and Kusha resumed:

Goutama gave Rama and Lakshmana
Many things that they hadn't seen before.
One night, Rama asked Biswamitra
How a piece of stone could turn to a woman
By the touch of his feet. Biswamitra
Explained, 'That woman is Goutama's wife,
Ahalya. Enchanted by her matchless

Beauty, Indra and Sun made love to her.
In effect, she gave birth to two sons,
Whom Goutama brought up with love.
Seeing this, Anjana Kumari was enraged;
She told the sage about Ahalya's infidelity.
The sage threw the babies into water
And cursed Ahalya to turn to stone.
Knowing about Anjana's foul play,
Ahalya too cursed her. In consequence
Anjana had illegal relationship with the Wind,
Resulting in the birth of Hanumanta.'

The reading was still continuing.
The listeners were drinking in the sweet
Words of the scripture. The Sun
Had ascended to the middle of the sky.
Still no one complained of thirst or hunger.

28

Marriage of Rama and his Brothers

Five days they spent in Goutama's hermitage.
Then, Rama and Lakshmana returned
To Mithila with Biswamitra.
Wherever they stopped on the way,
For rest and relaxation, Biswamitra
Would impart the teachings of various
Shastras on them. On the fourth day
Of their stay in Mithila, Janaka sent
A messenger, inviting them to visit
His place. Biswamitra called Rama
And Lakshmana and told them, 'Maharsi
Janaka is the King of Bideha. He has
A beautiful daughter called Sita.
He has a bow, Akalita by name, which
No king in the world was able to lift.
He has vowed to marry his daughter
To the one who can break it.'
When Srirama consented to go,

They set out for Bideha with the messenger.
Reaching there, Rama and Lakshmana
Bowed at Janaka's feet, while Janaka
Held Biswamitra in deep embrace.
The king blessed Dasaratha's sons
And fed them with delicious dishes.

To find a groom for his daughter,
Janaka held a *swayambara*, to which
Kings from far and wide were invited.
On the appointed day, they assembled
In the palace which was elaborately
Decorated. There was a chrystal platform
On which Sita was seated; the bow was
Placed near the kings. Rama wanted
To know more facts about the bow from
Biswamitra, which the sage told him.
Laba told Srirama in detail what
Biswamitra said. He also elaborated
On what Rama told Ravana when
He failed to raise the bow.

Ravana, while trying to pick up the bow,
Vomited blood, which flowed from
His ten mouths. Indisposed, he was sent
To Lanka with his charioteer. When it was
Rama's turn, he picked up the bow effortlessly.
While trying to string it, the bow remained
Steady, but when he pulled the string upto
His ear, it broke into two pieces.
Seeing the bow broken, Janaka's daughter
Came forward and adorned Rama

With a garland of golden lotuses.
Being informed by Srirama's messenger,
Dasaratha set out for Bideha with Basistha,
Gruhamedha and Lomapada, flanked by
His courtiers and soldiers. Bharata
And Shatrughna also accompanied him.
A huge number of chariots, elephants
And horses moved along among the sounds
Of bugles, trumpets and horns.
As they advanced, the mountains seemed
To be crushed under their feet. The sentry
Informed Janaka, 'King Dasaratha is coming
With a huge army. You may not be able
To entertain them all.' Janaka replied,
'I'll be glad to feed each of them,
And, in addition, offer them gifts.'
Arrangements were made accordingly
And the palace was decorated
So as to look colourful.

When Dasaratha arrived,
Janaka greeted him warmly and welcomed
Him into the palace. He fed all the guests
Well and gave away gifts among them.
Rama and Lakshmana bowed to Basistha,
Who blessed them, saying, 'May you achieve
Fame and fortune. May you destroy
The wicked demons from the world with
Your might.' Seeing Rama and Lakshmana,
Dasaratha took them in his arms, caressed
And kissed them. The four brothers sat
Near their father. When Biswamitra came,

Dasaratha lay prostrate before him.
With folded hands, he said, 'O sage!
I owe you a favour.' Biswamitra told
Him, ' Your son is a great warrior.
By virtue of his might, he won for himself
A bride who is a jewel among women.
Now see that the marriage takes place soon.'
Janaka interrupted, 'Rama got Sita
By virtue of a kshatriya's might. I've
Three other daughters. I wish to marry
Them to Dasaratha's sons. It'll be a great
Event for all of us.' Hearing this,
Dasaratha was filled with joy; the sages
Too appreciated it. The four daughters,
Decked in bridal robes and jewellary,
Were seated on the chrystal platform.
The marriage ceremony took place,
Rama was married to Sita, Bharata
To Alaka, Lakshmana to Urmila
And Shatrughna to Tara. Janaka gave
Five crores of gems to each couple.
He also gave them ornaments, expensive
Robes and a pot of gold, studded with gems.

Laba told Srirama about Janaka's
Advice to Rama. Looking at Basistha,
Srirama said, 'What they say is true.'
But he fell silent when Basistha
Gestured at him not to speak.

After the ceremony was over,
All of them joined the feast. The couples

Waited in the palace until the wedding
Was over. Thereafter, Dasaratha was
About to leave for Ayodhya when
Biswamitra told him, 'When I brought
Your sons from your palace, how sad
You were! Now you're going back with
Four daughters-in-law.' So saying,
The sage returned to his hermitage.

29

Parsurama's Embarrassment

Dasaratha proceeded to Ayodhya
With his people and army, among
The sounds of bugles, trumpets and horns.
The deafening sound brought Parsurama
To the scene, who, in anger, blocked
The way. Terrified, the soldiers ran for
Life. Dasaratha lay prostrate before him,
While Basistha persuaded him to be calm.
But all persuasions failed to pacify him.
He was roaring madly, 'Who broke
The Shiva's bow in Mithila?' It was then that
Rama reached there. Seeing his father
Thus humiliated, he lost his patience,
And shouted at Parsurama, 'Why do you
Use weapons, being a brahmin? Why
Do you show disrespect to your king?'
Srirama's words made him boiling mad;
He went on lecturing on his skills
And achievements. Srirama warned

Him, 'Stop your boastful words! Today
I'll expose you completely. Born as
A brahmin, you act as a kshatriya.
How dare you show your pride at this
Ripe age? My father has been lying
At your feet; doesn't it prick your
Conscience? I can teach you a lesson
Now, but I don't want to commit a sin
By taking a brahmin's life.'
Parsurama reacted violently, 'You feel
Yourself great for having broken
Janaka's bow. Don't think your
Heroism will work everywhere. That
Bow was far too old, eaten up by
Worms. That's why it gave way when
You picked it up. I challenge you
To string my bow; that'll prove how
Great you are!' Stretching his left
Hand, Rama took Parsurama's *Bijaya* bow.
With both hands, he fixed the string,
And when he gave a pull, it broke into
Two pieces. Embarrassed, Parsurama
Realised that he was no other than
Vishnu himself. He gave Rama
Another bow and taught him some *mantras*
Before he went on a pilgrimage.

Then, the journey resumed until
They reached the palace of Ayodhya.
While entering the palace, Rama killed
Kubuji. Dasaratha's queens welcomed

Their daughters-in-law cheerfully.
Srirama bowed at his mothers' feet,
Who blessed him. Dasaratha, with his sons
And daughters-in-law, lived in Ayodhya
Happily. Lomapada and Gruhamedha
Left for their respective places.'

Markanda added, 'O Pandu's son!
Sita's sons are telling the story
Of the *Ramayana* to Srirama, making
The hearts of the listeners flutter.
The Sun has already ascended the middle
Of the sky; still all were as attentive as before.'

30

Rama's Journey to the Forest

'O Pandu's son!
Listen to the events that followed,
As sung by Laba and Kusha.'

Dasaratha, the unrivalled King of Aydodhya,
Discharged his royal duties, as usual.
Noticing Rama's meteoric rise to fame,
He called Basistha and his courtiers
And instructed them, 'Find an auspicious
Day for my eldest son's coronation.'
When Basistha mentioned the day,
He called Rama and passed instructions
To him about the duties of a king.
He told him, 'The success of a king lies
Not in holding an *Aswamedha yajna*
Or donating a *gajaghanta*, but in
Devoting himself to the wellbeing
Of his subjects.' The news of Rama's
Coronation created many a ripple

Among the people. Golden urns filled with
Water were placed at the door of the palace.

Laba narrated how Manthadi,
Kaikeyee's maid, provoked her. Srirama
Spoke out, 'That Manthadi is the root of all
Evils. She is responsible for my suffering.
It's for her wickedness that my father
Died helplessly.' As he stopped, Laba said:

Provoked by Manthadi's words,
Kaikeyee prevailed upon her husband
To ordain her son the new king and banish
Rama to the forest for fourteen years.
Terribly shocked to hear this, Dasaratha
Fainted. Next morning, he told Rama,
'You'll have to remain in the forest for
Fourteen years. You'll live the life
Of a hermit, living on sweet potatoes,
Putting on saffron clothes, keeping long hair,
Holding a *kamandalu* and smearing
Your body with holy ashes.' Accepting
His father's instructions with alacrity,
When Rama told Sita about it, she readily
Joined him and Lakshmana too followed
Them. The threesome, before leaving,
Met Kausalya to have her blessings.
Unable to stand the sight, Kausalya
Let out a loud cry. She poured out
Her feelings in what she said to Rama.

Hearing this, Srirama asked
Basistha, 'O sage! How could these two

Know what my mother told me?' Basistha
Replied, 'It's because they are noble souls.
Now be patient and listen to them.
They're telling exactly what you did
And experienced in your life.' When
Rama became quiet, Laba sang:

When Rama left for the forest,
Bharata and Shatrughna were in their
Uncle's house. Agonised over Rama's
Exile, Dasaratha passed away that night.
A messenger rushed to Bharata
And Shatrughna and brought them back.

On reaching Ayodhya, they found their
Father dead and brothers missing.
His eyes tearful, Bharata asked,
'Where are our brothers?' Basistha said,
'The night before Rama's coronation,
Your mother asked the king to ordain
You the new king and banish Rama
To the forest. So Rama left for the forest
And Lakshmana followed him. As
A devoted wife would do, Sita joined
Him. Now it's your duty to cremate
Your father, and, then, take over the charges
Of the kingdom.' Infuriated, Bharata
Unsheathed his sword to cut off his head,
But Kausalya and Sumitra stopped him.
He, then, carried his father's body to Rama,
Who was staying in Chitrakuta. Twenty-one
Hundred queens, Basistha and the courtiers
Followed him.

Finding his father dead,
Rama broke down with grief. He cremated
His father there and completed ten days
Of funeral proceedings. When Bharata
And Shatrughna begged him to come back
To Ayodhya, he declined, considering it
An act of disobedience to his father.
All those who had gone there returned.
Bharata and Shatrughna launched
A scathing attack on Kaikeyee.

Laba told Srirama in detail
The arguments that went on between
Bharata and Kaikeyee.
He also added how Kausalya
Pined for Rama day and night.

31

Khara and Duhsana Eliminated

After a year's stay in Chitrakuta,
Rama went on a pilgrimage. Sita's sons
Gave a detailed account of the places
He visited, the rivers he bathed in
And the things he did during his journey.

Seeing Rama in the forest,
Maharshi Agasti expressed his sympathy
For him. He took him to the Panchubati
Forest, and, making him sit under
The overhanging *siuli* creepers, he left.

Laba reported Rama's meeting with
Jatayu and their conversation,
Which was explained elaborately by Kusha.
Srirama found each of the words
They said to be true.

One day, Lakshmana, looking for
Firewood, combed the whole forest,

But was disappointed not to find it.
To make matters worse, his right foot
Was pricked by a bamboo thorn,
And, while pulling it out with his left hand,
The wound bled profusely. He lay
There, almost unconscious. Wincing in
Pain, he accused Kaikeyee for all this.

As Laba was saying this, Srirama looked at
Lakshmana questioningly, who confessed
That to be true. Basistha silenced them
And allowed Laba and Kusha to go on:

Filled with anger, Lakshmana ran
Here and there until he came to a place
Where Japasura was in meditation,
His head down and legs upraised.
Mistaking his legs for wood, Lakshmana
Cut it down. His body cut into half,
The demon fell dead. Taking him for
A sage, he felt guilty and full of remorse.
When he told this to Rama, he arrived there
With Sita. Seeing Rama, Japasura was
Liberated. Coming back, the two brothers
Built a hut under the roof of *siuli* creepers.

Wishing to see her son, Suparnekhi[1] came
To the forest where Japasura was meditating.
Finding him lying dead, she rolled on
The ground, crying bitterly. When
She looked around, she found footsteps

[1] Subarnarekha.

With the signs of lotus and wheel. Following
The footsteps, she reached the hut and saw
Rama and Lakshmana talking to each other.
She heard Lakshmana narrating how
He killed Japasura. Seeking revenge,
She decided, 'I'll seduce Lakshmana
And be his wife. I'll please him by
Offering my body to him and kill him
When he'll fall asleep.'

Next morning, she came near the hut,
And, turning herself to a young woman,
Began to cry loudly. The noise brought
Sita there, who, out of sympathy, took
Her into the hut. At night, she went
To Lakshmana and begged for his love.
Irked by her behaviour, Lakshmana
Cut off her nose and ears. She fled
And complained about it to Trisira.
To avenge the insult, Khara and Duhsana,
Ravana's brothers mounted an attack on
Rama with fourteen hundred soldiers.
Rama killed all the demons and beheaded
Khara, Duhsana and Trisira.

32

Sita's Abduction

Returning to Lanka,
Suparnekhi, showing her nose and ears
To Ravana, complained against Rama
And Lakshmana. Hearing from her
About Sita's matchless beauty,
The Ten-headed one hurried to Panchubati.
But he dared not go to Rama's hut
For fear for Rama. He asked Maruchi[1]
To disguise himself as a two-headed deer[2]
And keep grazing near Sita's place.

Laba and Kusha read out to Srirama
How Sita, seeing the deer, prevailed on Rama
To fetch it for her.

Sriramachandra chased the deer
To catch it. Seeing Rama following it,

[1] Maricha.
[2] In Valmiki's *Ramayana* the deer had only one head.

It ran as quickly as it could. After
A chase of one hundred *yojanas*, when
He found it beyond reach, he shot at it
With a *babal* arrow that cut off its heads.
While dying, Maruchi cried out loudly,
'O Lakshmana! Save me!' Frightened
By the cry, Sita asked Lakshmana to go
And help his brother. Before leaving,
Lakshmana drew three lines with the tip
Of his bow and cautioned her, 'Don't
Cross over these lines. No men nor demons
Can reach you. Whoever passes over it,
Is sure to die.' Once Lakshmana left,
Ravana reached there in the guise
Of a sage, begging for alms.

As Sita went across the lines to offer
Alms to him, he caught her and pulled
Her away. Seeing it, Jatayu fought with
Ravana, while Sita escaped and hid
Under a banyan tree. With the *chandrahasa*
sword, Ravana severed Jatayu's right leg
and fetched Sita from under the banyan tree,
By pulling her hair. He pushed her into
The chariot and flew towards Lanka.
On the way, seeing Sugriba on the Risimukha
Mountain, Sita dropped a pair of her
Golden bangles and a piece of her clothing.
Reaching Lanka, Ravana held a meeting
Of his minister and courtiers. Bibhisana said,
By abducting Sita, he has dug his own grave.
Scared by his words, the Twenty-handed

Demon kept Sita in the Ashoka forest, with
Demonesses keeping guard over her.

Laba gave a detailed account of what
Bibhisana told Ravana. Srirama praised
Bibhisana for having done a great service
To him towards preserving his dignity.
While coming back after killing
The golden deer, Rama met Lakshmana
On the way. Reaching the hut, both of them
Looked for Sita, and not finding her there,
They cried bitterly. Accusing Lakshmana
For his negligence, Rama raised his sword
To kill him. Lakshmana told him,
'Why take pains to kill me? Before you do it,
I can cut off my head and give it in your
Hands. You're a victim to your indulgence
Towards your wife. Obeying her words,
You went away to catch the deer. Scolding
Me for my unwillingness to leave her,
She sent me to you forcibly. Ignoring
My request, she crossed the lines I had drawn.'

With a heavy heart, they went in search of
Sita, killing Yojanabahu on the way. They met
Jatayu who gave them the news of Sita's
Abduction by Ravana. Looking at Srirama's
Face, it breathed its last. After cremating
It, they reached the banks of the Godabari.
Seeing a *chakora* and a *chakori* in amorous
Playfulness, Rama asked them about Sita.
When they mocked him, Rama cursed them,

'If you mate at night, you'll die.' Then,
He met Tamrachuda bird whom he blessed.
Thereafter, they met the crane.

Reaching the Manmath forest, Lakshmana
Was overwhelmed to see a herd of cattle
Grazing there. He milked the cows,
And both the brothers drank the milk.
And took rest under a tree. They've been
Roaming through the forest for the last
Ten days. Fatigued, Rama fell asleep,
Resting his head on Lakshmana's thigh,
His bow still in his hand.

33

Making Friends with Sugriba

Sugriba had been there
To fight with Bali. Scared by Rama's
Radiance, he hid in the Risimukha mountain.
Seeing Srirama, Hanumanta came there,
And, finding him asleep, he climbed up
The tree. His movements shook the tree;
Some of the leaves fell on Rama that
Disturbed his sleep. Enraged, Lakshmana
Raised his bow and took aim at Hanumanta.
While doing so, his thigh moved and
Rama woke up. Looking at Lakshmana,
He asked, 'Who are you aiming at?'
Lakshmana replied, 'A red-faced monkey
Came from somewhere and shook the tree.
I was going to kill him.'
Rama looked up. He saw a monkey
Putting on a loin-cloth and a crown
On his head. Seeing Rama's face,
Hanumanta climbed down the tree,

And, holding his feet, lay prostrate before him.
At the time Sugriba reached there with
A pair of bangles and a piece of clothing.
Rama made friends with Sugriba
And killed Bali, by playing a trick on him.
He ordained Sugriba the king of Kiskindha
And married him to Bali's wife. Then,
Ramachandra spent the four rainy months
At the Malyabanta hill, sending Lakshmana
To Kiskindha to fetch Sugriba. When
Sugriba arrived, Rama sent for all
The monkeys who came and bowed at his feet.
Rama took a count of the monkeys.
Jambabana, the commander of bears,
Owed his allegiance to Rama.

34

Lanka Set Ablaze

In a bid to locate Sita,
Messengers were dispatched in all directions.
Jambabana, Satamali, Gandhamardana,
Hanumanta and Bali's son, Angada
Those five went southwards. Sitting down
On the seashore, they deliberated on how
To cross the sea. As no one came forward,
Hanumanta jumped over the sea.
And reached the land of Lanka.

Laba went on singing how Hanumanta killed
Ugratara and Simhikaka, how the Maninaga
Hill welcomed him warmly and how he
Destroyed Lanka. The people of Ayodhya were
Thrilled to hear it, as they did not know
Those before. They showered praises on him.

Thereafter, Hanumanta entered Lanka,
Spying on every nook and corner

Of the land, with a hope to find Sita.
Being tipped off by Tara that Sita was in
The Ashoka forest, Hanumanta met her there
And handed over Srirama's ring to her.
He gave her the news of Rama and Lakshmana.
She, in return, gave the ornament she wore
On her forehead to pass it on to Rama.
At parting, when he begged her for some
Food to eat, she advised him to go
To Madhubana and eat as many ripe
Fruits as he liked.

Entering Madhubana, the ten-*yojana*-long
Pleasure garden, Hanumanta ate all
The fruits and destroyed the whole garden.
Startled, the guards, eighty-four lakhs
In number, mounted an attack on him.
The battle lasted for a brief period,
In which Hanumanta finished off all
Of them. Being informed of it, Ravana
Sent Akshaya Kumar with his army.
A fight broke out between him
And Hanumanta, which ended with
Akshaya Kumar's pitiable death and most
Of his soldiers slain. Those who escaped,
Informed Ravana of Akshaya's death.
The Ten-headed One, then, sent Indrajita
With a large number of soldiers.
In the battle that followed, Hanumanta
Overpowered them. Realising that it was
Difficult to defeat Hanumanta, he planned
To win on the sly. Finally, Hanumanta was

Tricked into getting caught in the cobra
Snare set by Indrajita and was presented
Before Ravana. Considering the extent
For his mischief, Ravana ordered to kill him
Then and there. It was but for Bibhisana's
Request that his death penalty was postponed
To the next morning.

When it became morning,
Ravana ascended the throne, as usual,
And asked his order to be carried out.
Indrajita struck Hanumanta with
The *chandrahasa* sword. To their surprise,
Not a hair on his body was removed,
Rather, the edge of the sword turned blunt.
With a smile, Hanumanta said, 'You can't
Kill me like that. O Lord of Lanka!
Let me tell you how to kill me. Wrap a length
Of cloth around my tail, soak it with oil
And then, set it on fire.' When it was done,
Hanumanta wagged his tail. The fire
Spread all over Lanka and burnt it
Down. Then, he came back to Rama
And handed over Sita's ornament to him.

35

Preparations for the Battle

Following the advice of Baruna,
God of Water, Rama built a bridge
On the sea, with the help of Sugriba
And his monkey soldiers. Jambabana,
Satabali, Nala and Nila were busy
Piling matching boulders. Hanumanta
Alone fetched a mountain that covered
One hundred *yojanas*. The bridge completed,
Hanumanta entered Lanka with the army
Of monkeys. Rama stayed back in the Subalaya
Hill where Kanka and Dhanka used to live.
They rushed to Lanka and told Ravana,
'O King! A large army of monkeys
And bears is advancing towards Lanka.
Rama looks most formidable.' Scared,
Ravana mounted the Pushpak chariot,
Covering it with one lakh umbrellas.
Locating Rama, he stayed put in the midair
To watch his movements.

At the time, Rama, after bath, was offering
A handful of water to the sun. When
He looked up, he did not find the sun in the sky.
He asked Jambabana, 'How come, the sun was
So bright a moment ago, and now he is
Nowhere to be seen!' Jambabana replied,
'Ravana is watching you from above.
Because of the umbrellas on his chariot,
Chhaya's consort is hidden from sight.'
Without delay, Rama raised the *kodanda* bow
And shot at Ravana's chariot. The one lakh
Umbrellas covering his chariot were flung
Into the sea, exposing him to the sweltering
Heat of the sun. Learning from his charioteer
That Rama had struck off the umbrellas,
He fled straight to his palace, without
Turning back even for once.

Laba narrated through song
What thoughts went on in Ravana's mind
That moment, to which the people of Ayodhya
Listened carefully. Basistha thanked
Rama with a flurry of applause.

36

Bibhisana Seeks Refuge

Laba and Kusha continued:

As Ravana fled to Lanka in fear,
Kanka and Dhanka conspired to steal
Rama's bow. In trying to lift it, blood
Came out from their mouths. Failing
To do it, they cut the string. Suddenly
The bow gave a mighty jerk, both
Of its ends piercing through their chests,
Causing death. Rama reset the string,
And, using the bow and arrow, killed
Most of the followers of Kanka and Dhanka.
Those who escaped, informed Ravana
That Kanka and Dhanka were dead.
Seeing Ravana in dismay, Bibhisana,
With folded hands, suggested, 'O King!
If you do as I say, all your worries will be over.
Let's return Sita to Rama and live in Lanka
Without fear. If you don't, you'll lose

Everything you have.' Flying into a fury,
He kicked Bibhisana on his chest that
Made him faint. When he recovered,
He decided to take refuge at Rama's feet.
He met Rama and told him all that had
Happened to him. Rama took him into
His lap and caressed his head, assuring
Him to ordain him the King of Lanka.
Shocked at the news, next morning,
Ravana sent two messengers to Rama.
Disguised as monkeys, they mingled with
Other monkeys and spied on all the places.
Bibhisana could detect them easily;
He brought them to Rama as prisoners.
Rama pardoned them and welcomed them
With garlands. Surprised at Rama's treatment,
They went back to Ravana and told him
About Rama's magnanimity.

37

False Heads

Seized with fear,
Ravana, showing two false heads to Sita,
Said, 'Here are the severed heads of Rama
And Lakshmana. As your husband
Tresspassed on my kingdom,
The demon soldiers killed him,
Without my knowledge. You'd pinned
Your hopes on Rama and Lakshmana.
Now that they're gone, come with me
And enjoy your life as my wife.' Her head
Downcast, Sita said, 'I'm burning with anger
When I hear this. You're a despicable, wicked
Demon. Tell me, how did you kill my husband
And brother-in-law? No kshatriya in
The three worlds dare defeat Rama in war.
Who can kill Sumitra's son who is simply
Unbeatable? If what you say is true,
Remember, your days are numbered. Once
Hanumanta comes to know of it, He'll sever

Each of the ten heads you have. The monkeys
Are powerful enough to contain your
Demon soldiers. If they fail, I'm there.
I'll reduce Lanka to ashes.'

Laba and Kusha narrated through songs
How Sita encountered Ravana. The listeners,
While praising Sita, said, 'Rama was angry
With her unreasonably. She had nothing
Wrong in her. Had she any inclination towards
Ravana, she would not have said all this.'
Hearing this Rama sat still, his head bent down.
Bharata and Shatrughna broke down
With grief. When Basistha silenced the
Listeners, the singing resumed:

It became morning. The monkeys got onto
The ramparts of Lanka and destroyed
Everything that came to their sight.
Seeing this, the guards hastened to the Ashoka
Forest and told Ravana, 'O King of Lanka!
What're you doing here? The monkeys
Are going on the rampage at your land.
You kidnapped a woman and brought
Ruins on your great kingdom.'

38

The Battle Breaks Out

Hearing from the messenger
That the security of Lanka was under
Threat, Ravana proceeded to the battlefield
To fight the invading army. As the battle
Continued, both sides suffered heavy
Casualties. Lanka resonated with
War cries. Hearing the noise, Srirama asked
Jambabana, 'What is this noise for? I guess,
It's coming from the south.' Jambabana replied,
'A fierce fight is going on between us
And the Lankan army, headed by Ravana.
Most of our monkeys and bears have lost
Their lives. This noise comes from there.'
Impatient and furious, Rama rushed
To the battlefield, followed by Lakshmana.
As they reached there, Anjana's son bowed
To Rama and said, 'O Sita's consort!
When I'm there to serve you, should you
Fight on foot? Come, sit on my shoulders

And fight the demons. If you command
Me, I'll wring Ravana's head and gouge
His throat.' Rama restrained him, saying,
'No, you won't; that's exclusively my
Privilege. I'll kill him with my own hands
To keep my promise.'

Adorning Hanumanta's shoulders,
Rama and Lakshmana displayed their
Skills, killing many demons and creating
Panic among the demon soldiers.
Ravana's charioteer cautioned him,
'O King of Lanka! If you continue to fight,
Rama will surely kill you.' In panic,
Ravana fled; his soldiers ran away
In fear, most of them severely wounded.
After causing havoc in the battlefield,
Rama returned to the Subalaya.

39

Angada as Messenger

Sharing his thoughts with his minister,
Ravana stated, 'The monkeys gather
Strength by eating the fruits. We'll shut
The gates of Lanka and won't allow them
To enter inside. Hunger will make them
Weak, and then, we'll surround them
And finish them off easily.'

Seeing Ravana sealing the borders,
Indra sent a message to Rama, through
One of the *gandharvas*, to save the monkeys
From peril. Having received the information,
Rama assigned the task to Hanumanta,
Who folded his tail around the monkeys
To keep them safe and sound.
In consultation with his minister,
Rama sent Angada, Bali's son, to Lanka
As a messenger. Ravana was sitting
On the throne when Angada met him.

Not occupying the seat meant for him,
Angada curled his tail many rounds
And piled it higher than Ravana's throne.
He sat on it, his feet pointed at Ravana's
Chest. Enraged, Ravana shouted at him,
'Hey monkey! How insolent you are!
Have you no fear? You sit here, splaying
Your legs in front of me? Tell me,
Who is your father?' Angada replied,
'What? You don't recognise me? I was
The one who once tied you with a rope.
I'm Angada, the son of Bali, the King
Of monkeys. He brought you, seizing
You by the hair, and I tied you with
A rope and made rounds through
The kingdom. How don't you recognise
Me? I've come here as Rama's messenger.
Who prompted you to abduct Sita,
O wicked demon? Merciful Rama wants
You to give back Sita and surrender to him.'

Angada's words made Ravana
Boiling mad. He ordered the demons
To hold him down. When eighteen lakh
Demons seized him, Angada expanded
His body gigantically, and holding
All of them within the fold of his tail,
Wrung their necks. He shook the throne
So violently that Ravana fell off the throne
And lay on the floor, bleeding and senseless,
Giving him a kick, Angada wrested
The crown from his head and returned

To Rama. Placing the crown before him,
He narrated his encounter with Ravana.

When Ravana recovered, some of his soldiers
Informed him that many of his courtiers
Were killed by the monkeys. They said,
'Command us. We'll wipe out the monkeys
And kill Rama and Lakshmana.'
Incensed, Ravana sent seven commanders
To fight the monkeys. In the battle that followed,
All seven commanders were brutally slain.
When the news reached Ravana, he wept
Bitterly, quoting the name of each of them.

40

Indrajita's Fight

Seeing his father in tears,
Indrajita, with folded hands, consoled him,
'Father! I'm going to fight back today.
I'll slay the whole lot of monkeys
And bears. You send Narantaka
And Debantaka, the two brothers, with me
And relax yourself.' Brimming with hope,
Ravana anointed his son with *kumkum*,
Aguru, musk and sandalwood paste.
He adorned him with crown, earrings
And a necklace of one hundred pearls.
Among the sounds of bugles, trumpets
And horns, Indrajita set out for
The battlefield. With spears and maces
In their hands, Narantaka and Debantaka
Strode along, followed by Indrajita's chariot.

Staying in the air, Indrajita supervised
The proceedings of the battle, while

Narantaka and Debantaka went on slaughtering
Monkeys and bears. When Rama's commanders
Blocked their way, they held them by the legs
And crushed them to the ground. Seeing
The two brothers advancing towards him,
Rama shot them to death using *krutantaka*
Technique. Finding them dead, Indrajita
Showered arrows from above indiscriminately
That put many to death. When Rama
Came forward to attack, he pulled up
His chariot before him and struck Rama
And Lakshmana with a *mohana* shot
Frightened, Bibhisana left the battlefield.
After wiping out Rama's soldiers,
He thought of killing Rama and Lakshmana.
Just then, the sun, which was in the middle
Of the sky, disappeared behind the Meru
Mountain. As darkness fell, Indrajita
Returned to his palace. He told his father
That Rama's army was completely routed
And all his soldiers slain. When Ravana
Heard that Narantaka and Debantaka
Have laid down their lives in the battle,
He was terribly upset.

After Indrajita was gone,
Bibhisana, hiding in the Subalaya hills,
Came out. He broke down to see
Sugriba's head severed, and Angada
And the other commanders lying dead,
Their bodies mutilated. Only Rama,
Lakshmana, Jambabana and Hanumanta

Were in a state of unconsciousness.
Taking Jambabana into his lap,
Bibhisana said tearfully, 'How I wish
I died with you! When Bibhisana's body
Touched Jambabana's, he woke up.
Wiping his eyes, he looked around in
Wonder. Bibhisana, between sobs, asked,
'What'll we do now? How to save the lives
Of Rama and Lakshmana?' Jambabana
Replied, 'Go to Hanumanta and bring
Back his consciousness. Get him here.
He only can bring the leaf of a medicinal
Plant by which the dead can get back
Their lives. Bibhisana hurried to
Hanumanta, and, chanting Rama's name,
Began to caress him, that brought back
His life. He broke down with grief
To hear Rama lying unconscious.
Jambabana, the King of Bears, told him,
'Listen, Maruti! Hurry to Hemabanta mountain.
Ask him to give you the leaf of the plant
Which will revive Rama and Lakshmana
To life.' When Hanumanta flew into
The air, the gods sent a *gandharva*
To Hemabanta with Indra's message.
Hemabanta, in trying to hide himself,
Hastened into the sky, when Hanumanta
Caught sight of him. He pulled the mountain
Back and carried it to Jambabana,
Requesting him to get the plant from it.
Hemabanta offered the leaf to Jambabana
Who gave it to Hanumanta, asking him to fan

Everyone with it. Hanumanta first went
To Rama and Lakshmana who regained
Their consciousness, being fanned with
The leaf. He fanned the monkeys, bears
And the commanders who got back their
Lives in a moment. Observing the miracle,
The gods in heaven cheered and strewed
Flowers on Rama. They sent a *gandharva*
To hand over a *sisirakiran* gem to Rama.

Laba and Kusha expressed through song
What Rama said to Jambabana, after
Receiving the gem. When Srirama
Attested to what they said, Basistha
Asked him to be calm and said,
'What happened during the battle
Is best known to you.'

41

Rama and Lakshmana Caught in Cobra Snare

When the news
That the King of Lanka would come to see
The dead soldiers next morning reached
Bibhisana, he rushed to Srirama
And told him, 'Ravana is coming to see
The dead bodies of our soldiers.
I've an idea. We'll lie in the battlefield
As if dead. When Ravana and his soldiers
Enter the field, we'll rise to our feet
And slay the demons.' Consenting to it,
Srirama held a meeting of the commanders
Of monkeys and bears and addressed them,
'All of us will lie down in the field with our
Eyes shut. No one will murmur a word.
When Ravana enters the place with
His soldiers, we'll capture and kill them all.'
In obedience to Rama's instruction,
The monkeys and bears lay in the field,
Withdrawing their breath.

Ravana arrived in a chariot with
His soldiers. As they got into where
The dead ones lay, the monkeys and bears
Sprang to their feet, and, raising war cries,
Started a fight, slaughtering the demons.
Thereafter, the monkeys invaded the palace,
Releasing the captive *apsaras* free
And destroying whatever came their way.
Ravana could not escape as Rama blocked
His way with *parvata bana*. Soon, Indrajita
Joined him and the battle resumed.
The fight between Hanumanta and Ravana's
Two sons, Kalanageni and Janughanta,
Ended tragically, Hanumanta wringing
Their heads and hurling them into the sea.
Seeing his sons' death, Ravana, full of remorse,
Left the battle and fled with Indrajita.

Reaching the palace, he was dumbstruck
To see the demonesses raising a loud cry,
Their noses cut. The *apsaras*,
Whom he had held captive, were nowhere
To be found. In bitter agony, he let out
A wail. Indrajita, with inspiring words,
Told him, 'Father! Today I'll capture
Rama and Lakshmana in the snare
And bring them to you.' Forgetting the loss,
He ordered Indrajita to go immediately.

Indrajita, with his demonic power,
Created a woman, looking exactly like Sita.
When it became night, he took her to Rama.
Mistaking her for Sita, Rama was extremely

Upset. Taking the opportunity, Indrajita
Attacked Rama and Lakshmana, his arrows
Turning to a cobra and binding them.
This way, he bound others too, except for
Bibhisana who escaped into the Subalaya hills.
Indrajita could have killed Rama then,
Had not Goddess Durga intervened.
She prevailed on him not to do so.

Returning, he told his father
That all were caught in the cobra snare.
Exceedingly happy, Ravana sent a message
To Trijata, in charge of the Ashoka forest,
To take Sita to the battlefield. Accompanied
By demonesses, Trijata carried Sita
In a chariot and flew to the Subalaya hills.
Seeing Rama bound and helpless,
She burst into tears. After showing
To her Rama's predicament, he returned.

Invoking Goddess Durga, Rama sought
Her help. She asked him to call Garuda.
When Rama called him, he arrived there.
Seeing Binita's son, all the snakes fled
In fear. Looking at Srirama's face,
The King of Birds said, 'Command me;
I'll kill Ravana and get Sita back.'
Rama forbade him, saying, 'I'll kill him
With my own hands because he is
My enemy. Relieved, Garuda
Returned to the Ramyak islands.

As Laba and Kusha narrated it in detail,
The listeners plunged into despair.
His eyes tearful, Bharata banged his head
Against the ground. Lakshmana held him
By both of his hands, while Basistha
Reminded him, 'Weren't you demanding
To go to the forest with Rama?
What would have you done there, when
You can't bear to hear this? Imagine,
What an ordeal Rama and Lakshmana
Might have passed through during
Their stay in the forest! Don't you know
That they are invincible! Now, forget
Your sorrow and listen to the scripture.'
Turning to Laba and Kusha, he said,
'Now enlighten us with the news
Of the war.' When silence was restored,
Laba and Kusha began singing.

42

The Killing of Indrajita

When it became night,
The King of Demons reached
The Ashoka forest to find Sita still
Weeping. With consolatory words,
He told her, 'Why do you mourn for
Rama and Lakshmana? From today,
You are my life. My son has trapped
Them in cobra snare. They'll be killed
As soon as it becomes morning. Your
Hopes for them are fading. Be my wife
And enjoy your life thoroughly.
I'll love you more than I love Mandodari.
I'll do as you say.' Her head downcast,
Sita bawled him out for his arrogance.
She said, 'You despicable wicked demon!
My husband is the greatest of all
The kshatriyas. If Dasaratha's son dies,
Do you think, I'll ever remain alive?'

Laba gave a detailed account
Of how she hurled abuse at Ravana.
Kusha explained when it needed
To be elaborated.

The night passed;
The day began on a cheerful note.
The monkeys jumped over the ramparts
And killed the gatekeepers with stumps
And stones. A great noise arose that filled
The air. Soon a messenger carried the news
To Ravana, 'All the monkeys are moving freely;
Rama and Lakshmana have freed themselves
From the snare.' Hearing this, Ravana left
The Ashoka forest and hurried to the palace.
Sitting on his throne, he sent for Indrajita.
When he came, Ravana scowled at him
And said that cobra snare had failed to work.
Indrajita assured him, 'This time I'll fight
Face to face. I'll kill the monkeys, the bears,
Rama and Lakshmana.' Saying this,
He held a *yajna* which Rama's commanders
Destroyed as soon as it began. They punished
The brahmins who took part in it.

Then, Indrajita entered the battlefield
And launched an attack on Rama's army.
Seeing this, Rama sent Lakshmana to face
The challenge. Lakshmana shot at him
With a *brahmasara* that killed him
Instantly. When Ravana heard the news,
He rolled on the ground, crying bitterly.

43

The Killing of Kumbhakarna

Kumbhakarna was having a deep sleep
When Ravana's minister woke him up.
Annoyed, he asked the minister,
'Why did you wake me up? Have you
No fear for death?' The minister replied,
'Do we have the guts to disturb your sleep?
But it's the king's order, and we daren't
Disobey it. Your brother has committed
A grievous mistake. He kidnapped Sita,
Srirama's wife. Hanumanta came to Lanka,
Looking for Sita. He destroyed the Madhubana
And killed Akshaya Kumar. Indrajita
Tied him and brought to the king. He tricked
Your elder brother into wrapping his tail
With cloth, soaking it with oil
And setting fire to it. In consequence,
He burnt down the whole of Lanka.
Returning to Rama, he informed him
Of Sita's captivity. Rama built a bridge

Over the sea and attacked Lanka.
In the battle that followed,
We suffered heavy casualties. Rama's
Brother killed Indrajita. In this situation,
The king needs your help. Had it not been so,
We wouldn't have come here to disturb you.'

Kumbhakarna got up and went straight
To Ravana. He bowed at his feet and found
His brother in tears. They held each other
In deep embrace and began to weep.
Ravana told him, 'Listen, brother!
I've lost all my soldiers by now.
Bibhisana, the sinner, has left me.
He has caused a great loss to me.
Lakshmana, Rama's brother, killed Indrajita,
The bravest of my sons. Brother!
You're my only hope. I'm sure you will kill
Rama and Lakshmana. Rama dares us
With the support of Sugriba, Bali's brother,
Who commands the army of monkeys.
Hanumanta has also become my enemy.'

Kumbhakarna replied, 'Why do you blame
Others? Why don't you admit that it is
Your fault? As a precaution, you wrote
Everywhere you won't kidnap Sita.
Why did you do it, then? Isn't it because
Of your self-pride? Now, listen to what
I say. Let's give Sita back to Rama
And surrender to him with all humility.
That'll bring an end to our sufferings.'

Enraged, Ravana rebutted, 'Why do you
Say all this? Think seriously. See,
If both of us are killed by Rama, we'll
Live happily in Vishnu's abode everafter.
What is the use of living a demon's life?
Don't you remember anything about our
Previous birth?' After much deliberation,
Kumbhakarna agreed and sat down to eat.
He ate sixty *pautis* of cooked rice, equal to
A man's food for six months, fruits,
Many sheep, goats and buffaloes.

As Kumbhakarna walked into the battlefield,
Many monkeys and bears lost
Their lives under the weight of his feet.
Realising Kumbhakarna's might,
Ramachandra got ready to shoot at him.
It was then that Bibhisana interrupted
Benignly, 'O Lord! Allow me to have a word
With him. I'll try to prevail on him
Not to fight.' Srirama remarked,
'If he does as you say, he'll certainly
Deserve to be the King of Lanka.'

Laba told through song the conversation
That went on between Kumbhakarna
And Bibhisana. Turning to Basistha,
Srirama said, 'See, how virtuous
Bibhisana is! That's why he
Became the King of Lanka.'
Basistha asked him to stay calm
And not to ask questions while listening to

The scripture. Srirama said to the boys,
'Kumbhakarna turned down Bibhisana's
Request. What happened, then?
Tell it for everyone to listen.' Laba sang:

After meeting Kumbhakarna,
Bibhisana told Rama all that he said.
Suddenly Kumbhakarna charged at them.
Rama shot a *babal* arrow at him that
Cut off his head which fell to the ground,
But Kumbhakarna, having his head
Replaced, resumed fighting with
Renewed vigour. Acting on Bibhisana's
Advice, Rama treated him with *brahmasara*
That severed his head. Then, with
Pabanasara his bones and skins were
Crushed into powder that floated in air.

44

A Duplicate Sita

Shocked at the news of his brother's death,
The King of Lanka realised he was
In a difficult situation. He hid Sita
In the netherworld and kept a duplicate
One in her place. Putting Jambomali
In charge of the Madhubana, he engaged
Himself only in warfare. Unable
To take on Rama on equal terms, he played
A trick on him. He cut off the duplicate
Sita's head, and showed it to Rama.
Seeing it, Rama was upset, though
It was not recognisable. To verify
The truth, he sent Hanumanta to the Ashoka
Forest. Hanumanta returned with
Mandodari, holding her by the hair.
Embarrassed, Rama paid her due respect.
He asked Hanumanta, 'Why did you fetch
Ravana's wife? She is a chaste and pious
Woman. There is no glory in showing

Disrespect to women. This young woman
Doesn't deserve to be treated like this.'
Mandodari bowed at Rama's feet,
As a sign of her gratitude to him.
When Rama wanted to know from her
Where Sita was, she said, 'Kumbhakarna's
Death scared Ravana so much so that
He hid her in the netherworld where
None can reach. Handing over a gem
To Rama, she said, 'I'm giving you this gem.
Only Hanumaṇta can go there with the gem
Held in his hand.'

Rama gave the gem to Hanumanta
And told him to leave Mandodari at her
Place first and then, to visit Sita
And come back with her news.
Hanumanta made her sit on his outstretched
Palm and dropped her in the palace.
Holding the gem in his hand, he entered
The netherworld. He met Sita and gave her
The news of the war. Glad to hear it,
She gave him a ring as a token of her love
To Rama. While leaving, he closed the
Entrance with a boulder and headed
For the Subalaya hills.

Golaka, the gatekeeper of the netherworld,
Informed Ravana, 'O Lord! The monkey
Who had burnt Lanka went into
The netherworld and met Sita there.'
Ravana thanked his luck that Hanumanta

Had not taken her away. He rushed
To the netherworld and brought
Sita back to the Ashoka forest.

45

Lakshmana Wounded Lethally

Raising war cry, Ravana fought ferociously,
Killing a number of monkeys and bears.
Seeing it, Sumitra's son confronted him.
Unable to retaliate, Ravana, invoking Brahma,
Shot an arrow at his chest; so deadly
A shot that Lakshmana lapsed into
Deep unconsciousness. Seeing Lakshmana
Passing out, Srirama mounted an attack
On Ravana's army, shattering the chariots
And killing his elephants, horses and soldiers.
Thoroughly exhausted, his hair awry
And clothes torn off, Ravana left the battle
And ran away to save his life.

Returning to Lakshmana, Srirama took him
Into his lap and began to weep. The arrow
Had pierced through his chest.
When all attempts by the commanders
To pull the arrow out failed, Jambabana

Said, 'Unless the arrow is removed,
We can't apply any medicine to it.'
Hearing this, Srirama, with his left hand,
Pulled it out effortlessly and hurled it
Into the air. The arrow removed,
They found a deep wound on his chest.
Jambabana said, '*Bisalyakarani* is found
In Girisrunga mountain. It'll heal
The wound, if applied for once.'

Carrying out Ramachandra's order,
Hanumanta left for the mountain.
When the news reached Ravana, he sent
Trijata to stop Hanumanta from reaching
His destination. Disguised as a sage,
Trijata sat on the way, worshipping
A *linga*. Seeing Hanumanta, he called out
To him. Mistaking him for a sage,
Hanumanta bowed to him, and, following
His advice, he took a bath and sat in meditation
In the Ganduki river. A crocodile which
Lived there, picked him up and sank deep
Into the river. Pulling it back to the bank,
Hanumanta tore its chest apart. As he did it,
An *apsara* came out of it. She said
She was turned to a crocodile by
Indra's curse. She told him, 'The sage
Whom you see there is Ravana's man,
Disguised as a sage.' So saying, she left
For heaven. Returning to Trijata,
Hanumanta held him by the hair
And spun him round and round,

While he groaned and grunted.
He landed a lethal blow on his head
That left him dead.

While Laba was narrating it,
Srirama, turning to Basistha, said
'O sage! How can I forget Hanumanta
Who did so much for me! Had he been
With me, he would not have allowed me
To send Sita to the forest. Since he went
With Gorekh to the Kadali bana,
Everything has gone wrong with me.'
Basistha consoled him, 'The inevitable
Must happen. Who can alter it?'
When they stopped, Laba began:

As soon as Hanumanta reached
The Girisrunga mountain, the *gandharvas*,
Who had been living there by Indra's order,
Waged a war against him. Hanumanta
Killed all of them, but they soon revived
To life when the air coming from the divine
Plants touched them. Hanumanta tied
Eighty thousand *gandharvas* to his tail
And uprooted the mountain. While leaving
With the mountain, Indra sent another
Group of *gandharvas* whom he beat
To death with his tail. Throwing them into
Water, he proceeded on his way.
He killed the demons Ravana had sent.
While passing over the Subahu bana
With a great noise, Kaikeyee's son shot

At him with a catapult. It struck
His forehead and he fell down unconscious
Before Bharata. Recovering next moment,
He asked Bharata how much of the night was
Left. Bharata asked him sympathetically,
'Why are you worried about the night,
Forgetting that you might have died
A moment ago?' Hanumanta replied,
'I won't hesitate to die while doing my
Master's work. Curse on me! Why did
I choose this way? Had I taken some other
Way, I could have already delivered
The medicine to him.' When Bharata asked
Him what was the medicine for,
Hanumanta explained, 'The battle between
Rama and Ravana is going on.
Enraged by the loss of most of his kins,
Ravana struck Lakshmana with a deadly
Arrow. Rama had sent me to Girisrunga
To fetch the medicine and return as quickly
As possible. Due to many obstructions
On the way, I'm already late. If I don't
Reach before sunrise, Lakshmana will
Succumb to injury.' Hearing this,
Bharata wailed 'O brother!'

Laba and Kusha gave details
Of what Hanumanta told Bharata,
Feeling sorry for Hanumanta, Srirama asked
Bharata, 'How come Hanumanta did not tell
Me all this?' With folded hands,
Bharata replied, 'When he was rushing

Through the air with the *bisalyakarani*,
The noise terrified me and I shot at him
With a catapult. He fell down before me
And informed me about Lakshmana's
Condition. I was sorry to have hit him.
I told him not to intimate Rama about it.
That's why he didn't reveal it to you.'
Srirama praised Hanumanta for his love
Towards his brothers. When Srirama told
Laba to continue, he said, 'How will our
Song be heard when there is so much noise?
When a scripture is being read, all should
Listen to it mindfully.' As soon as
Silence prevailed there, Sita's sons sang:

When Bharata came to know he was
Rama's messenger, he embraced Hanumanta
And kissed him on his forehead.
Leaving Bharata, Hanumanta reached
The Subalaya hills with the mountain
In his hands. Rama was sitting mournfully,
With Lakshmana in his lap. Exceedingly
Happy to see Hanumanta returning,
He asked him if he had brought the *bisalyakarani*.
Hanumanta replied, 'I couldn't identify
The plant, so I carried the whole mountain
With me. Let Jambabana find it out.'
Hearing this, Girisrunga handed over
The plant to Srirama and said, 'Since long
Indra had commanded me to preserve
This plant and not to give it to anyone.
He had said anyone who touched it

Would die. One day Vishnu would come
To the earth as Srirama; give it only in
His hands. For that reason I wasn't giving
It to Hanumanta.' Saying so, Girisrunga
Went back to its place.

Rama showed the plant to Jambabana
Who said, 'It's a divine plant.
There is one thing else. We've to bring
Tara who lives in Ravana's palace.
Send Hanumanta to fetch her.
She will grind its leaf
With the milk from her breast.
Only she will apply it to Lakshmana's
Wound. That'll heal the wound in a moment.'
Hanumanta fetched Tara from the palace
Taking the *bisalyakarani* from Rama's hands,
She ground it with her milk and daubed
Lakshmana's wound with it. It worked
Like nectar; in a moment Lakshmana
Recovered. Seeing Rama's face, Tara
Felt herself blessed.

Laba described through song
What Lakshmana had told Rama
When he regained consciousness.
Kusha elaborated wherever it was
Felt necessary to do so.

46

The Killing of Mahiravana

Bihoda demon, one of Ravana's spies,
Reported from the battlefield the details
Of how Lakshmana was cured of the injury.
Expressing anger at what Tara had done,
Ravana prepared himself for the battle.
Just then, Mahiravana approached him,
'Father! Command me to take on the enemy.'
Glad to hear it, Ravana sent him to fight,
Nominating him as the commander.

With staff, *kamandalu* and umbrella
In his hands, a *rudraksha* garland around
His neck, his forehead smeared with
Holy ash, he disguised himself as a sage,
And went to Rama with seven demons.
With sweet words, he won Rama's confidence,
And, offering him some holy ash, said,
'All of you smear it on your foreheads.
It'll save you from the fear of arrows

And swords. It'll make your bodies
As strong as thunder.' When everyone
Rama, Lakshmana, Jambabana,
Satabali, the commanders, the monkeys
And the bears – did as the sage had said,
All of them fell unconscious. Mahiravana
Carried away Rama to the netherworld
And hid him there secretly. But he daren't
Kill him as he was terrified by his vigour.

Rama's absence from the battlefield
Filled Ravana with joy. Disguised as
Rama, he entered the battlefield,
Attacking the monkeys and killing
Many of them. Mistaking him for Rama,
No one raised weapon against him.
Watching the proceeding on the battlefield,
The gods called out to Bibhisana loudly.
They told him, 'Wipe the holy ash
From your foreheads; that will bring back
Your consciousness.' All of them wiped
Their foreheads clean; soon their
Former sense revived. Lakshmana was
Now sure that Ravana was fighting
In the guise of Rama. Infuriated, he ran
To him, accompanied by Hanumanta.
Realising Lakshmana's prowess in war,
Ravana quit the battle and ran away.
The commanders of monkeys and bears
Destroyed the demons active in the battlefield.

Rama's disappearance filled Lakshmana
With sorrow. Bibhisana informed him,
'Mahiravana, the wicked son of Ravana,
Came in the guise of a sage and gave
The holy ash which we smeared on our
Foreheads. He has taken away Rama
And kept him in the netherworld secretly.'
Seeing Lakshmana worried, Hanumanta
Volunteered himself to go there and bring
Back Rama. When Lakshmana consented,
He went away and entered the netherworld.
Killing Lohapada, he searched for Rama.
Knowing his intent, the demons there
Disguised themselves as Rama, putting
Hanumanta in utter confusion. Using
The *jnanabanta* gem, he could identify
His master when he saw the ring on his hand.

Laba and Kusha narrated
How Rama killed Mahiravana and how
He was rescued from the netherworld.

Suchimukha, the demon, who was fighting
In the battlefield, informed Ravana
That Mahiravana was dead.

47

Jambomali's Battle

While mourning his son's death,
The King of Lanka sent for Jambomali.
He told him, 'O uncle! This is my kingdom.
I ask you to go and eliminate the monkeys
And the bears.' Jambomali joined Ravana's
Army and battled hard. When he pounced
On Hanumanta, Sugriba caught him
And threw him into the sea. He got out of it
Without getting wet and continued
To battle. Tying him to his tail, Sugriba
Carried him to the Vindhyagiri forest.
Not finding Sugriba in the battlefield,
Rama asked Hanumanta to look for him.
Hanumanta found him in the Vindhyagiri
Forest and conveyed to him Rama's concern
For him. Not being able to kill Jambomali,
Sugriba was lost in despair. He asked
Hanumanta what to do about it.

Acting on his advice, they placed
A mountain on him and went back to Rama.

When Ravana got the news, he sent
Jambomali's two sons in search of
Their father. Mukha and Drumukha
Came to Vindhyagiri. Standing on
The mountain, under which
Their father was buried, they called
Him at the top of their voice. In response,
Jambomali let out a roar. Recognising
It to be their father's voice, they removed
The mountain and rescued him. Returning
To the battlefield, the threesome put up
A brave fight, making Rama's army suffer
A lot. When Rama aimed his arrow at
Jambomali, Bibhisana fell at his feet
And said, 'If you kill him, I'll die.
Our lives are tied to each other.'
Pardoning Jambomali, Rama tried to prevail
Good sense on him. Jambomali agreed
To quit the battle.

Sita's son sang elaborately about
The relationship between
Bibhisana and Jambomali.

48

The Killing of Ravana

Hearing about Jambomali's withdrawal
From the battle, the King of Lanka hurried
To Paulasti's hermitage. Bowing at
The sage's feet, Bisraba's son said,
'O sage! I've lost all my sons and brothers
In war. My uncle, who was my last hope,
Deserted me, affirming his allegiance to Rama.
What should I do now? How will I kill
Rama and Lakshmana? All the glory
And wealth I've are because of your
Blessing. I've come here to seek your advice.'
Paulasti replied, 'Listen. None in the three
Worlds can challenge Rama to fight.
Besides, it's not desirable on your part
To fight against the monkeys; they are,
In fact, the incarnation of the gods.
If you do as I say, you'll enjoy your life
As a king. There'll be no damage done
Either to your glory or to your wealth.

Your family will grow as luxuriantly
As the plantain tree. Give back Sita
To Rama, it'll pacify his anger.
If you are scared of him,
I'll give you my company. Let's go
Together; I'll talk to Rama on your behalf.
Don't have second thoughts.' Ravana
Reacted, 'O sage! Did I come here for this?
If I submit myself to Rama, won't it be
An insult to the position I hold?'

Returning to the palace, he met his mother
And sisters-in-law. He complained
To his mother, 'Your brother has betrayed us.'
Naukesha advised him to return Janaka's
Daughter to Rama. Heedless to her words
He arranged a *yajna* under the Nikumbhila
Banyan tree, with a purpose to succeed
In war. To please God, he offered sacrifices
Of goats, buffaloes and hens. The fire
Of the sacrificial pit gave rise to so much
Smoke that it covered the sky and kept
The sun out of view. Fireballs showered
On Rama's army caused concern
To Rama. Carrying out his order,
His commanders destroyed the *yajna*,
Making the brahmins flee. In anger,
Hanumanta uprooted the banyan tree
And placed it before Rama. Receiving
Brahma's message through a *gandharva*,
Rama asked Hanumanta not to destroy it,
But to shift it to Gomanta mountain.

Watching the tree being removed,
Ravana made elaborate arrangements for
The battle. He collected fifty crore renowned
Warriors, and, offering them flowers
And sandalwood, he told them, 'I would like
You to share my fate. Let's wipe out our
Enemy or lay down our lives and go
To heaven.' Motivated by his inspiring
Words, they got their horses and chariots
Ready. Ravana mounted the Pushpak with
Kumbhakarna's two sons. The warriors
Battled hard, but all of them were
Put to death by the mighty monkeys.

A fierce battle ensued between
Ravana and Rama. The exchange of arrows
Covered the sky, hiding the sun from sight.
The earth shook by the twangs
Of the bow-strings. Unable to fight Rama
Face to face, Ravana stationed himself
In the sky, shooting *ripudahana* arrows
At Rama's army, causing heavy casualties.

Seeing Rama's disadvantage of fighting
On foot, Indra sent Matali with
Chariots: Nandighosa for Rama
And Mangalajana for Sumitra's son.
Finding two young warriors attacking him
From Ravana's chariot, Rama asked Matali
Who they were. As Matali could not answer,
Rama wanted Bibhisana to accompany
Him. Matali protested, 'This is the chariot

Of the gods. How can I allow a demon
To occupy it?' Rama replied, 'He is someone
Whom I love. He has become a part of my life
Since the day I sheltered him.' Pleased,
Matali made Bibhisana sit by his side.
When asked, Bibhisana said that they were
Kumbhakarna's sons, Kumbha and Nikumbha
By name. They were as mighty as their father.

Rama slew them, firing *babal* arrows.
At this, Ravana pulled up his chariot
In front of Rama and fought with
A greater effort. Rama chopped his head
Off nine times, but a new head sprang up,
As soon as it was severed. In despair,
Rama gave up his bow. Bibhisana told
Him, 'Ravana has *akshaya linga* in
His heart, so shoot at his chest. Strike
Ten arrows at his ten heads.
That's the only way to kill him.'
Ramachandra fitted eleven arrows
To his bow. The *brahmasara* hit his
Chest and the rest ten severed his heads.

A great cheer went up from the gods
In heaven. The *apsaras* ululated
And showered flowers on Rama
Narada, the great sage, danced around,
Waving his staff. Brahma, Indra,
Dikpalas and *yogis* rejoiced at the news.

After being killed in Rama's hands,
Ravana was conveyed to heaven. He was

Welcomed by the *apsaras* who danced
And played cymbals and *mridanga*.
Indra offered him a seat in his court.

The listeners were excited when
Sita's sons went on singing.
Turning to Basistha, Srirama said,
'O sage! The boys told exactly the way
I killed Ravana. Was he, who taught them
The scripture, present in the battlefield?
Was he someone who could foresee things?
Was he Brahma or Saraswati?'
Basistha replied, 'The virtues of the previous
Birth can reward one with such wisdom.
He must be born in the most auspicious
Moment. These boys belong to a noble family,
Let the scripture finish first.
Then we'll know all about them.'
Quite happy, Rama took them into his lap
And kissed their foreheads.

49

Sita's Trial by Fire

Looking at Laba and Kusha,
Basistha said, 'We learnt about how
Ravana was killed. Tell us in detail
What Dasaratha's sons did thereafter.
All of us are eager to hear it.' Laba began:

Upset about Ravana's death,
Bibhisana wept bitterly, muttering,
'O brother! Why did you take away Sita?
Blessed with immortality, you ended up
Dying so prematurely. You let your sons
And grandsons die.' Expressing sympathy,
Rama took him into his lap and said,
'Don't weep. It rattles me.' Hurt by his words,
Bibhisana moved a little away from him,
Lying on the ground and sobbing. Rama
Raised him with his hands. He ordered
Sugriba not to punish the demons
Who survived the war, but to take care

Of them. He told him, 'They are no more
A threat to us. The one who was my enemy
Has already been killed.' Sugriba collected
The demons and produced them before
Bibhisana. To him Rama said,
'It's time to cremate Ravana's body.
See that it is done properly.'

After the cremation completed,
Bibhisana's coronation as King of Lanka
Took place; Mandodari was made
The chief queen. With his minister holding
The golden staff and the umbrella,
Bibhisana went on a tour around
The city. Returning, he begged Rama,
'Now that you've killed
Your enemy and made me the king,
There should be no delay in bringing
Sita back.' Irritated, Rama replied,
'She is a fallen woman. She has betrayed me.
I'd to kill Ravana only to save myself
From public criticism. She made me
Suffer without end. In spite of wiping out
The enemy, I'm still not happy.'
Bibhisana explained, 'Sita is blameless.
It was God's desire that Ravana would
Abduct her, and, thereby, fall from
The grace of goddess Lakshmi. We'll bring
Sita back from the Ashoka forest.
Let's gloss over her silly mistakes
And cling only to her virtues.' Seeing
Rama unmoved, Bibhisana and Mandodari

Fell at his feet. The commanders, too,
Followed suit. When Rama asked
The commanders what they wanted,
They said, 'We want Sita to come back,
Seeing her, we'll forget our sufferings
During the battle.'

Following Rama's order,
Hanumanta brought Sita from the Ashoka
Forest. Fuming with anger, Rama
Told her, 'To prove your innocence,
You've to hold one hundred *palas* of hot
Copper in your hands.' Sita retorted,
'Why so? Why not consign me to fire?'
Approving of it, Rama confined her
To fire for seven days and seven nights.
She emerged from the fire unhurt;
Not a single hair on her body was burnt,
Nor her wet clothes had become dry.
Still, Rama did not believe her.
He, however, cooled down when he
Remembered how his father loved her.

50

The Dead Soldiers Regain Life

When Ramachandra told Bibhisana
To remain in Lanka with Mandodari,
He asked, 'O Lord! Who shall I live with?
If I leave, my kingdom will stand completely
Empty. My store-house is full of wealth
And gold, more than what you expect
To find in the abode of the gods. Having
No soldiers under my command,
Who'll safeguard it? Suggest me a way
To handle the situation.' Srirama replied,
'Well! If that is your concern, I'll bring back
All the dead soldiers to life.'

When Sugriba heard this,
He prayed to Rama, 'O Lord!
Many of the monkeys who had come
With me, leaving their families, have died
In war. When I go back, their wives,
No seeing them with me, will cry their

Eyes out. Can I stand such a sight as this?
As I see, I'll have to leave my kingdom
For elsewhere.' Srirama consoled him,
'Friend! All those monkeys who are
Dead will wake up again.' Learning this
From Sugriba, Jambabana went to Rama
And fell at his feet. He begged him,
'O Lord of Ayodhya! I've lost sixty-seven
Crores of bears in war. I pray to you
To bring them back to life.' Srirama
Assured him, 'Your wishes will be
Soon fulfilled.'

Looking upward, Rama invoked Indra,
'O God of Rain! Have mercy on me!
Give back life to those who died in war.'
Merciful Indra rained nectar on Lanka.
Ravana's sons, grandsons, warriors,
The monkeys and the bears – all got back
Their lives.

Turning to Bibhisana,
Srirama said, 'Now take over the charges
Of your kingdom and rule Lanka
With the help of your soldiers.'
Bibhisana replied, 'I wish to go with you
To Ayodhya and see your mothers.'
Mandodari expressed her wish to serve
At Sita's feet. Srirama restrained
Them with soothing words. Jambomali,
Having lost his son, was feeling like
Dying. Rama brought back his son's
Life by praying to Brahma.

51

Return to Ayodhya

Thereafter, Rama and Sita
Set out for Ayodhya in the Pushpak chariot,
Followed by the army of monkeys and bears.
They watched Lanka from above
And saw the prisoners of war
Being set free. They had carried with
Them Baruna's golden staff from Lanka.
While passing the sea, Rama told Lakshmana,
'Look at the bridge we had built
To enter Lanka. We destroyed the demons
And defeated Ravana. Now it is necessary
To destroy it.' In response to Rama's order,
Lakshmana, tucking Baruna's staff under
His arm, fired three arrows that demolished
The bridge. When they reached the land,
Rama sent the monkey soldiers to their
Forest homes. Accompanied with Sugriba
And Jambabana, they went to the cowherd,
Who had given Lakshmana three pots

Of milk in exchange for a gem. After
Spending a day with him, they left for
Nandigram from where they picked up
Bharata. Then they reached the Nandika
Forest to fetch Shatrughna.

With his brothers and friends,
Rama reached Ayodhya. While entering
The palace, he obliged Madhubati,
The wife of Gandhamaya, who prayed to him.
Going inside, he bowed to his mother.
On an auspicious day, Rama's coronation
Took place, in which seven sages took part.
Sugriba, Jambabana and Satabali attended
The ceremony as guests of honour.
When the ceremony was over,
They went back to their respective places.

Rama asked Hanumanta to stay in Ayodhya.
For long past, seven gems had been lying
In the store-house, unused. Rama made
Them into a necklace and tied it around
Hanumanta's forehead. Hanumanta
Perched himself on a banyan tree on
The sea beach. He spent his time recounting
The events of the recent war. Meanwhile,
The sea rose and the tree was surrounded
With tide waters. A shoal of fish, driven from
The sea to the shore gathered under the tree
For food. Hanumanta plucked some fruits
And dropped it into water, which
The fish swallowed merrily. Hanumanta

Went on feeding them until the tree was
Shorn of fruits and leaves. Having
Nothing else to offer, he took off the necklace
From his forehead and dropped it down,
To be swallowed by the fish. With the fall
Of the tide, the fish disappeared into the sea.

Moments later, Hanumanta could realise
What a grievous mistake he had done.
His courage failed when he thought of
Meeting Rama without the necklace.
He climbed down the tree and hid in
The forest. Having not seen him for
A long time, Rama asked Basistha,
'Hanumanta is not to be seen.
Where is he?' Basistha replied,
'He has dropped the seven gems
Into water, and is now hiding in
The forest.' Rama sent his three
Brothers who fetched Hanumanta.

After meal, Rama, accompanied by
Hanumanta, went to Baruna,
God of Waters. Scared to see Rama
Getting ready to shoot at him,
He came out with the seven gems
And began to worship him. In addition,
He offered Rama one lakh gems. Returning
To Ayodhya Rama had ornaments made for
Hanumanta with one lakh gems.
Those seven gems were kept back in

The store-house. On an auspicious day,
Pusyaviseka was held, participated by
One thousand sages; it was decided
To hold *Aswamedha yajna* soon.

52

Rama's Commendable Actions

Hearing that Rama had killed Ravana,
Labana flared up. Being informed
Of Labana's anger, Rama sent a messenger
To him with a gift of five gems, as a gesture
Of friendship. Appreciating the gift,
Labana was pacified. To bring him to book,
Rama sent Shatrughna who remained
In the forest, waiting for an opportunity.
When, one day, Labana went hunting,
Leaving his lance behind, Shatrughna attacked
Him unawares. They boxed and wrestled
With each other; the fight ended with Labana
Winning a victory and Shatrughna kicked
Unconscious. Tucking Shatrughna under his arm,
Labana proceeded to the palace. At Lion Gates,
Regaining his consciousness, Shatrughna pulled off
The demon's head that fell to the ground.

Pleased with Shatrughna's heroic performance,
Rama was full of praises. After Labana's death,

Shatrughna renamed the kingdom as Madhubana
And set up a settlement for one lakh brahmins.
Hearing all this, Rama paid a visit to Madhubana
And held Shatrughna's coronation soon.

Laba narrated how Rama severed
A sudra *yogi's* head and how he gave back
Life to a brahmin's son.

One day a dog, hit by a brahmin came
To Rama, seeking justice. Happy to see
Punishment being meted out to the brahmin,
The dog spoke of his previous birth.
With Basistha, Sugriba, Jambabana
And Sita, Rama went on a pilgrimage
To Prayag, Ganga, Varanasi and many other
Religious places. During that period,
He fought with Singhanada. After teaching
Rama the ways of *yoga*, Singhanada
Breathed his last. He performed *Aswamedha
Yajna* in Varanasi and gave away
A large amount of donations. At home,
He fed a number of poor and needy people.
All this simply added to his virtues.
His subjects, too, followed him.
As a result, no one in Ayodhya died
Prematurely. Even those dying a natural
Death, were allowed to sit in Indra's court.
Finding his court overcrowded, Indra,
Puzzled, asked Brihaspati what to do
About it. Brihaspati said, 'This can be
Stopped if Rama and Sita are separated

From each other. He will be forsaken by
Goddess Lakshmi, then. The depression for
Missing Sita will bring his virtues
To a nought.' Then, Indra, accompanied
By other gods, met Brahma. To address
Indra's grievance, Brahma asked Saraswati
Impel the people of Ayodhya, so that
To spread scandal against Sita. Hearing
This, Rama will start despising her,
And finally banish her to the forest.'

53

Sita in Exile

As desired by Brahma,
Goddess Saraswati won over the people
Of Ayodhya. She also prevailed on
Rama to change his impression on Sita.
Lest she might take it amiss, he did not
Speak out his mind to her, but he always
Nursed a secret desire to abandon her.

Sita's sons sang how Gorakhnath
Imparted the spiritual teachings on Hanumanta
In the Kadalibana. Hearing about
The decision of the gods, Srirama mused,
'Unfortunately the gods
Turned hostile to me. They tricked me
Into banishing my wife. Forgetting how
Ravana, the grandson of Paulasti
And the monarch of the three worlds,
Forced them into slavery, they took revenge
On me! They induced me to kill Ravana

And later banish my wife.' Looking at Laba
And Kusha, Basistha said, 'Go on singing,
Boys! Let everyone hear it.' Laba and Kusha,
Then, began with usual aplomb :

Saraswati filled Rama's mind with
Evil thoughts. He stooped to leaving
The palace and walking along the roads
Of the city, in the darkness of the night,
To know what people think about Sita.
He stopped near the house of Sukeshi,
The milkmaid[1] whose husband had
Gone out to milk the cows, while she was
Sleeping with her paramour in the house.
Rama could overhear the passionate talks
Going on between them. After some time,
Harisa, the milkman, arrived there
With a load of milk. He called out to
His wife again and again, but overcome
By deep sleep, she failed to respond.
Opening the door, he entered inside.
He could hear his wife breathing deeply.
He lighted a lamp and found his wife
Sleeping with another man. He held
Both of them by the hair when his wife
Woke up and pushed him away. Providing
A safe passage for her paramour to escape,
She began to scold her husband harshly:

'You, low-born cowherd!
You should know that milkmaids are

[1] The story is an innovation by the author, not found in Valmiki's text.

Equal to prostitutes. We go from
Door to door, selling milk and curd.
Attracted by our youthfulness, men make
Amorous advances. Firstly, as young women,
We've a strong inclination to sex, secondly,
When we see men, we're more and more
Excited. It's for this reason, women
Of good families are not allowed to remain
Outdoors. Can't you bear with whatever
I did? Why do you create a scene here?
Many great men ignore such mistakes
Made by their women. Look at King Srirama,
Whose fame spreads across the world.
The King of Lanka took away his wife
And kept her there for fourteen months.
Didn't Ravana make love to her, she being
So young and so beautiful? Rama built
A bridge to Lanka with the help
Of monkeys and bears. He destroyed
The demons, killed Ravana and rescued Sita.
She was with him when his coronation
Took place. Didn't he know that she was
Unfaithful to him? Did he complain?
No, he kept it a secret.'

Terribly shocked at what she said,
Rama returned to the palace with
A heavy heart. Lying on the bed with
A vacant look, he spent the night sleeplessly.
In the morning, he called his brothers,
His minister and his priest and told them
How people make demeaning remarks about
Sita, which was supported by his spies.

A few days later,
He overheard a washerwoman making
Caustic remarks on Sita's character.
He was in a dilemma; he could neither take
Any step against Sita, nor live in peace.
One night, while on bed, he heaved
A deep sigh. Sita, who was pressing his legs,
Said, 'What do you sigh for? What're you
Worried about? Is it because we're
Issueless? You'll be happy to know that
I'm three months pregnant.' Seemingly
Happy, Rama wanted to offer her anything
She would ask for. Sita begged, 'I've
Nothing to do with wealth and riches.
I'll be happy, if you allow me to go
To the forest.' Hearing her words,
Rama said to himself, 'What an irony!
Now the sinner is caught in its own snare.
She wishes to go to the forest, why shouldn't
I allow it? If it's written in her fate
To suffer, how can I stop it?'

Rama called Lakshmana and told him,
'Take her to the forest now. Leave her
In the densest part of the forest and come back,
Don't show mercy to her.' Carrying out
His instruction, Lakshmana set out for the forest
With Sita. It was a long walk; the Sun moved
Slowly in the sky, unwilling to leave Sita
In such a state. Extremely tired, she sat
Under a *bahada* tree and fell fast asleep.
Lakshmana wrote the allegations against

Her on a leaf and hung it from a branch
Of the tree under which she slept.

Laba described what thoughts were passing
Through Lakshmana's mind after he left
Sita in the forest. Now all eyes flew to
Lakshmana, who was sitting silently,
His head bent down and tears streaming
From his eyes. When he admitted all
That the boys said about him, Basistha
Told him, 'They're telling what you've
Really done. No one would be so
Cruel to do such a heinous work.'
Lakshmana replied regretfully,
'I couldn't disobey Srirama's orders.
I'm pained when the boys narrate it.'

54

Sita in Valmiki's Hermitage

Looking at Laba and Kusha,
Basistha said, 'Continue your song
And tell us elaborately what happened
Next.' Laba began:

By the time Lakshmana returned, leaving
Sita in the forest, it was afternoon.
The sun stayed in the sky.
Chhaya Devi's husband wished Rama
would come and take her back. He decided
To remain in the sky until Lakshmana
Returned and reported to Rama. Then,
He would move past the Meru Mountain.

Hearing from Lakshmana that Sita was left
To her fate, Rama broke down with grief.
Soon he was surrounded by his minister,
Courtiers and his mothers. Basistha,
Srirama's priest, advised him to have
An idol of Sita made with five *bisas* of gold.

Laba and Kusha told through song
What had exactly happened after Sita was
Sent into exile. Brahma's daughter was
Influencing them; they were only reproducing
Her words. They did not have the faintest
Idea who Basistha or Valmiki or Sita
Or Janaka or Srirama or Dasaratha was.
They did not know which period of time
They were talking about. They were too
Small to make out friend from foe. But
The way they presented the events seemed
To be an eye-witness account. Feeling
Restless, Srirama asked them,
'Lakshmana left Sita in the forest.
To whom did Janaki go, then? Was he
A man of noble birth? A pious man?
Did he pardon a woman's failings?'
Laba and Kusha resumed singing:

Tired of the long journey,
Sita had fallen asleep, while in Ayodhya,
Rama had golden idols made. The Sun,
Disappointed, disappeared from the sky.
Meanwhile, Sita woke up and looked
Around. Not finding Lakshmana where
He was, she cried out, 'O Lakshmana!
Where are you? Where will a lonely woman,
Such as I'm, go? You're the only one
I depend on. You brought me here as
My husband wanted it. Did you get killed
Somewhere in the forest? Have you fallen
Prey to wild beasts? Without you,

The world seems dark to me.' It was only
When she went through Lakshmana's letter
That her doubts were dispelled.
She kept sitting there helplessly, crying.
When the beasts caught sight of her,
They took her for a prey and came to her.
Amazed by her beauty, they asked her
Whose wife she was. When they heard
She was Srirama's wife, they changed
Their minds and kept guard over her
All night, promising to help her.

When it became morning,
They led her the way to Valmiki's hut,
Which was an arduous journey
Of four months. Valmiki welcomed her
To the hermitage and sent the beasts
Away. Sitting beside her, he wanted
To know what led Rama to banish
Her. When Sita pleaded innocence,
The sage sat in meditation and came
To know everything. After ten days
Of her stay there, Valmiki took
Her to Janaka's palace.

55

Birth of Laba and Kusha

Led by sage Valmiki,
Sita trudged along. After a journey
Of eighty days when they were only
One *kos* behind the kingdom
Of Bideha, Sita sat down under a *sal* tree,
Her body beset with labour pains.
Valmiki was worried, not knowing
What to do. Wincing in pain,
She was chanting Rama's name,
Tears pouring down from her eyes.

Seeing Sita in a precarious condition,
Valmiki caressed her head and said
Soothingly, 'Don't weep. Hold these
Siali creepers tightly with both of your hands.'
No sooner did she clasp the creepers,
Than she gave birth to a son, looking like
The rising Sun. When she had labour pains
Again, the sage gave her grass rings to rub

Over her belly, which, he said, would relieve
Her of the pains. As she did it, another son
Was born. Both the babies looked alike.

Hearing this,
Srirama felt a surge of unease in him.
He was sitting with his head bent low,
His face ablaze and tears dropping down
From his eyes. Turning to Basistha,
He lamented, 'There can't be a greater
Sinner than I in the world.
O sage! My sons would have been
In a better environment to grow, had they
Been here. I can't imagine what suffering
Janaka's daughter was destined to bear.
What a pity that she gave birth to babies
As animals do! I punished her for nothing.
My sons are the light of my clan. How shall I
See them? What shall I do?' Basistha told
Him, 'I'd cautioned you much before,
But you didn't listen to me. What use
Repenting now? Well, let's listen to
The scripture and think about other
Things later.' Rama, then, asked Laba
And Kusha anxiously to tell him what
Sita did after giving birth to her sons.'

56

Sita at her Father's House

Laba and Kusha burst out singing:

Casting a fond look on the babies,
Sita was filled with joy.
The twins took after their father
And looked alike. As they fell to the ground
From their mother's womb, they let out
A loud cry. Valmiki fetched a bamboo blade,
And asked Sita to cut their umbilical cords
With it. When it was done, the sage bathed
Them with the water from his *kamandalu*.
He made the bed with young *sal* leaves
For the babies to sleep. He told her,
'At the cost of all your sufferings in the forest,
You've given birth to two idols of gem.
A look at their faces will make you forget
Your sorrows. Don't burden your mind
With past memories and remain happy.'
Putting the sleeping babies down on the bed

Of leaves, Rama's queen lay beside them,
Covering them with the end of her saree.

Hearing this, Srirama looked above in despair.
He felt like a tree burning by the fire
Spreading from its hollow. He mused,
'Janaka's daughter used to sleep on a bed
Of silk clothes, as soft as the body
Of a swan. Her sons are now lying on leaves!
What a pity!' Collecting himself, he implored
The boys to tell him what Sita did thereafter.
Laba sang:

Thoroughly exhausted,
Sita fell asleep, Maharsi Valmiki sitting
Beside her. Seeing a *sabara* collecting
Sweet potatoes, he called out to him
And asked him his whereabouts. When
He said he came from Bideha, Valmiki told
Him confidentially to go back to Janaka
And bring him there immediately.
The *sabara* left in a hurry and informed
Janaka, 'Sage Valmiki was coming to you,
But too tired to proceed further, he is resting
On the way, waiting for you.' Glad to hear it,
Janaka and his disciples set out for
The forest, led along by the *sabara*.
Reaching Valmiki, they bowed at his feet.
Janaka said, 'O Brahma's son! It's my
Privilege to have your blessings.
You're tired of the long journey. So,
Let's go to my palace where I'll have

The opportunity to serve you.'
Valmiki interrupted, 'I must let you know
Why I was going to your house. Don't be
Panicked to hear what I'm going to say.
Your daughter, who was Srirama's wife,
Has been languishing in the forest after
Her husband abandoned her. The beasts
Of the forest brought her to my hermitage.
Since she was a heavily pregnant woman
And needed care, I was bringing her to you.
On the way, she had severe labour pains
And it was here that she gave birth to twins.
So I am stranded here, looking for you.'

Finding Janaka anxious to see her, Valmiki
Led him to her. Seeing his daughter lying
Asleep with her babies, and, unable to stand
The sight, he fainted. Sprinkling some
Water on his face, Valmiki brought him
Round. But, when his eyes fell on her,
He passed out again. Recovering,
He began to cry. The noise woke Sita up;
She was surprised to see her father crying,
His face looking as pale as the waning moon.
She said, 'Father! I'm as thick-skinned
As the wild beasts. I'd to wander through
The forest with noone to accompany me.
But for the great sage such as Valmiki,
My life is still protected.'

Srirama felt guilty
And full of remorse to hear this.

The listeners burst into tears. Bharata
And Lakshmana too cried. Some expressed
Their anger against the injustice done
To Sita. Srirama said to himself,
'No other man can be cruel as I am.
How did I stoop so low to take such an
Action, by trusting a rumour?
Even a common man wouldn't do
Such injustice. O I'm cursed!
She has been rotting in the forest
And I'm dying here. I'm responsible
For the misfortune that had befallen her.'
Realising Srirama's agony, Basistha told
Laba and Kusha, 'What did Janaka do
With the children? Read out the *Ramayana*
To us. Enlighten us with the holy words
Of the scripture.' Then the reading resumed:

To console Janaka, Valmiki told him,
'I had cautioned you to take the matter
Patiently. But you started crying
As soon as you saw your daughter.
Now, let's move to your palace with Sita
And her sons. By living with her mother
Her sorrow will be assuaged.' Following
His advice, Janaka took them to the palace.
The nurses took care of the babies.

The rites related to the birthday were
Observed ceremonially. The babies were
Put down on the swing on the twentieth
Day; the sages named them as Laba

And Kusha. As they grew up,
They looked like Rama, more and more.

These words created a ripple
Among the people in the hall, their eyes
Pinned on Laba and Kusha. Some said,
'These boys must be Srirama's sons.
They look exactly like Rama.'
Others questioned, 'Is it possible that
A king's sons have become singers?'
There were still others who sighed,
'Rama's brothers are enjoying the company
Of their sons. But Rama is too unlucky
Even to see his own sons.' Soon the murmur
Grew into a loud noise. It continued
To be so until Basistha interfered.

57

The Second Trial by Fire[1]

When the noise subsided
And silence was restored,
Laba burst into song:

Six months crawled by.
One day Janaka called Sita and asked her,
'What was your fault which outraged
Srirama so much so that he turned
You out from his palace? He belongs
To a reputed family of the Sun clan;
He himself is wary and benevolent.
Why should he forsake you if you are
Not guilty?' Sita replied, 'I'm sure
I've committed no offence. I never
Failed to show greatest respect to my
Husband and elders. Kaikeyee, Bharata's
Mother prevailed on the king that Rama

[1] The Second Trial is an addition by the author.

Would go into exile for fourteen years
And Bharata be ordained the king.
In spite of his unwillingness,
The king ordered Rama to leave.
To honour his father's promise
Rama went to the forest. Lakshmana left
Ayodhya and joined him. I too followed
Him, being a faithful wife who would not
Take her meal until she worshipped
At her husband's feet. We, threesome,
Went to the forest, coming across,
On our way, many places of pilgrimage.
We'd to bear immense hardship during
The course of our journey. Seeing us,
Maharsi Agasti led us to Panchubati
Where we settled. Lakshmana, while
Wandering in the forest in search of
Firewood, killed Ravana's nephew.

Finding her son, Japasura, killed,
Suparnekhi was furious. Seeking revenge,
She disguised herself as a young woman
And won my confidence. Lakshmana
Turned down her proposal to marry her.
Knowing her evil intent, he cut off
Her nose and ears, in anger.

Seeking revenge, she complained
To Trisira about what had happened to her.
Khara and Duhsana, with fourteen commanders,
Launched an attack on Rama. The battle
Ended when Rama killed all of them.

When the Ten-headed demon knew it,
He sent Maruchi in the guise of a deer
With two heads. Delighted to see it, I urged
My husband to fetch it. He chased it for
Some distance, but when it tried to slip
Away, he chopped off its heads. While dying,
It cried out 'Lakshmana! Save me!'
When the cry reached my ears, I sent
Lakshmana forthwith to help Rama.
Just then, Ravana, disguised as an ascetic
Appeared there, begging for alms.
At first I didn't respond to him.
But, when he threatened to kill himself,
I came out and offered him sweet potatoes.
Suddenly he grabbed the end of my saree
And took me to Lanka in his chariot.
I was kept in the Ashoka forest,
One thousand demonesses guarding me.

After killing the deer,
While Rama was returning, he saw
Lakshmana on the way. Not finding
Me in the hut, both the brothers combed
The whole forest. Rama made friends
With Sugriba and killed Bali, the king
Of the forest. With the help of an army
Of monkeys, Rama built a bridge.
To cross the sea. He placed Lanka
Under a virtual state of siege.
He killed the demons and slew Ravana.
Rama put me to a test by fire that

Continued for seven days and seven
Nights. Then, his anger was pacified.

We returned to Ayodhya, riding
The Pushpak. Our coronation took place;
Kings from far and wide owed their
Allegiance to Rama. Following Basistha's
Advice, we went to Varanasi to worship
Lord Shiva. Returning, we spent
Our days in Ayodhya merrily. When
I was three months pregnant, my husband
Wanted to fulfil my wishes. It was
Stupid of me to ask for his permission
To go to the forest. Carrying out
My husband's order, Lakshmana
Took me to the forest and left me there.'

Sage Janaka said, 'Well! If you are
Confident that you're true, that you've
Done nothing wrong, take a test by fire.'
Sita replied, 'If this be your desire,
I'm ready to take the test now.'
Janaka raised a fire and Sita remained
Inside it for three days and three nights.
The roaring fire left her untouched
And Janaka's doubts were removed forever.

Thereafter, Sita lived at her father's house
With peace and honour, devoting herself
Entirely to the wellbeing of her children.

58

End of the *Ramayana* Recitation

By the time the *Ramayana* was finished,
It was midday. Soon after the recitation,
The Sun hastened to the western horizon.
Srirama was lost in thought: O God!
Why are you so unkind to me? How long will
Sita's sufferings continue? Led by
Suspicion, I abandoned my wife. I'm solely
Responsible for the humiliations inflicted
On her. Had she been here, her sons
Would have been of these boys' age. I think,
I'll send them to Janaka's house, but
Something in me pulls me back.

Returning from faraway thoughts,
Srirama looked at Laba and Kusha
And said, 'Are you Sita's sons? You're
Of the same age and you look alike.
Your words are full of nectar. Where
Have you come from? Who are your

Father and mother? Who is your guru
Who taught you this scripture?'
Laba replied, 'We go from house to house
Everyday, singing from the *Ramayana*.
Whatever we get, it goes to our guru.
You'd ordained me the scripture-reader.
I've completed the task assigned to me.
The Sun was in the middle of the sky
When the reading finished. Now it is
About to set. We've no time to answer
To your queries. We've got to go.
Give us our fees or ask us to leave unpaid.'
Srirama was quiet. Basistha told the boys,
'You must be paid for your services.
He who doesn't contribute towards listening
To the scripture will be born in a poor family
In his next birth. He'll be a victim to diseases
And deafness, and he'll be deprived of
Lakshmi's blessing. Srirama is the king
Of this kingdom. He is righteous, so are his
Minister and courtiers. The listeners
Consist of young women, sages, brahmins,
Common men and housewives. They'd
The privilege of listening to the *Ramayana*.
Each of them will contribute according to
His capacity. You've made the king unhappy
By not answering his questions.
It's not desirable to disappoint the person
Who called you here. Now, come on, boys!
Tell us, who are your father and mother.
Then, collect your fees and leave.'

Kusha looked at Laba. He told him,
'If they so insist, let's tell them what
They wish to know. If it'll be dark,
We'll carry weapons with us to protect
Ourselves from the fear of lions, tigers,
Elephants and bears. You'll be behind
Me; I'll take care of the rest. When the sage
Blesses us, why should we fear?
We're able to kill demons in war.'

59

Revelations by Laba and Kusha

Addressing the gathering,
Laba said politely, 'Listen, everybody!
We'd asked our mother where our father
Was. I'm telling you what she replied.
She said our father died soon after
She conceived. She, then, came to stay
In her father's house. The name of her
Father is Janaka. My mother's name is Sita.
Her father calls her by that name.
We were born into the clan of Sun.
Sage Valmiki taught us the scriptures.
Our mother didn't tell our father's name
To us, for reasons not known to us.'

His throat clogged with emotion,
Srirama could not speak a word.
He took them into his lap and began
To shed tears. Bharata and Lakshmana
Were rolling on the ground, crying.

The people there wailed bitterly.
Their cries sounded like the roar of the sea
That reverberated across the sky.

Taken by surprise, Laba said,
'What foolishness is this! Why do you make us
Sit in your lap and cry, when we're
Someone else's children. We've never
Heard of such a thing. Have all of you
Taken leave of your senses? How can we
Expect you to pay to us, when all of you're
Busy crying. We don't need our fees.
It annoys us to see your crying faces.
O Mahatma! Let's go back to our mother
To get some peace.'

Basistha stopped them, saying,
'Have patience, O Sita's sons! Let me tell
You that Srirama is the son of Kausalya
And Dasaratha, the famous king of the Sun clan.
This is Kaikeyee's son, Bharata.
Lakshmana and Shatrughna are Sumitra's
Sons. After killing Labana, Shatrughna was
Ordained the King of Madhubana.
Your mother and Janaka's daughter is
Srirama's wife. Misled by a rumour,
He abandoned her. You were born in
The forest. Janaka is your grandfather.
The sage who taught you is Brahma's son,
Valmiki. He has sent you here to sing
So that you can meet your father.
He can have the most precious things

Of the world in the twinkle of an eye.
Does he need your alms at all?
Bideha is eighty-four *yojanas* from
Here. The wind, at Brahma's command,
Brings you here in a few moments.
I knew who you were when I first saw you,
But I kept it a secret from Srirama.
To relieve the gods of oppression,
He has descended to the earth as
The incarnation of Vishnu. Being
A kshatriya king, he brought disgrace
To his clan forsaking her for no fault
Of hers. For her sufferings in the forest,
And, for the hardship she underwent
To give birth to you, he had to bear
The blemishes. Being a king's son, you had
To experience insurmountable suffering,
Taking shelter in Janaka's house
And living away from your father. By virtue
Of reading the *Ramayana* you're able to see
Your father. Hearing the scripture,
All his sins are expatiated. The people who
Listened to it, will be conveyed to heaven.
They'll be reborn on the earth
With wealth and riches. They'll be
Remembered for their noble deeds.
Being Brahma's son and a Maharsi
Myself, I'm wasting my life by sitting
In the king's court. The sin of neglecting
My divine responsibilities were
Atoned by listening to the holy book,
From no other than Vishnu's son.'

He, then, kissed them, and, taking off
His gem-studded earrings, adorned
Laba with it. He, then, took off his gem-ring
And gave it to Kusha. He appealed to everyone
To contribute, each according to his capacity.
Soon the hall was filled with gold and finery.

When Basistha told the boys that
Srirama was their father, their eyes
Turned misty. Srirama too could not
Hold back his tears. Basistha told him,
'Take your sons into the palace. Let Kausalya
And Sumitra see them.' Srirama held Laba
Against his chest while Lakshmana took
Kusha into his arms. The crowd rushed into
The palace and informed Kausalya,
'Your daughter-in-law whom Lakshmana
Had left in the forest, has been staying
In her father's house. She is blessed with
Two sons who are well-versed in scriptures.
Yesterday the eldest one came to read out
The *Ramayana*. Today he came with his brother.
Now Srirama is arriving here with them.'

Tears of joy flowed from Kausalya's eyes.
Kaikeyee, Sumitra and all the women
Of the palace gathered there. As Srirama
Arrived with his sons, they welcomed
The boys with hugs and kisses. Laba
And Kusha bowed to Srirama's mothers
Respectfully. In return, they blessed them,
Saying, 'May you enjoy your father's wealth!

May you live long!
May your enemies be wiped out!'

The women, their eyes locked on
Laba and Kusha, found them looking
Exactly like Rama. They showered praises
On Sita for giving birth to such
A pair of beautiful sons.

60

Welcoming Laba and Kusha

Thereafter Rama adorned the throne
With Laba and Kusha on his lap,
His arms folded around their waists.
Srirama's mothers welcomed them,
Burning gem-studded lamps
And anointing them with sandalwood paste
And musk. The three sons of Bharata,
Lakshmana and Shatrughna sat nearby.
All the children were looking alike.
The mothers strewed holy grass
And sunned-baked mixed
With turmeric on their heads.

Srirama ordered a city-wide celebration,
No holds barred. The people of Ayodhya
Spilled onto the street, determined to make
Most of the wild time in hand. They revelled
In robbing houses, frolicking with dust,
Pushing each other and smearing one another

With a mixture of lime and turmeric.
No one regretted; no one grumbled, no one
Grieved – all of them were in high spirits.
The king compensated for the loss of property
And other valuables of those who were
Affected. Everyone had a decorated gate
In front of his house and a white flag
Atop it. The sound of conches, bugles,
Drums and *mridangas* filled the air
And reverberated across the sky. At some
Places, singing and dancing went on.
The gods were bathed with milk; wealth
And clothes were donated to the brahmins.
Sacrifices of goats and buffaloes were
Offered to the goddesses. Srirama himself
Bathed the presiding deity of Ayodhya.
The women of the palace smeared the five
Princes with *kumkum* and sandalwood paste,
While Srirama put a mark of musk on
Their foreheads. He adorned Laba and Kusha
With Sita's jewellery. He put the gem
And pearl necklaces around their necks
And gem-studded rings on their ears,
Which gave them the look of the full moon.
The maids decked them in finery and decorated
Their heads with jasmine and chrysanthemum.

After an early bath, Srirama and his sons
Sat together to have their meals.
Seeing a golden idol placed
Near them, Kusha told Laba, 'Doesn't this
Idol look exactly like our mother?'

Hearing this, Srirama explained to them,
'Listen, my sons! After I banished
Your mother to the forest, I had her
Idol made. It makes me remember her
All the time.' Laba and Kusha fell silent.
The thoughts of their mother flashed through
Their minds. She had told them to return
Soon, but they were detained there till then.
It was late afternoon already;
And she must be anxiously waiting for
Them. It was fine that they met their
Father, but, in the process, they made
Their mother suffer. Lost in thought,
They shed tears incessantly. They sat
With long faces drawn downwards.
The food in their hands got stuck there;
They forgot to take it to their mouths.

After meal, Srirama washed his hands
And sat on his bed, studded with nine
Kinds of gem, with his sons on his lap.
He took camphor and betel for himself
And offered the same to his sons.
Looking at their father, Laba and Kusha said,
'O Lord, the greatest kshatriya of the Raghu
Dynasty! O monarch of the world!
You banished our mother for no fault
Of hers. You made her suffer without
End. We wander from place to place,
Reading out the scripture. We can't tell
Friend from foe. We came to know
Everything from sage Basistha. The alms

We collect go to Valmiki. Our mother
Used to wait for us at the palace door
Until we returned. After receiving us,
She would go for bath and take food.
Today, in our absence, she must be
Going without food. When we left home,
She had asked us to visit nearby
Places and return early.' He added,
'As you ordained me the scripture-reader,
I had to bring Kusha to help me.
By virtue of the noble deeds we did in
Our previous birth, we met you.
Now allow us to return to Janaka's house.'
Srirama said sorrowfully, 'What'll
Happen to me if you go away?
Ever since Sita left, my life has been
In doldrums. It's my good fortune
That I heard the scripture from you.
He who hears it from his son, his fourteen
Generations achieve salvation.
You're the pride of the Sun clan.
I've to tell you one thing. I couldn't
Go against God's Will. You've to take
Me to Janaka's house and show my wife
To me. I'll convince her and bring her
Back. We'll rule the kingdom
And live happily everafter. With
Folded hands, the sons said,
'As you please! You're the preserver
And the destroyer of her life.
We can't say you yes or no. We can
Only obey what you say.'

61

Rama's Journey to Bideha

In response to Rama's call,
Basistha, the minister, the courtiers,
The vaisnavas, the learned men
Of Ayodhya, Bharata and Lakshmana
Assembled in the King's court. Looking at
Basistha, Srirama said, 'We've to leave
For Bideha now. We go by the Pushpak
Chariot and bring back Sita from there.
We can't do it ourselves; you're the only
One who can prevail on her to agree
With us.' Basistha replied sternly,
'Don't you remember what you did
Earlier? You didn't do as I said.
I don't think it's the right time to go
To Janaka's house. A virtuous
Woman as Sita is, you made her life hell.
You did neither think of the past nor
Care for the future. One who, hearing
Allegation against his wife, abandons her,

Is bound to pass the rest of his life
In sorrow and regret.' Srirama said,
'No use crying over what is already gone.
Let's start for Bideha with my sons
Without delay.' So saying, he invoked
Kubera who sent the chariot immediately.
Srirama boarded it with his sons,
Basistha, The courtiers and his brothers.

With an irrestible desire to see Sita,
Kaikeyee, Kausalya and Sumitra,
Followed by their maids, reached there,
Hoping to get into the chariot. Seeing it,
Basistha told Kausalya, 'It's not
Necessary for you to leave the palace.
We'll fly to Bideha by the chariot
And return today itself. Attend to
The royal duties until we come back.
Don't take my words amiss.'
Kausalya pleaded, 'Allow me and my
Sisters to go and have a look of Sita.
That'll relieve us of our agony.
She passed her life in the forest miserably.
She was pregnant then, and her
Husband was not with her. I'll try
To persuade her. I believe, she'll forget
Her anger, once I speak to her. After all,
A woman can understand another better.'
Dissuading her, Rama said, 'Mother!
What you said is true. She is no doubt
An embodiment of virtues. After
Killing Ravana in Lanka, to remove my

Suspicion of her, I asked for a trial
By fire. She spent seven days and seven
Nights inside fire. The fire didn't touch
Her, nor her wet clothes got dried up.
I sent Sugriba and Angada to her, but
She didn't speak to them. When I went near
The fire, she came out and talked to me.
I'm sure she has no ill-feeling towards me.
Sage Basistha is there; he'll persuade
Her. Bharata, Lakshmana and the courtiers
Will try their best to influence her.
Laba and Kusha will also help us
In this regard. She, being virtuous, won't
Turn down the request of so many of us.
Why should you take pains to go there?
You better remain in the palace.'
Convinced, Kausalya and others
With her, returned to the palace.
The Pushpak took off and flew to Bideha
At the speed of the wind."

Glory to the Enchanter of the gopis,
Who was born into Yadu dynasty
And brought up in Nanda's house!
Sitting under the *kadamba* tree,
You played the flute amorously,
Inflaming the gopis with the passion of love.
They ran to the arbour, leaving their
Household chores. You enchanted
Each of them, one after another, either
By embracing or kissing or making
Fun or consoling or talking passionately

Or laughing or clapping or biting her lips
Or piggybacking her or taking her into
Your lap. Some of them sang, others
Danced. The display of your divine
Dalliance went on throughout the night.

May I lie at your lotus-feet,
O my Lord!
Help Siddheswar Das cross over
The sea of the mundane world.

62

Sita's Waiting

Bowing at sage Markanda's feet,
King Yudhisthira, his four brothers
And Draupadi said, 'We learnt that
Laba and Kusha finished the *Ramayana*.
By midday, the recitation was complete.
Now it is late afternoon already.
But they still had not started for home.
Tell us, how did their mother feel
As time ticked away.'

Markanda replied, 'Listen, everyone!
Waiting long at the palace door for
Her sons' return, Sita climbed down
The steps impatiently and looked at
The sky. The sun was sinking in the west.
Her face turned pale, her heart palpitated.
She said to herself, 'How frolicsome
My sons are! As long as they are with
Me, they'll obey each word I speak.

But when they are away, they'll fall out
With each other on the way. All day
Long they remain outdoors, leaving
Me alone. It's what sage Valmiki had
Asked them to do, and he won't tolerate
If his order is not obeyed. He was
Of great help to me when I was passing
Through hard times. It's my bad luck
That he is unkind to me, separating
Me from my sons. They're at an age
When they should eat, play and make
Merry. But they pass their days,
Wandering through the deep forest
And singing to others to make them happy.
Being king's sons, they are subject to
Intense hardship. Why were they born
To me who is not able to make them
Happy? For her past sins, Kausalya
Had not yet been able to see
Her grandsons. She can see them
Only if God favours.'

She could neither sit nor stand.
Like a doe separated from the herd,
She was looking around. She prayed
To Lord Biswanath to protect her sons.
Her eyes swam with tears. She said,
Anger creeping into her voice, 'Let them
Come back. I'll tie them and beat
Them. I won't allow them to enter my
Father's house. He who stops me will face
The consequence. Whom shall I complain

Against them? Why are they so late?
Did they quarrel with each other and didn't
Come in fear of being rebuked? Or
They didn't have enough alms today?
Singing the same songs again and again
May be the reason for less collection.
People worship the second day moon;
The full moon does not attract them.
Everyone loves the woman who is young,
And the cow which gives milk.
They are fond of clothes and ornaments
If they are new. Similarly, they prefer
New songs to the old. This might have
Accounted for the fall in the quantity
Of alms. Fearing that the guru may be
Displeased, they probably went to distant
Places in search of fortune. Did they
Fall prey to the wild beasts?
Or had they gone to the same house
As yesterday? Did they forget to come
Because of the honour and treatment
They received there? As children,
They're likely to cling to the place where
They find love and affection.'
Sandwiched between emotions of sorrow
And anger, she added, 'Let them come.
I'll die because of them. The earth will crack
And I'll sink into it. They're of no use
To me. They rather create troubles for me
From time to time. Their father made my
Life miserable; now his sons are adding
More to it. It's no use sitting here

And waiting for them. Let me go
To the forest and look for them.'

She called Kanchana and Ratna
And told them, 'Let's go to the forest
And bring back my sons. If I don't find
Them, I'll hang myself.' She remembered
Sovana who was looking after her when
She was a child. During that period,
She had given birth to Kanchana and Ratna.
They were so named because
Of their complexion and beauty.

They proceeded to the forest
At a time which was most inauspicious.
Stopping at a banyan tree in the forest,
Sita said, 'My sons used to return
This way. Yesterday Laba made me sit
Here, while he climbed up the tree.
From the top of the tree he called out
To Kusha loudly who came running
Towards us. Here, two roads diverge
In two directions. You take a road
Each and look for my sons, while
I rest under this tree.' She sat down
And undid her hair that spread
Over the ground around her.

Listen, Yudhisthira, it is from
One of the books of the *Ramayana*,
Entitled 'Uttara Kanda'. When the Creator

Completed Sita's idol, he found it
Perfect in all respects. He wanted
To add something odd to it. So He gave
Her a fuzz of long and bushy hair.

63

The Meeting between Sita and Rama

While the Pushpak was flying over
The forest of Bideha, Laba and Kusha,
Looking below, spotted their mother there.
They told Srirama, 'Our mother is looking for
Us in the forest. She is sitting alone
Under that banyan tree.' Srirama could
Recognise her easily. Basistha told
The boys, 'Alight from the chariot carefully
And hurry to your mother. She seems
To be angry. She'll be happy to see both
Of you. We'll hide ourselves behind
The creepers. We'll meet her only when
We find her comfortable. Then, we'll tell
Janaka everything and take her back
With us to Ayodhya.'

O Yudhisthira! Basistha is one of those
Who has witnessed the deluge that

Hit the earth seven times since its creation.
Whatever he says, it goes to Srirama's
Benefit. He is omniscient. He knows, now
The time has come when Sita will disappear
Into the earth. Now, listen!

Leaving the chariot,
Laba and Kusha went to their mother
Who was sitting under the tree angrily.
They lay prostrate before her, holding
Her feet. Seeing her sons, she was
As delighted as a blind man getting back
His eyesight or a poor man receiving
Wealth. Tears poured down from her eyes.
She forgot that, moments ago, she was angry
And was thinking of killing herself.
Kanchana had gone southwards;
She returned after the boys arrived.
Sita took her sons into her lap. Seeing
Them adorned with jewellery, flowers,
Sandalwood paste, musk and finery,
She asked, 'Where did you get these from?
When you left, you promised to return
Early. Lured by the jewellery,
You forgot me. I've been going without
Food since you left. Without you,
The world seemed dark to me.
Have you stolen these from somewhere?
Where had you been until sunset?
The sin of thievery is never pardoned.
One who donates cheerfully in this birth,
Will reap the benefit in the next birth.

Who is that pious man who gave you
These rare gifts?' Too shy to speak,
They stood there as before.
Ratna had gone to the east;
She now returned. She felt relieved
To see the sons. She said to Laba angrily,
'Do you realise your mother's agony?
What have you been doing till now?
From the time you leave home, your mother
Sits at the door waiting for your return.
As you grow up, you become more
Insensitive to your mother's feelings.'

Provoked by Ratna's words,
Sita ordered her, 'Get me a stick soon.
I won't get peace until I beat them.'
She held the boys by the arm and raised
The stick to beat them, when Kanchana
Begged her, 'Don't beat them unnecessarily.
Be calm. Let's know from them what
They've to say. Ratna is an ignorant fool.
She is adding salt petre to milk.
Didn't you see, when she brought the stick,
How tears dropped down from your sons'
Eyes? Poor boys! How tired they must be!'

Her anger pacified,
Sita asked her sons soothingly,
'These ornaments of pearl, sapphire,
Gold and ruby are rare and not available
To all the kings. When I was in my
Husband's palace, I had seen them

In his store-house. If I'm not mistaken,
These ornaments look like mine.
Who gave you all these rare ornaments?'
Laba replied, 'Mother! Won't you be angry
To hear it?' When she assured him
Not to worry, he said, 'Listen carefully.
Can we ever tell lies to you? We'd been
To the same place as yesterday.
It's Ayodhya where Rama is the king.
Bharata and Lakshmana are his brothers.
He has one more brother, Shatrughna,
Who is now the King of Madhubana,
After he killed Labana. Rama has
A priest called Basistha. Saying that
We are his sons, he took us into the palace.
Srirama is Kausalya's son, Bharata
Is the son of Kaikeyee, and Lakshmana
And Shatrughna are the sons of Sumitra.
Dasaratha had twenty-one hundred
Queens. All his widows gave us
Hugs and kisses. Your three sisters
Were happy to see us. Each of them
Has a son. All their sons look alike.
Rama brought these ornaments from
His store-house and put them on us.
Most of the contributions we received
Went to the brahmins and the rest were
Kept in reserve. We'd our meals together.
Had we not been his sons, why should
He allow us to eat with him. When we'd
Asked you about our father, you said
He was dead when we were young.

We'd taken it for granted. Now we saw
Our father with our own eyes. Now tell us
The truth. One's mind knows the sins
One has committed. A mother knows
Who the father of her children is.'
As she heard it, she began to sweat.
She sat down on the ground, tears
Rolling down from her eyes. She said,
'By God's grace you could go there.
I'd told you a lie. Kausalya is Srirama's
Mother. Kaikeyee and Sumitra are her
Sisters. These three were the chief queens
Among the twenty-one hundred wives
Dasaratha had. Bharata is Kaikeyee's
Son; Lakshmana and Shatrughna are
Sumitra's sons. As my sisters have
Sons, the Sun clan is going to live long.
My father will be happy to learn that
All of his daughters are blessed with sons.'

Basistha told Srirama, 'Now that Sita is
Angry no more, I think, it is
The right time we should go to her.'
Srirama forbade him, saying,
'You take Bharata and Lakshmana
With you for the timebeing. I fear,
She might not like to see me.'

Accompanied by Bharata and Lakshmana,
Basistha went to Sita. Sita was happy
To see him, but the sight of Lakshmana
Seemed to make her furious. She mused,

'I can't bear to see his face. He took me
To the forest and left me there.
It's true, he was doing what my husband
Asked him to do, but he should have
Told me the truth. He is the cause of my
Misery. What brings him here?'
Basistha told her, 'Don't be cross with
Your husband. He is the lord of your
Life. A husband who is cruel to his wife,
Suffers all his life. By being unjust
To you, Srirama has been passing
His days miserably. A virtuous
Woman does not take revenge on her
Husband. Whatever has happened,
It was by God's will.' These words
Made her more angry. She got up
And bowed to him. The sage blessed her,
'May fortune favour you! May your sons
Rule the world! Don't be angry with
Srirama anymore.' Seeing Sita
Enraged, Srirama appeared there
With the *kodanda* in hand.

64

Sita Sinks into the Netherworld

Seeing Srirama,
Sita was ablaze with anger,
Like flames fed with ghee. Looking at
Laba and Kusha, she roared out,
'You have brought this devil to me!
From the moment you met your father,
Your mother has been dead for you.'
So saying, she invoked the Sun,
'You are witness to the sufferings
Inflicted on me. Need I see his face?
Of what use is my life now?
If my loyalty to my husband is absolute,
If frailty has never been my way,
O Earth, split into two parts. O mother!
Take me into you.' As she said this,
The Earth cracked and she sank into it.
Panicked, Rama threw away the *kodanda*
And pushed his hands into the crack

To pull her out. But she slipped further,
Leaving tufts of her hair in Srirama's
Hands. Soon she was conveyed
To Vishnu's abode.'

Glory to Janaki, born from fire!
You were born to restore peace and order
To the world. Named as Sita, you grew up
In Janaka's house. You married Srirama.
While in Panchabati, Ravana took you away.
O lotus-seated! For you, the monkeys
And the bears went to Lanka. For you,
Rama killed the demons and Ravana.
He made Bibhisana the King of Lanka
And came back to Ayodhya with you.
You continued to live with Rama peacefully.
Thirty-three crores of gods hatched
A conspiracy and sent Saraswati
To Ayodhya to prevail on Rama to take
Wrong decisions. He banished you
To the forest. He showed you no mercy.
Even though you were pregnant.
You had to undergo immense sufferings
To give birth to your sons. You named
Them Laba and Kusha. Sage Valmiki
Taught them the *Ramayana*. Seeing them,
Srirama's sins were redeemed.
He came to know they were his sons.
They brought Srirama to you. Seeing him,
You boiled mad with anger. At last
You lived in Vishnu's abode as his consort.

I pray at your lotus-feet! Save me
From the sea of the mundane world,
Says Siddheswar Das.

65

Mourning by Rama and Others

His eyes awash with emotion,
Pandu's son asked, 'O sage!
What did Rama do after Sita disappeared
Into the bowels of the earth?'
Markanda replied, 'Listen, O Kunti's son!
She lived with Vishnu in his abode.'

With Sita's hair in his hands,
Rama slumped onto the ground, unconscious.
Not seeing their mother, Laba and Kusha
Beat their chests and lay on the ground.
Bharata and Lakshmana burst into tears.
At the time the minister and the courtiers
Arrived there. Recovering,
Rama took his sons into his lap
And said mournfully, 'O Janaki!
Where did you go, leaving behind your
Dear sons? You endured untold
Miseries while in the forest

And gave birth to sons, looking like
Idols made of gem. How could you
Think of deserting them? Before you
Buried yourself under the earth,
You didn't look at me even for once.
What my mother was saying when
I came, was true. Had I brought her with
Me, we could have returned with Sita.
I always fail to take the right decision
At the right time. Because of my stupidity
I lost my wife.' Saying so, he wept,
To be joined by Basistha and others.

Kanchana and Ratna, who were present
There, saw how Sita plunged into the earth.
They cried out, 'Why did you leave us,
O Janaka's daughter! How will we convey
The news to your father? You brought us
With you to look for your sons.
How could you be so unkind to them?'
Returning to the palace, they met Janaka
Who was sitting gloomily with his disciples,
Surrounded by the women of the palace.
Still crying, they told him, 'Your daughter,
The mother of Laba and Kusha, had been
To the forest with us in search of her sons.
She sat under the shade of the banyan tree
And sent us to find them out.
Laba and Kusha had been to Ayodhya
To sing the *Ramayana* to Rama. When
They introduced themselves, Rama knew
They were his sons. He took them into

The palace and decked them in finery
And ornaments. When they were returning
With Rama, Bharata, Lakshmana
And Basistha in a chariot, they spotted
Their mother sitting under the tree.
While all others hid behind the creepers,
Laba and Kusha went to their mother.
Seeing them, her anger dissipated
Into happiness. When she asked them
About the ornaments on them, they said,
'At Ayodhya, we sang the *Ramayana*
To Rama. Claiming us to be his sons,
He gave these to us.' Soon Basistha,
Bharata and Lakshmana came out
From their hiding and reached there.
The sight of Lakshmana rattled her.
Basistha, however, tried his best to console
Her. Just then, Rama came. Not caring
To look at him, she prayed to the earth
To split off. The earth cracked
And your daughter jumped into it,
Now Rama is sitting there with his sons.'

No sooner did they finish,
Than Janaka fainted. When the news
Reached the queen, she too passed out.
After a while, Janaka woke up and said
Weepingly, 'Where did you go,
O my unfortunate girl! Forsaken by
Your husband, you came to live here.
How can I live without you? I wish
I died this moment!' All those who were

Present there let out a loud wail.
The noise brought Valmiki to the scene.
Trying to soothe Janaka, he told him,
'Stop worrying about your daughter.
She went there where she had come from.
She had come to the earth with a purpose,
To relieve the gods of oppression.
Now that Srirama is here, we ought
To go and see him. A look at his face.
Washes away one's sins.' Janaka replied,
'Should I meet someone who has tortured
My daughter without reason? Being
Righteous, how could he be so wicked?
Now I need no meditation; I feel
My life is of no use. Surely I'll kill
Myself today.' Valmiki persuaded him
Not to be swayed away by emotion.
He said, 'Don't be angry. Rama is
The incarnation of Vishnu who descended
To the earth for the good of the people.
He killed Ravana and the demons.
Seeing that all the sinners in Ayodhya
Turned to noble ones by seeing him,
He decided to go back to heaven.
He separated himself from Sita
Simply because the *Tretaya Yuga* will
Not come to an end as long as Sita
Stays with him. Let's invite him
To your palace. If he refuses,
We'll hand over his sons to him.'
With valuable gifts, Janaka and Valmiki
Went to the forest where they found

Rama sitting with Basistha and others.
They were as silent as flies in oil.
Janaka caressed Laba and Kusha
And cried bitterly. Seeing this,
Rama could not hold back his tears.
Valmiki consoled him, 'If you lose
Patience, what will happen to others?
You need to control yourself in such
A situation. No one can defy the dictates
Of fate. If you cry your eyes out,
Will Sita ever come back?'

Crying no more, Rama got up
With the *kodanda*. A *ripudahana* arrow
Fitted to it, he aimed at the earth
And cried out, 'Now I'll destroy the earth,
It has killed my wife.' Seeing it,
The gods in heaven were panicked.
They thought if the earth is destroyed,
All the livingbeings on it will be perished.
They called out, 'O Rama! Drop your
Weapon. Don't shoot at the earth. You'll be
Accused of killing all the lives on the earth,
Led by a rumour, you banished your wife.
She was subject to immense suffering
In the forest. What are you going
To do in this old age? Be reminded of
What the scriptures say,
O Lord of the Universe!'
Rama dropped his bow and sat down
Under the tree. Janaka came
To him and offered the gifts he had

Brought with him. He said,
'The sun has set. It's dark already.
Come with me to my palace. Your presence
In my house will make me forget
The sorrows of my daughter's death.'
Rama replied, 'I'm the cause of your
Daughter's death. How can I go to your
Palace? What will the women there tell me?
How will your subjects take it?
Won't I be ashamed?' Valmiki pleaded,
'It's dark already. Stay in Janaka's
Palace tonight and leave for Ayodhya
Tomorrow morning with your sons.'
Rama replied, 'No, it can't be.
I'm burning like wild fire. When
My wife is dead, what for shall I go
There? It'll be embarrassing for me
To show my face to others.'
Basistha told Janaka, 'We'll go back
To Ayodhya in the Pushpak and reach
There in a short time.' Janaka, then,
Brought Laba and Kusha to him
And said, 'Look after these motherless
Children. They spent their childhood
In my house. Sage Valmiki was kind
Enough to teach them. See that
They don't lament for their mother.'
So saying, Janaka returned home,
The memory of Sita haunted him
Day and night. He could neither eat,
Nor sleep. He became weaker day by day.
Valmiki advised him, 'Have patience.

Make your mind steady through
Yogic practices. Then only you'll find
No difference between joy and sorrow.'
Valmiki, then, left for his hermitage.
Remembering Valmiki's words,
Janaka forgot his sorrows.

66

Mourning in Ayodhya

Srirama seated himself in the Pushpak
Chariot, his sons in his lap, Bharata
And Lakshmana by his side and Basistha
And others around him. The chariot flew
At a breakneck speed. All were sitting in
Gloomy silence. The moon was waning;
There was darkness everywhere.
In a short time, they reached Ayodhya.

Presuming that Sita has come back,
The men and women of Ayodhya flocked
To the palace. They informed Kausalya,
'Your son has returned with Sita.' Hearing
The news, she came out with her sisters,
Followed by twenty-one hundred queens
And the palace maids. They proceeded
To the Lion Gates where the Pushpak had
Landed. With a golden lamp in her hand,
Kausalya went to the door of the chariot.

No one came out; there was not a murmur
Inside the chariot. She asked Basistha,
Sitting at the door, 'Where is Sita sitting?'
There was no response,
No one said if she was there or not.

Breaking the silence,
Basistha spoke out, 'You were right.
I tried my best to prevail on her to come
With us, but she didn't listen to me.
She didn't even look at Srirama's face.
In anger, she sank into the netherworld.'
Shocked at the news, Kausalya fainted.
Those who were present there let out
A wail. Recovering, Kausalya told
Basistha accusingly, 'Didn't I urge
You to take me to Sita? I could have
Persuaded her with easeful words.
That would have prevented her from
Taking such a step.' Having heard her,
Srirama alighted from the chariot
With his sons. He sat down on the ground,
His head bent down and drops of tears
Falling from his eyes. Kausalya told
Him, 'Listen to me carefully. I didn't
Give up my life in the same pyre my
Husband was cremated. Instead,
I went on worshipping goddess Durga
After you went to the forest. It's due to
Her blessing that you returned safe
And became the King of Ayodhya.
You went on a pilgrimage and gained

Virtues by serving the poor and the needy.
Still, you could not get away with the sins
Of your previous birth. Rattled by
A rumour you banished the most virtuous
Sita to the forest, refusing to accept
Anyone's advice. I had a hope to see
Your sons; that hope is now fulfilled.
Seeing my grandsons, the sins of my
Hundred births are atoned. My sisters
Too are blessed with sons, which is
A pride for your clan and my father's clan.
There are five sons in your family.
Look after them and rule the kingdom well.
Now prepare a pyre; I'll consign myself
To it.' Srirama told her mournfully,
'How can you say it, mother? My sons
Have no mother. You'll look after both
Of them.' She replied sternly,[1]
'Don't dissuade me. God will take care
Of those who have no one to help.
I had persuaded you to take me
To Sita. But you didn't allow me to go.
As a result, you lost her forever.
I hate to see your face. You never
Obeyed my words. When your father
Ordered you to go to the forest,
I forbade you to do so. Paying no heed
To my words, you left for the forest.
In regret, your father breathed his last.
You had a hard time while in the forest.

[1] Kaushalya's long speech is another innovation by the author.

It was stupid of you to go after the deer.
After sometime, Lakshmana went away
To help you. Seeing Sita alone in the hut,
Ravana kidnapped her. It is for you
She suffered. It's because of the powers
Of the monkeys that you were able
To kill Ravana. On your arrival in Ayodhya,
You asked me, in the presence of others,
Why I have not yet consigned myself
To fire. I could have done it, hadn't
My husband forbidden me before he died.
Those women who sacrifice their lives
In the pyre with their husbands are
The most fortunate ones. It destroys
Their husbands' sins and makes them
Unite with their husbands forever.
Now I shall do it. Why should I care for
Your request? If you don't arrange
A pyre for me, you'll be held responsible
For my death. I will either jump into
A well or immolate myself.' Looking at
Basistha, Srirama said, 'Did you see,
O sage, how misfortune never comes alone?
Having lost Sita, I was in a state of gloom.
Seeing my mother, I thought, I would forget
Sita.' Basistha replied, 'Women don't
Change their minds so easily. Old women
And young women who are widows
And from noble families never falter
In their commitment. Why would she
Obey you? If you don't do as she says,
You'll commit a sin.' Hearing this,

Srirama called his brothers and Sumanta
And ordered them to prepare a pyre.
Then came the other queens who said,
'After our husband died, Kausalya
Meant everything to us. She was
The only source of our happiness.
She used to take care of us. How can
We live after she is gone? All of us
Want to sacrifice our lives in fire.
You look after the five sons.'

Accordingly, two pyres were prepared,
With piles of wood and sandalwood,
Aguru, camphor, ghee, oats and sesame
Added to it. All the queens reached there
After bath. People threw flowers,
Gems and gold on them while the sound
Of drums and trumpets filled the air.
A huge crowd gathered there to witness
The event. Srirama's mother arrived with
A coconut and her dead husband's ring
In her hand. She first prayed
To the sun, and, then, going round
The fire three times, she jumped into it.
She was followed by Kaikeyee and Sumitra.
The three sisters were burnt in one pyre,
And the rest in another. After death,
All were conveyed to Indra's court,
Where they joined Dasaratha.
They were felicitated by Indra himself.
They lived with their husband everafter.

67

The Preparation for the Funeral Rites

Listen, O Pandu's son!
Overcome with grief, Srirama entered
The palace. He lay on the bed with
His sons; Bharata and Lakshmana
Sat a little distance apart. All night
He lay awake, folding his sons in his arms.

When it became morning,
All of them woke up. Not finding their
Mother, Laba and Kusha started crying.
Rama's condition was no better.
The memory of Sita haunted him, he felt
As if his body was on fire. Seeing
Basistha arriving with the courtiers,
Srirama told the sage, 'It's all
Too much for me to take in. Keeping
My sons in charge of the kingdom, I wish
To leave this place forever. I'll go on

A pilgrimage and die unlamented.'
Basistha replied, 'Don't despair. Stop
Feeling sorry for yourself. Your mother
And all the queens consigned themselves
To fire. Sita, the other half of your life,
Is now no more. This is not the right
Time for you to leave the kingdom.
You need to purify yourself before
You go on a visit to holy places
And eat outdoors. On the top of it,
Your sons have lost their mother lately.
Your absence will bear heavily on them.
Had your mothers been alive,
They would have taken care of them,
Or had they been in Janaka's house
They would not have felt your absence.
What do they know about administration?
They also need to purify themselves
As their mother has died. How can
They do their mother's rites without
Having wives? You've to wait for
One year for that. You'll get
Them married, ordain them kings
And then, think of going on
A pilgrimage. Send a messenger
To Shatrughna; he is not yet informed
Of his mother's death.'

Srirama called Madhukeshi, the charioteer,
And ordered him, 'Hurry to Madhubana
With my letter to Shatrughna.
Don't tell him about my mother's death.

He may be too shocked to bear it.
Tell him to come with you forthwith,
Assigning his duties to his ministers.'
Madhukeshi sped fast, and reaching
Madhubana, met Shatrughna who was sitting
On the throne. Seeing the messenger's face
Turned pale, he was apprehensive that
Something unpleasant might have
Happened. He asked him, 'What brings
You here, Madhukeshi? Why do you
Look so sad? Had Rama any news of Sita?'
Madhukeshi handed over Rama's letter
To him. After going through it, he ordered
His ministers to attend to the affairs
Of the kingdom until he returned.
They told him, 'We're better off than
What we were during Labana's rule.
You're as benevolent as God. How can
You disobey Srirama's command?
Try to return as early as possible.'

With Shatrughna onboard,
Madhukeshi drove the chariot as quickly
As he could. Reaching the palace,
He found Rama sitting gloomily,
Surrounded by Basistha, Sumanta,
Bharata, Lakshmana, Laba, Kusha,
Their sons and the courtiers. There was
A stony silence all around. Previously,
When he came, Rama would
Welcome him ceremonially; women
From every house would greet him

With flowers and lamps, and the mothers
Would sprinkle holy grass and sunned-baked rice
Mixed with turmeric on his head.
But, that day, nothing of that sort happened.
He was frightened that something has gone
Wrong. Pointing at Laba and Kusha,
He asked Bharata, 'Who are they?
I've never seen them before. Whose sons
Are they? They look exactly like Rama.
They look the same in age and appearance.'
Bharata replied, 'They're Srirama's sons.
Sita gave birth to them in the forest.
They used to collect alms everyday
And give it to their guru every evening.
One day Laba came to Ayodhya,
Singing and begging for alms.
He read out the *Ramayana* to Rama
Next day he brought Kusha with him.
All of us heard the *Ramayana* from them,
From beginning to end. The scripture
Revealed that they were Srirama's sons.
With them, we went to Sita. She didn't
Even look at Srirama's face. She sank
Into the earth and was lost forever.
We brought her sons here last night.
Shocked at the news of Sita's demise,
The queens sacrificed their lives in fire.
Since you need to know all this
We sent a messenger to fetch you.'

Unable to bear with the loss of kith and kin,
Shatrughna fainted. When he came round,

He cried bitterly and complained
To Bharata, 'Why didn't you let me know
That you were going to Janaka's kingdom?
I could have fallen at Sita's feet
And prayed to her to come back. To me,
She didn't fall short of a mother.
What use regretting now? Whatever
God wishes, must prevail.' So saying,
He embraced Laba and Kusha,
Who bowed to him in respect. He said
To Rama, 'Our mothers passed away.
So did Sita. Who will look after these
Children now? Basing on a rumour,
Spread by people who do not count,
You forsook Sita. You subjected her
To injustice, humiliation and shame.
You listened neither to Basistha
Nor to us. God's wish can't be altered.'

In deep regret, Rama held his head
In his hands. Basistha consoled
Rama, saying, 'Your brothers have
One son each. Suratha is the son of Bharata
And Alaka, Bidhangsarath, the son
Of Lakshmana and Urmila and Birabara,
The son of Shatrughna and Tara.
Now all the members of your family
And all your relatives should take a bath.
That will relieve you of stress
And freshen you up.'

While bathing, Sita's sisters mourned
For her. They recounted her sufferings

In the forest and in Lanka. They praised
Her for her virtues. Returning
To the palace, Rama lay on bed with
His sons, all night awake. When
It became morning, the relatives
And the scripture-readers came
And consoled him. They persuaded him
To eat a little something. When
He finished, his brothers, their wives
And the children took their meals
And felt somewhat better.

68

Annual Rituals for the Dead

Ten days of bereavement passed,
During which Rama and his brothers
Observed the rites enjoined by the Vedas,
Each offering cooked food to his mother
And donating wealth and riches to brahmins.
On the eleventh day Basistha purified
Their bodies with holy water.

Srirama said to Shatrughna,
'You may leave for Madhubana now,
But come back again to attend the annual
Rites. Then, we'll finalise the marriage
Of our five sons. After ordaining Laba
The King of Ayodhya, I'll leave.
I'm of no use here any longer.' With
Folded hands, Shatrughna asked, 'Why do
You send me to Madhubana? What for
Shall I go there? If you go to the forest,
Leaving me here, I'll surely kill myself.'

Bharata added, 'You're right. How can we
Live happily without him? Three of us
Will follow him wherever he goes.'
Srirama fell silent, pleased with those
Soothing words. The four brothers decided
To stay together in Ayodhya, their hearts
Broken and minds burdened with thoughts.

Srirama kept a count of days;
A year seemed to him like an age.
He drew a line on the wall to mark
The passing of a day. When twelve months
Elapsed, he called his priest
And ministers and told them, 'You know
My wife and mothers have left for
Their heavenly abode. Arrange for
The annual rites to make them happy.'

When the ministers set everything
Ready, the rites of the anniversary
Started. Srirama offered cooked rice
To Kausalya, Bharata to Kaikeyee,
Lakshmana to Sumitra, Shatrughna
To the twenty-one hundred queens
And Laba to Sita. The brahmins were
Paid more than they expected.
The relatives and people of Ayodhya
Were well fed. They offered clothes
And ornaments to priests, ministers
And courtiers. The anniversary
Ended on a happy note.

69

The Marriage of the Princes

Finishing his morning constitutionals,
Srirama sat on the throne. He consulted
With his priest and ministers about
Finding brides for the five princes.
Basistha called a meeting of the courtiers
And asked them, 'Do any of you
Have daughters worthy enough to be
Brides for the five princes? Don't
Tell lies; if you do, it will be viewed
Seriously by the King.' After much
Deliberation, they said, 'Sumanta's
Son, Sribanta and his daughter-in-law,
Rupamayee have two daughters.
For their beauty and virtues, they are
Named Chandrakanti and Gunamati.'

They considered the two girls
A perfect match for Laba and Kusha
Respectively. Sukeshi, the daughter

Of Bhagadatta, one of the ministers
And Pravabati was chosen for Suratha,
Bharata's son. The courtiers,
Gunakar and Pravakar had a daughter
Each. Kusumarekha, the daughter
Of Gunakar and Sachisila, was as
Beautiful as Sachi; she was found
Suitable for Lakshmana's son,
Bidhangsarath. Shatrughna's son,
Birabara was to marry Madanabati,
The daughter of Pravakar and Kamasena.

The marriages of the princes were held
On the tenth day of the bright fortnight
Of Magha. It was a Thursday, star
Rebati and lagna *Mithuna*. They were
Performed according to Vedic customs,
Such as tying of the hands of
The couple and worshipping the sacrificial
Fire. The newly-weds entered the palace
Among the sounds of ululation by
The women of the palace. Alaka,
Urmila and Tara welcomed them
By sprinkling the holy grass and rice,
Mixed with turmeric on their heads.
In the night of the day of the wedding,
The princes and their brides went
To bed in pairs. Next morning,
The sons left the bed early and bowed
Down first to Rama and, then, others,
Holding their feet. In return,
They received parental love and blessings.

70

The Partition of the Inheritance

Srirama held a meeting with
Basistha, his ministers, courtiers,
Brothers and the five sons to propose
A division of power among his sons.
With folded hands, he prayed to the sage
To find a suitable day for Laba's
Coronation as the King of Ayodhya.
Basistha suggested, 'The third day
Of the bright fortnight of Magha
Is the most auspicious. It's a Friday
Ruled by star *Pusya*.' Srirama replied,
'There is no time for delay. A look
At the palace disheartens me. It
Looks desolate with my mother gone.
I'm dismayed when I think of Ayodhya.
I had Sita's idols made to make me
Feel better, but now, like a dagger,
They pierce my heart. Listen everybody!
If Shatrughna goes with me to the forest

Who will be the King of Madhubana?'
The conquest of Madhubana has become
A burden on me now. If I don't provide
A substitute, I'll fail in my duty.
Basistha suggested,
'Your youngest son, Kusha will be
The King of Madhubana. He will be
Assisted by the sons of Lakshmana
And Shatrughna.'

On the appointed day,
Laba's coronation took place with
Pomp and ceremony. He was as handsome
As Kamadeva, as judicious as
Yama and as forbearing as the Meru
Mountain. When he entered the palace,
After his ascension to the throne,
Women of the palace welcomed him
Warmly. Taking Kusha into his lap,
Rama told him, 'You've to move to
Madhubana now. Bidhangsarath
And Birabara will accompany you.'

x x x x

Be gentle in your manners. Never be
Egoistic. Maintain discipline.
Don't hesitate to give away donations.
Don't displease your ministers
And courtiers. Don't dilute your principles.
Don't be harsh to those you sheltered.
Don't ignore the minister's advice.
Be nice to others while you speak

To them. Don't let your enemies
Prosper in your kingdom.

x x x x

Srirama ordered Ratnakar,
The son of Madhukeshi, to carry Shatrughna
To Madhubana. Kusha, his brothers
And their wives on board,
Ratnakar drove the chariot as quickly
As he could. When they reached Madhubana,
They were greeted by a huge crowd.
While Kusha proceeded towards the throne,
Their wives went inside the palace.

Kusha adorned the throne; Bidhangsarath
And Birabara stood on each side
Of him, with fans in their hands.
The ministers and courtiers thronged
To greet him. He offered them gifts,
Such as finery and ornaments.
The subjects celebrated Kusha's
Coronation with mirth and jubilation.

After sending off Kusha,
Srirama gave Laba some tips on how
To rule the kingdom, 'Love your
Subjects as you love your sons.
Worship God of Fire everyday.
Be aware of what's going on in your
Neighbourhood. Don't ever punish
The innocent ones. Award of penalty
Should be proportionate to the gravity

Of the crime. Kill him who destroys
The wealth of the kingdom.
Take care of your ministers and brahmins.
Address to the grievances of the people.
Help the poor and the needy. Service
To the poor is the only way to keep
The evil spirits away. Pay respect
To the gods and brahmins. First, worship
The gods and then, ascend the throne.
Treat Suratha, Bharata's son, as your
Own. My father had made Bharata
The king, but, for his love for me,
He left Ayodhya for the Subahu forest.
Dressed in ochre clothes and living on
Sweet potatoes, he spent his days
In meditation. It was only when
I came back, he returned to Ayodhya.
He is always obedient and respectful
To me. Send messengers to Madhubana
Daily and collect the news of Shatrughna.
If you come to know your ministers
And courtiers are wasting wealth,
Never mind.' He, then, proceeded
To discuss with his courtiers
And relatives the issues related
To the welfare of the kingdom.
Sugriba, who was in Kiskindya,
Came to see Srirama. He bowed to
Srirama, holding his feet. Rama raised
Him to his feet and fondly embraced
Him. Hanumanta, leaving the Kadalibana
Also arrived there. Caressing his head,

Srirama told him, 'Since your departure,
Misfortunes, one after another,
Befell me. Driven by evil thoughts,
I abandoned Sita. I didn't even
Listen to Basistha's advice. She had
A harrowing time in the forest.
There she gave birth to two sons.
Sage Valmiki took her to Janaka's house
And taught her sons the best of all
Scriptures, the *Ramayana*. One day
Laba and Kusha came to Ayodhya,
Singing the *Ramayana*. They described
Your heroic exploits in the war.
They told about the past and the future.
When they introduced themselves,
I came to know they were my sons.
With them we went to Sita.
Not wishing to see my face,
She sank into the netherworld.
We returned with her sons. Too shocked,
My mothers sacrificed their lives in
The fire. We performed their annual rites
And we got all our sons married.
Kusha was made the King of Madhubana.
He went there with the sons of Lakshmana
And Shatrughna. Laba, the apple of my eye,
Became the King of Ayodhya.
It's fine you came here. I am glad
To see my friend, Sugriba after
A long time. Hearing the whole story,
Sugriba and Hanumanta were taken aback.

71

Going on a Pilgrimage

Rama announced, 'It's time for me
To go on a pilgrimage. It's of no use
Staying here any longer.'
Sugriba told him, 'I remember
The day on which Indrajita shot at
Us with the *mohana* arrow; some
Of us were dead and others dying.
It was Hanumanta who fetched
The medicinal plant from Hemabanta
Mountain, which brought back our
Lives. Because of his tireless effort
We were able to kill Ravana
And return to Ayodhya. You
And your brothers were given a leaf each,
On the day of coronation. Angada,
Hanumanta and Jambabana had
One leaf each. It made Hanumanta
Immortal. If Jambabana had known
About your journey, he would have

Joined us. Hanumanta and I would
Go with you and serve you all along.
What will we do, staying here?'
Rama told him, 'Listen, my friend!
You're here without the knowledge
Of your wife, ministers and courtiers.
If you leave, who'll take care of
Kiskindha? As for myself, I'm not
Returning to Ayodhya again. Joy
And happiness are not written in
My fate. I've lost my wife and mother.
For whom shall I come back?'
Sugriba replied, 'Bali is the real
King of Kiskindha. As he is dead,
The kingship is due to Angada,
His son. I was the king because of
Your mercy. When you're leaving
For the forest, why should I be here?'

He ordered Brukshasimha, a monkey
Who accompanied him, to go to Kiskindha
Forthwith. He said to him, 'Tell Tara
Not to worry. Tell Angada that
Rama wants to see him as the king
Of Kiskindha and Tara as the king's
Mother. Tell them to take care of
The subjects.' Brukshasimha hastened
To Kiskindha and passed on the message
To Angada and Tara. Both of them
Regretted and cursed themselves
For missing the opportunity to go
With Sugriba and see Rama.

Tara, with the help of the minister,
Held Angada's coronation soon.
Srirama begged Basistha,
'My sons are young. They will do
As you say. The responsibility
Of my kingdom rests on your shoulders.
Take care of my subjects and see that
Laba doesn't pine for me henceforward.'

The four brothers changed into ochre
Clothes, while Sugriba and Hanumanta
Dressed themselves as hermits.
Srirama put on Sita's hair which
Was with him on his head.
All of them wore *rudraksha* around
Their arms, garlands of wooden beads,
And copper earrings, and held staff
And *kamandalu* in their hands.
They smeared their bodies with holy ash.

Alaka, Urmila and Tara,
The three sisters, came out of the palace,
Ready to go with their husbands.
Seeing this, Basistha forbade them,
Saying, 'You don't need to go
To the forest. Stay in the palace
And attend to the affairs of the kingdom.
You can help your husbands in no way.
Living in the forest is never easy.'
Srirama added, 'Stay here and do
Your duties as the king's mothers.
Your company will create problems

For us as we've to move from place
To place. You know what trouble
I was in by taking Sita with me
To the forest. Ravana, the sinner,
Kidnapped her, for which his whole
Clan was destroyed. I killed Ravana
And took her trial by fire. Basing
On a rumour I banished her
To the forest. She was so angry with
Me that she sank into the netherworld
Without looking at me. I lost her
Forever. For what happiness
Should I stay here? My brothers
Insisted on going with me. Take
Them back, if you can, or return
To the palace.'

The three sisters went back
In grief. They were sure that
Their happy days had come to an end.
With Srirama, the incarnation
Of Vishnu leaving them forever.
Before parting, Rama bowed
To sage Basistha, who blessed him,
Saying, 'May your wish be fulfilled.
Descend to the earth in every age
To destroy the wicked.'
Then, they left.

72

Journey to Heaven

Listen, O Pandu's son!

With his three brothers, Sugriba
And Hanumanta, Dasaratha's son
Visited many places of pilgrimage.
Through vigorous *yogic* practices,
He could bring control over his mind.

There, in heaven,
Brahma, Indra, all other gods, Devarsis,
Rajarsis, dikpalas, sages, the cow-goddess,
The Sun and the Wind had assembled
In Indra's court. Seeing from a distance
That Rama was coming towards them,
They whispered among themselves,
'He has killed Ravana, Bisraba's son
And Paulasti's grandson, who, through
His unflinching devotion to Lord Shiva,
Received a boon that made him

The monarch of the three worlds.
Srirama has committed the sin
Of killing a brahmin, which is grave.
None of you will look at his face,
Nor speak to him.' All of them were
Sitting silently, their heads between
Their thighs. Just then, Rama entered there.
He looked around; from their indifference,
He could guess what they were thinking.
He told Sugriba, 'Look at the gods.
See, how they behave with me!
It's because I've killed Ravana.
They forget the days when Ravana was
Using them as slaves, it was down to
them to wait for his orders. My fault is
That I saved them from humiliation
And brought back their honour.
It'll be unwise to be angry with them.
One should not stay at a place, even
For a moment, where one is not treated
Honourably.' Sugriba replied,
'You're right. One should not help
Those who don't deserve it. Those
Who are ungrateful are destined
To go to hell. They will be reborn as
Beasts. Only by worshipping Lord Shiva,
They can be rescued from hell.'

Leaving Indra's court,
The six of them went to the abode
Of Vishnu, the Supreme Reality into whom
All earthly lives disappear.

Srirama inhabited Vishnu and went
To the Milky Sea. There, he lay on
The coiled Ananta Cobra,
Lakshmi pressing his feet.

Sita reached there with a gem-studded
Lamp in her hand to welcome him.
She said respectfully, 'O Lord!
You suffered immensely on the earth.
When you insulted me and sent me
To the forest, I had no option but
To leave you. Forgive me for my fault.'

Sitting beside Vishnu,
She began playing the *veena* with
A melodious note. The snake's hood
Served as the umbrella overhead.
The wind blew mildly. Soon
Sri Jagannath fell asleep.

Thus, the story of the *Ramayana*
Comes to an end.

73

Epilogue

Listen, O Pandu's son!
You've listened to the seven books
Of the sacred text, the *Ramayana*.
It gives the same result as performing
One hundred *Aswamedha Yajnas*.
It will liberate both the Soma clan
And Bhoja clan. No sin will touch
You in future. Now it's time I must
Be paid my fees. Let Draupadi
And all your brothers pay too.

A grass-ring on his finger,
Yudhisthira held a conch containing
Water and sesame seeds aloft and said,
'I vow to give you one hundred pieces
Of gold, one lakh healthy cows,
And one lakh pieces of clothes.
I'll feed one lakh brahmins and provide
Settlements for one thousand brahmins

Once I become the King of Hastinapura.
Bhima, Arjuna, Nakula and Sahadeva
Took an oath to offer one lakh gems each.
Draupadi was in a dilemma. She said
To herself, 'What'll I give to the sage?
Being married to five persons, I'm viewed
As a sinner by the society. If I don't
Pay anything, how shall I expiate my sins?'
She took off her gem necklace, and, offering
It to the sage, she said, 'When my
Husband will kill the Kauravas and become
The King of Hastina, I promise to give you
One thousand pieces of gold.' The sage
Blessed her, 'May your wish be fulfilled.'
The Pandavas, then, lay prostrate before
Him, holding his feet. Caressing
Yudhisthira's head, he told him,
'Do as I say. You've one more year
To live in secret. Go and stay at Birata,
The capital of Macchhya kingdom.
Take care of your brothers. As soon as
The period of your exile is over,
Declare war against your enemy.
Ask those wise men, brahmins,
Vaisnavas and others who came with
You to go back.'

Yudhisthira told him, 'You can
See my plight with your own eyes.
Defeating me in dice by fraud,
Duryodhan occupied my kingdom
For twelve years. If we are exposed

Before our term of exile ends,
We'll have to go into exile again.'
He asked the men who had come with
Him to leave. Markanda advised them,
'Chant Hari's name and remember
The holy words of the *Ramayana*.'

The Pandavas took leave of the sage
And left. Markanda left for Dwaraka,
Then to Indra's abode. When Indra
Wanted to know about the Pandavas,
He said, 'They're still in hiding, waiting
For one more year to pass, when
The term of their exile will be over."

To bring relief to the earth,
Hari descends to the earth in human form
To destroy the demons. He is the Preserver
And the Destroyer. Meditating on Srirama
Is holier than taking a dip in Ganga.
His devotee is rewarded with wealth, honour,
And happy family life. Fortune favours
The woman who listens to the *Ramayana*;
She'll be born into a noble family
In her next birth.

How can a feeble man, such as I am,
Fathom out the *Ramayana* which is as
Deep as the ocean? Can a man whose
Mind is not steadfast, who is born
Into a sudra family, and whose habits
And actions are unrefined, produce

Such a scripture in its purest form?
O brahmins, vaisnavas, noblemen,
The wise and the learned ones!
Don't mind my mistakes.
I'm Siddheswar Das,
The author of the *Ramayana*.
I narrated the story of Laba and Kusha.
The readers may consider my effort
A misadventure and laugh at me.
An unseen power instructs me to write.
He inhabits me and shows me the way.
O noble ones! Do I deserve to write this?

Listening to the *Ramayana*
Makes one's wishes fulfilled.
Hari, Hara and Brahma are one
And the same. The *Ramayana* is the Supreme
Wisdom. Listen to the story of Laba
And Kusha and Srirama's journey
To heaven. Rama's name is recorded
In the Vedas and Puranas. Chanting
His name, one can avert the fear
Of Death. Siddheswar Das reproduces
The *Ramayana* written by Valmiki.

Glossary

aguru	:	a kind of perfume
Ananga	:	Kama, God of love
apsara	:	a celestial damsel
Aswamedha yajna	:	Horse sacrifice performed by emperors in ancient India
Basudeva	:	Krishna
Benu	:	One of the six emperors in the golden age of Hindu mythology
Bighnaraj	:	Lord Ganesh
bimba	:	a creeper; its fruit looks shining red when it ripens
bisa	:	a unit of weight in ancient times
brahmachari	:	One who practises continence and studies the Vedas in the preceptor's house after investiture
brata	:	a religious practice for fulfilling one's wish
chakora	:	also chakrabaka; a bird which is said to be living on moonlight
charu	:	a bundle of rice, sweetmeats etc. offered to the sacrificial fire

dambaru	:	a small double-faced drum in the shape of an hour-glass
dikpalas	:	the gods ruling the ten directions. According to Manu, they are Kubera, Indra, Yama, Baruna, Fire, Moon, Sun, Wind, Brahma and Vishnu. The Vedas mention five dikpalas and the Buddhists four
Dwapara	:	One of the four Ages of Hindu mythology
gajaghanta	:	the bell hanging from an elephant's neck
Gajanana	:	Lord Ganesh
Gananath	:	Lord Ganesh
Garuda	:	a huge mythological bird, the carrier of Vishnu
Gayatri	:	the holiest of all mantras, composed by sage Biswamitra
gandharva	:	a demi-god
Gorekh	:	Gorekhnath; a Natha yogi and a powerful exponent of yoga marga
graha	:	planet
jaba	:	hibiscus
yajna	:	the sacrificial and ceremonial rites enjoined by the Vedas
jui/jai	:	types of jasmines
kamandalu	:	an earthen, wooden or metallic ewer with a handle (as in a bucket), used by ascetics.
Kodanda	:	name of Rama's bow
kos	:	two miles (approximately)
kshatriya	:	one of the four castes in Hindu society
Kubera	:	the custodian of wealth in heaven
kumkum	:	a type of cosmetic
Lambodara	:	Lord Ganesh
lata	:	creeper

linga	:	(Hinduism) a symbol of divine generative energy, especially a phallus and phallic object symbolising Lord Shiva.
Madana	:	Kama, God of love
Mahatmani	:	feminine gender of Mahatma, a great soul
Manu	:	1. a unit of time comprising 71 x 4320000 years of man. 2. Brahma's son, the progenitor of man.
Meru	:	the Meru mountain of mythological fame. It is also called Sumeru, Hemadri, Ratnasanu and Amaradri. It is eighty-four thousand yojanas in height, of which sixteen thousand yojanas are submerged. It has three mounts. In modern geography, it is North Pole located in the Arctic circle.
Nanda	:	King of Gopa; foster-father of Krishna and Balarama
Om	:	a sound syllable which symbolizes the infinite
pala	:	a unit of weight in old times
pauti	:	a unit of measurement in old times. One pauti = 20 gaunis, one gauni = 8 or 10 seers
Pusyaviseka	:	the ceremonial investure of a king during Pusya snana conjunction
Ratishastra	:	the science of sex-works
Rudraksha	:	the seeds of a tree with the same name, regarded holy and used by ascetics.
sabara	:	a tribal man
Sachi	:	the consort of Lord Indra
sal	:	a tropical tree
Saraswati	:	Goddess of Learning
Sashankasekhar	:	Lord Shiva

satwa, raja, tama	:	represent creation, preservation and destruction
shastra	:	scripture
Skanda	:	Kartikeya, the eldest son of Lord Shiva
sloka	:	a couplet of a Sanskrit poem
Sri Bhagabate Basudevaya	:	Invocation to Lord Krishna
Suparnekhi	:	Subarnanekha, sister to Ravana
swayambara	:	a form of marriage in which the bride chooses her husband from among assembled suitors
tirtha	:	a holy place
Tretaya	:	one of the four Ages of Hindu mythology
Trilochana	:	one with three eyes; Lord Shiva
Uttara Kanda	:	one of the seven books of Valmiki's Ramayana which describes Rama's life after his return from Lanka.
yojana	:	a distance of eight miles